Paradoxical Wisdom: Just **B.E. K.I.N.D.**

Paradoxical Wisdom: Just **B.E. K.I.N.D.**

Sayers R. Brenner, M.D.

Paradox Books
Sarasota, Florida
2015

PARADOXICAL WISDOM: JUST **B.E. K.I.N.D.**
Copyright © 2015 Sayers R. Brenner, M.D.

Paradox Books
2027 Rose St.
Sarasota, Florida 34239

Author: Sayers R. Brenner, M.D.
Editor: Charlotte T. Brenner

All rights reserved. No part of this book may be reproduced or transmitted in any form, or by any means, electronic or mechanical, including photocopying, recording or by any information storage and retrieval systems, without the prior written permission from the author.

ISBN 978-0-9640827-1-7
Library of Congress Control Number: 2015912871

10 9 8 7 6 5 4 3 2 1
First Edition

Printed in the United States of America
Serbin Printing, Inc. — Sarasota, Florida

DEDICATION

To Charlotte, whose love, wisdom, strength, and joy I still try to emulate. I'm a lucky guy.

To our loving children and grandchildren

Contents

Summary
    Part One 1
    Part Two 10

Chapter 1. The Cosmic Con-Game
    Part One 17
    Part Two 29
    Part Three 41

Chapter 2. Paradox
    Part One 54
    Part Two 69
    Part Three 80

Chapter 3. Resistance to Change, To Awakening
    Part One 94
    Part Two 107

Chapter 4. The Inner Congress
    Part One 123
    Part Two 134

Chapter 5. Integration 147

Chapter 6. Just **B.E. K.I.N.D.**
    Part One 157
    Part Two 169

Contents

Chapter 7. Insight
    Part One 179
    Part Two 196

Chapter 8. B & E: Balance and Embracing
    Part One 204
    Part Two 220

Chapter 9. Disillusionment
    Part One 233
    Part Two 250
    Part Three 260

Chapter 10. Deflation
    Part One 268
    Part Two 280

Chapter 11. The Present Moment/Eternity of Now
    Part One 295
    Part Two 309

Chapter 12. The Secret Victory of Self-Defeat, Revisited
    Part One 320
    Part Two 334

Contents

Chapter 13. Romantic Love's Illusions

    Part One 348

    Part Two 359

Chapter 14. Love's Fierce Teacher: The Manipulator

    Part One 370

    Part Two 385

Chapter 15. Paradoxical Romantic Love

    Part One 397

    Part Two 409

    Part Three 418

    Part Four 429

Chapter 16. Final Musings 443

About the Author and Editor 451

SUMMARY

PART ONE

Forty-four years and over eighty thousand psychotherapy sessions. This or any other challenging endeavour can unveil life's secrets. It turns out that amidst the interpersonal process of insight-oriented psychotherapy, patients inevitably reveal profound, universal, encoded, and paradoxical truths which they, themselves, don't endorse or even perceive at a conscious level. They challenge me, thereby, to attempt to harmonize with their resistances and collaborate with their inner and most profound selves. Together, we can decipher these codes and help them to return to their own most ultimately wise, paradoxical, and healing insights.

To accomplish this, I must go beyond psychotherapy's already abundant and helpful knowledge and integrate it with the little I know of the perennial and deepest wisdom of the world's seemingly disparate philosophies, religions, literatures, meditations, sciences, and arts. I'm always educating myself. It's the best we humans can do. We have so much to learn and so little time, no matter how deeply we go into any discipline.

Don't just practice your art. Force yourself into its secrets.
　　　　　　　　　　Beethoven

Twenty-seven years ago, my first book explored the intricacies of how human nature so often bypasses profound and fulfilling reason, success, and happiness; and pursues, instead, superficial and insatiable irrationality, self-defeat, and misery. The childish part of the unconscious mind tricks and seduces us to dance, like marionettes, to its unheard, wishful thinking, instinct-driven, and siren song misassumptions, or illusions. This intricate and often life-long self-deception is called the "repetition compulsion".

We're all the unknowing playwrights, directors, actors, victims, victimizers, audiences, promoters, and critics of these self-deceptive, self-confirming, self-aggrandizing, and, therefore, inevitably self-defeating scripts which we use to act out the compulsive psychodramas of our lives. Plato's ancient "Cave Allegory" comes to mind as an illustration. Chained with our backs to the cave's distant opening, we make it all up from the dance and play of mere shadows on the back wall of the cave. It's both an inner and outer con-game.

All that we see or seem is but a dream within a dream.
　　　　　　　　　　Edgar Allen Poe

Everything is not as it seems, nor is it otherwise.
　　　　　　　　　　The Buddha

In addition to this self-inflicted pain and suffering; what about the intrinsic and inescapable agonies and afflictions which inevitably occur throughout life, whether we're awakened or not? This book attempts to explore both types of suffering by applying the nearly inexpressible, inexplicable, and poetic insights of paradoxical wisdom.

The lengthy task of compiling this audacious book entails the linear, lengthy, either-or, and compartmentalized rationale of mere prose, but that's only part of how we humans think. At a more fundamental and often subliminal level, we experience reality in all-at-once images, thoughts, and gestalts, apart from and beyond normal language. We perceive in instantaneous, here-and-now frames of multifaceted, multidimensional, integrated, fused, and even poetic consciousness.

I wish I could transcend the limits of prose, altogether. I'd express myself, instead, solely within playful metaphors, poems, parables, tales, riddles, songs, art, and dance. These would best reveal and conceal the tiny portion of what I can comprehend of the sacred, central, and paradoxical essence of deepest reality. The poetic logic and humor of paradox allows us to crack the code, break Plato's chains, redirect our gaze towards the light, travel to the cave's opening, and manage to decipher the fullness of reality clearly for the first time. It enables us to emerge from a life of chasing after merely limited, inaccurate, superficial, unfulfilling, and elusive mirages. We graduate, thereby, to a life of enjoying gloriously expanded, authentic, profound, fulfilling, and enduring insights.

I would name this poetic language "Paradoxese." Ideally, its every phrase would express the contradictory, balanced, and integrated essence of nature itself, which wordlessly and unceremoniously displays and conceals the entire array of its secrets within each moment.

In an effort to more clearly reflect this elusive, exquisite, present moment, and healing integration of opposites; and in order to bridge the gap between poetry and prose; I sometimes use slashes when I try to write in "Paradoxese." Examples include "creative/destruction," "successful/failure," "foolish/wisdom," "earnest/indifference," "cynical/optimism," "present moment/eternity," "mis/understanding," "honest/hypocrisy," and so on.

Some ancient and present thinkers go so far as to theorize and even calculate that the entire universe is comprised solely of pure consciousness, itself. This seemingly preposterous and counter-intuitive proposition might be taken by some to imply or even prove the notion of a universe or god with conscious intention. Instead, I think of the universe as a giant, non-personified, self-renewing, self-propagating, and un/conscious paradox. I posit that at the ultimate center of paradox, ... substance and consciousness, as well as randomness and design, are essentially coexistent, synchronous, integrated, interchangeable, and even identical.

The cosmos can thus be envisioned as one big, balanced, self-contradictory, and ever-dynamic whirlpool of fused material and conceptual paradox. It dances and reverberates impartially, carelessly, mindlessly, and seamlessly at astronomical and microscopic levels, and between such extremes as positive and negative, creation and destruction, light and dark, mass-energy, particle-wave, fusion-fission, and so on. Indeed, the vast intricacies of paradox may hold the key to the very meaning of the enigma of life, itself.

> *Stop acting so small. You are the universe in ecstatic motion.*
>
> Ranier Maria Rilke

The universe thus integrates, coordinates, and unifies infinite numbers of apparently opposing and mutually exclusive pairs of extremes. Such is the definition, majesty, essence, and enigma of paradox. What little we mere humans can comprehend of the most profound fullness of truth lies in the seemingly still, stable, pinpoint, integrated, expanded, and sacred center of paradox. It's always in the center; and yet it harmonizes and integrates with the entire periphery, as well. They are one. This calls to mind the black holes at the centers of galaxies.

We humans have the small-minded arrogance and audacity, however, to attempt to improve on reality by trying to permanently split apart these essentially fused and identical polarities. This gives us the preposterous illusion that we're seeing these artificially separated aspects clearly, distinctly, and completely. This is our fatal flaw; ... our collective, basic, dualistic, this-or-that, contradictory, and extremist confusion, conceit, or "sin."

If we attempt to define, refine, and distill truths, they remain forever embedded within the confusing, enigmatic, and non-linear format or matrix of paradox. Alas, after all analysis, a poem remains a poem. The most poetic and profound integration of any paradox can't possibly yield what we really want, which is the illusion of a tidy, either-or, split-up, and single-pointed answer, truth, or clarity. We mistakenly think that this is the only way to preserve a pristine and comforting sense of organization, clarity, structure, focus, certainty, and hope. Reality, however, is served up only in centered, integrated, and fused packages of self-contradictory paradoxes or dilemmas. The simple truth is that there are no simple and one-sided truths.

The very process of an individual's maturation from concrete to abstract reason is the journey from a split-up, contradictory, and extremist awareness, with its artificially amped-up, melodramatic, confused, and clashing emotions; to a paradoxical, integrated, centered, fused, and compromised consciousness, with its profound, harmonious, and serene inner peace. The very resolution of our split-up, reverberating, and contradictory cosmic con-game confusion, therefore, is to drop into the illuminatingly/baffling paradox of the cosmic confluence of fusion, or "CON/FUSION."

*My aim is to teach you to pass from a position of
disguised nonsense to something that is patent nonsense.*
        Ludwig Wittgenstein

The enigma of paradox inspires endless, authoritative, learned, articulate, impressive, and contradictory interpretations and misinterpretations. Consequently, any deeply integrated and profound truth can be spun and promoted in multiple accurate and inaccurate directions. Freud mentioned that neurosis, itself, stems from the inability to tolerate life's inherent, inescapable, and paradoxical ambiguity.

Perhaps, I should emulate the seemingly careless and neglectful silence of the non-personified and uncanny universe. It knows how to keep its secrets. Unlike arrogant, self-important, and self-aggrandizing humans, it provides no narration, manual, or justification. Maybe ultimate secrets are best left as obscure hints within symbols, metaphors, postures, and actions. Detailed and impressive explanations often obscure the most profound, sacred, and useful truths all the more.

He who knows does not speak,
and he who speaks does not know.
                                    Lao Tzu

Believe those who are seeking the truth; doubt those who find it.
                                    Andre Gide

The hubris, folly, audacity, and urgency of old age move me, however, to "pull a Lao Tzu," so to speak. After all, at the end of his life, he broke his silence by trying to condense ultimate truths into a brief collection of poems. I, too, will attempt to distill and convey all the nearly ineffable and incomprehensible secrets that I've grasped so far in a simple, paradoxical, poetic, compassionate, light-hearted, and applicable way. Maybe next week or year, I or someone else will find a better, shorter, simpler, more profound, more articulate, and more poetic way to express it.

I have no illusion that scores will immediately awaken upon reading these words, any more than I did when I studied all too few of the world's masters. It took me decades to find, decipher, resist, misunderstand, misapply, understand, teach, misunderstand again, reconcile, integrate, and remain open to their further hidden and simple harmonies. This recurring, ever-spiraling, and "stumbling-and-fumbling-towards-enlightenment" process still takes place for me. After all, the objective is to discover, over and over, just what kind of fools we are. I still find, study, quote, and re-quote the masters. I even have the audacity to edit them. It's all been spoken and unspoken, quoted and misquoted, understood and misunderstood, applied and misapplied, countless times before. This book does all of that.

It turns out that each of us must become an ultimate Plato, Rumi, Aristotle, Shakespeare, Kierkegaard, or Kafka. We are the oracle. Each mortal is destined to retrace and reinvent humanity's generic, ancient, proverbial, and experiential pathway towards deeper wisdom, each in our own way, one person at a time, and one moment at a time, whether it's conceptualized, articulated, organized, literate, educated, clever, world-wise, or not. The notion that humanity as a whole makes permanent progress in matters of ultimate wisdom is simply indefensible.

Once we discover the elusive secret of paradox; we then see, experience, and enjoy it literally everywhere. How could we have missed it? Incidentally, this is also how psychotics feel about the sometimes profound revelations imbedded within their irrational delusions. The initial gap between sanity and madness can be as thin as a spider web. Both are intricately woven, self-justified, convincing, and sometimes widely sanctioned. Starting one micron apart, wisdom and madness can lead to starkly contrasting universes. They can also occasionally lead to the same profound and paradoxical center of universal enlightenment. After all, several of the world's greatest religions were started by individuals whose most enduring, worthy, and inspiring revelations derived from hallucinations and delusions.

This seems so backwards and uncanny. It's consistent, however, with modern theories of physics, which calculate the existence of parallel or serial universes and multiple invisible dimensions, one of which may, incidentally, be another dimension of time. It reminds me of what Carl Jung said about a delusional patient: that she didn't think she lived on the moon; she lived on the moon.

A funny and exasperating thing happens on the way to paradoxical wisdom. The cosmos inevitably and repeatedly pulls the rug out from under us. It's nothing personal. That's its job. Each day, it unthinkingly uses this seemingly cruel technique to confront and awaken us within the adversity of calamities, or what I call "calamortunities." These obnoxious and painful opportunities can get our attention and shake us loose from our self-defeating attachment to our most earnest, cherished, split-up, limiting, and disastrous misassumptions or illusions. The universe graciously and sadistically invites us, thereby, to have an awakening or epiphany, to catch on to the cosmic con-game, and to graduate into paradoxical realms, as much as we can. Isn't that the point?

When life hurts our feelings; when it crosses us up and confronts us with these creatively/destructive "fierce teachers;" when it benevolently and malevolently strips us of all our illusions; when it betrays us; when it causes the most profound pain and confusion; when it rips away everything we think we can't live without; when it breaks us; and when it pushes us to the brink; ... that's when it's actually presenting us with exquisite opportunities to awaken, forge, anneal, enlarge, and strengthen ourselves all the more. Against our wills, it endows us, thereby, with precious, profound, centered, "CONFUSED," and sacred paradoxical truths.

Thus, enlightenment is free, but it costs us everything. That is, it strips us of all our preconceived notions and assumptions, ... all of them! This painful crucible induces a required detachment, a "first step," a necessary loss, or a therapeutic disillusionment. Even so and thereby, the universe gives us back exponentially more, ... much more than we could ever imagine. Like the Phoenix, we must die to our small, self-aggrandized, and mistaken selves. We must choose to fall for the cosmic con-game and lose everything; so that we can be reborn and reincarnated in the present moment; and so that we can gain an exponentially enhanced and pleasurable experience of the centered and integrated fullness of paradoxical reality.

Most humans are understandably reluctant to enter into such a glorious and terrible crucible. We're reluctant to pay the exorbitant and painful price of admission. We just don't come wired for this "jumping-into-the-fire," "falling-for-the-cosmic-con-game," and "losing-everything" sort of endeavour. It seems too weird, confusing, backwards, unprofitable, agonizing, unendurable, and downright suicidal. It's certainly a reluctantly acquired taste. It'll never be popular.

In fact, reality must drag us all against our wills, ... kicking, screaming, and digging in our heels on each painful step of the way towards our own small measure of uncommon, hard-earned, openly revealed, and yet elusive enlightenment and happiness. We just can't get there the easy, straightforward, and apparent way. No mortal is exempt.

This creatively/destructive crucible must catalyze the recapitulation of eons of humankind's revelations and pack them into each tiny little lifespan. There's so much to learn and so little time. And yet, this instant is also an eternity, if we just choose to drop in. Remember that other dimension of time. There's really plenty of present moment/eternity to let it unfold. There's no need to rush.

SUMMARY

PART TWO

    If our striving for paradoxical or integrated wisdom seems to be easy, clear, fast, acceptable, popular, and natural, we're likely deceiving ourselves, as usual. We're good at that. In fact, self-deceit may well comprise humanity's most exquisite and extensive form of genius. We're compulsive self-confirmation machines, especially while we're racing headlong in precisely the wrong direction.

    It takes most of us nearly half a century to come full circle and arrive merely where we started. We then realize that we possessed all we ever needed within, all along. We were already in paradise, or paradox. We were pre-endowed and "pre-disastered." We have and/or will spend decades struggling to accomplish endless, self-imposed, and yet required, practical, and realistic external objectives and responsibilities. Nevertheless, we inevitably find that there's nothing out there that's wholly admirable, heroic, fulfilling, or meaningful to accomplish or acquire.

    You can never get enough of that which you really do not want.

Erick Hoffer

The paradox is that we must consent to take these outer, circular, and futile journeys; get on this externalizing and busy bus of life's "occupational therapy;" choose one of life's many worthy meanings; and collect impressive and sanctioned accomplishments and destinations along the way; ... all in order to experience enough disastrous, instructive, and transformative failures and tragedies to foster an inner awakening; an abandonment of our entire and customary way of looking at things; a detachment from our impossible illusions; and a discovery that the ultimate destination is merely and gloriously within.

It's an inside job; nevertheless, outer quests are necessary, too. If we manage to awaken, our usual preoccupation with mere and single-pointed externals comes to feel empty and meaningless. It's time for us to move on from such childish and adolescent ways. After all, our ultimate achievement is simply a reunion with our quiet, ordinary, sacred, and integrated self, within. That's when the limited, two-dimensional, this-or-that, confused, and conflicted perspective of so-called normality expands into the centered, multidimensional, harmonious, illuminated, and "CON/FUSED" pleasure of paradoxical wisdom. We must choose to jump into the fire, in order to transcend confusion and replace it with "CON/FUSION."

> *Life is a spell so exquisite that everything conspires to break it.*
>
> Emily Dickinson

There are no ultimate, permanent, and universally accepted answers to life. Most miss the boat amidst the abundant, well-meaning, and yet more-or-less misinterpreted wisdom of any discipline. Moreover, there's no elite utopian land, group, or retreat where all have arrived and where we can bask in the womb-like warmth of pure, absolute, certain, shared, confirmed, and sanctioned enlightenment. Each individual must take the journey alone, although good and bad company can be equally illuminating. It's this inner awakening that's the point. Consciousness and substance merge, remember?

There's no utopian escape from the essential risk, confusion, and messiness of inner human nature, either. Its foibles and errors are never wholly eradicated and tidied up, no matter how deeply into wisdom we may go. After all, nothing about the self goes away, not even the seemingly dispensable, childish, foolish, or even traumatized aspects. Rather, all parts of our multidimensional selves must be fully accepted, welcomed, embraced, integrated, utilized, respected, and even revered. Split-up and contradictory confusion becomes an integrated and reconciled "CON/FUSION."

> *It is easy enough to praise men for the courage of their convictions. I wish I could teach the ... young ... the courage of their confusions.*
> John Ciardi

Hang on. We need patience, humility, and an enduring sense of humor. In fact, integrated consciousness engages the very same paradoxical reasoning as does a kindly, gentle, playful, resigned, and ironic (not sarcastic) sense of humor.

> *We should call every truth false which [is] ... not accompanied by at least one laugh.*
> F. Nietzsche

> *Man is most nearly himself when he achieves the seriousness of a child at play.*
> Heraclitus

Laughter is carbonated holiness.
> Anne Lamott

If we're predominantly humorless, extremist, perfectionistic, exclusive, superior, proud, self-aggrandizing, self-absorbed, power-hungry, attention-seeking, outside-focused, magical, preachy, negative, pessimistic, afraid, hopeless, nihilistic, critical, angry, pushy, complaining, long-suffering, angst-driven, chest-beating, duty-bound, and unhappy; we're failing to catch on to the cosmic con-game. There's no honor or merit in such self-imposed and supposedly heroic misery, or masochism.

It takes uncommon humility, tolerance, humor, and, most of all, forgiveness to realize that we've been so terribly and thoroughly hoodwinked about nearly everything that really matters in life, ... hoodwinked, that is, by our own wired-in, compulsive, well-intended, but disastrously mistaken misassumptions. Moreover and preposterously, it's even imperative that we consent to this hoodwinking many times along the way. That's how the ever-patient, non-personified, and indifferent cosmos teaches us. It's an enlightening and benevolent cosmic con-game.

At the end of the day, we discover just what kind of fools we are. We realize what kind of childish and misguided inner repetition-compulsion melody we've been unknowingly dancing to.

No delusion, no awakening.
> Zen saying

Life is a long lesson in humility.
> Max Shulman

Only two things last: shoes too small and foolishness.
> Minon Drouet

This hoodwinked/awakening, foolish/wisdom, mistaken/astuteness, endarkened/enlightenment, failure-ridden/success, confused/clarity, argumentative/collaboration, and condensed/expansion; ... these comprise our most profound and ineffable paradoxical solutions. This is how we learn to catch on to the cosmic con-game, in order to think, speak, experience, and behave in the most profoundly mastered dialect of Paradoxese. In essence, we become life-long students or beginners.

As Buddhists say, the cause of our suffering is attachment. Each day and moment, even over sixty or eighty, we must think like beginners and detach from our most cherished, wired-in, traditional, grandiose, pleasurable, and "forbidden fruit" ambitions, or illusions. We must free ourselves as much as possible from all our self-imposed, precious, and "splitting-up-of-fused-reality" shackles. This is how we recover from our tidy, split apart, partitioned, and miserable "knowledge of good and evil." It's how we get back to the centered, fused, integrated, and enlightened garden within.

The confidence we have in our beliefs is preposterous-and it is also essential.
                                    Daniel Kahneman

These disappointing disillusionments produce our most ultimate healing awakenings. This is when we transcend the limits of normal human nature and find out what kind of fools we really are. This is when we find the real treasure: our elusive, uncanny, paradoxically wise, and integrated self, within. It harmonizes with the universe's paradoxical con-game. Our paradoxically wise self hides cleverly and predominantly in the most deceptive place of all: right out in the open and amidst the merely modest, ordinary, routine, obvious, trite, mundane, humble, solitary, unpopular, uncool, kindly, and amusing. It can't be that simple, ordinary, playful, and unimpressive, can it? We demand our impressive drumrolls, trumpets, and melodramas. The ingenious universe displays and hides its uncanny secrets with such modest, understated, open book, and encoded treachery.

It is not at all easy to understand the simple.
E. Hoffer

So, take this humble inner journey with me. Let these concepts harmonize with and nurture your own already abundant, profound, paradoxical, and ultimate wisdom. It's wired in. We can best embrace the agony and ecstasy of life by being still, quiet, open, and alert, ... to the treasures within.

Don't worry. These obnoxiously/liberating pearls of wisdom are free and equally accessible along any path to everyone, everywhere, ... in any language. No one has a leg up. We all possess everything we need within, and yet we also need a helping hand. There are no shortcuts to take, no bribes to pay, and no clergy or scholars to hire. We each must do this ourselves, one step at a time. No one else can awaken to our collective, humble, inner, paradoxical, and integrated self.

The catch, however, is that we must spend decades searching for and earning that which is so freely and openly given to us from the very start. It's a pre-endowed, yet hard-earned and elusive enlightenment.

The heavens cannot open for the soul; they are already open.
James P. Carse

What you seek is seeking you.
Rumi

The world will freely offer itself to you to be unmasked, it has no choice, it will roll in ecstasy at your feet.
                                    Franz Kafka

Beyond a certain point, there is no return. This point has to be reached.
                                    F. Kafka

Here's hoping you choose to walk with me towards this weird, terrifying, mortifying, naked, amusing, glorious, and eye-opening point of no return. This uncanny and quietly ecstatic awakening is not just a mildly interesting academic exercise for extra credit. Rather, it's required. It's audaciously ambitious. It's beyond therapy, and yet it's not. It changes everything. It lands us not only on the moon, but into an entirely alien parallel universe; and yet, nothing on the outside needs to change. It's an invisible makeover. In fact, the more it shows, and the more we crow, the more it's not really so.

The following chapters outline a simple, boots on-the-ground, and practical method, which condenses into a simple mantra-mnemonic: "**B.E. K.I.N.D.**" It's designed to yield nothing short of an abundant, enriching, enduring, resilient, and quiet form of inner happiness, serenity, love, hope, fulfillment, meaning, balance, and peace, ... all amidst the inevitable maelstrom of confounding, desperate, frustrating, painful, and even un/bearable inner and external elements of reality.

None of the negative goes away. We must strive to use, embrace, revere, and even celebrate it, equally. Life's a fully balanced catastrophic/ecstasy. The ultimate goal is the emotional jujitsu of what I call "unreasonable happiness," or "unconditional happiness;" that is, a quiet, present moment, humble, war-torn, and finely centered serenity which transcends so-called normal, dualistic, and split-up reason. It's a clarifying/ "CON/FUSION."

This weird and backwards enlightenment thing is well worth it. We can do this. This should be fun.

CHAPTER 1

THE COSMIC CON-GAME

PART ONE

The gods too are fond of a joke.
           Aristotle

The universe is like a safe ... But the combination is locked up in the safe.
           Peter DeVries

Life is like playing a violin solo in public, and learning the instrument as you go along.
           Samuel Butler

We focus ... through ... a prism from which we can never be free except by exchanging prisms.
           Joseph Chilton Pierce

Many men go fishing all of their lives without knowing that it is not fish they are after.
           Henry David Thoreau

Dear Lord, please forgive me for all the terrible things I have done, and then maybe I'll forgive you for the terrible trick you played on me.
Robert Frost

The world wants to be deceived.
Sebastian Brant

The non-deified universe places us in a giant and elaborate enigma, maze, paradox, or practical joke, which I call "The Cosmic Con-Game." The cosmos then waits to see who among us can manage to decipher it. The con goes like this: It doesn't matter about our particular rearing, childhood, culture, language, nationality, religion, politics, skin pigment, era, or even century. After all, our species hasn't changed in any basic way for thousands of years. All multiracial humans on this tiny, insignificant, and accidental speck in the universe learn one of a few dozen versions of the same basic game, although each of us inevitably suffers from the conceit that our game is the correct, superior, and most up-to-date game for all people and for all time. This seemingly inconsequential and egocentric error of logic is woven seamlessly into all that is base and divine, horrible and sublime, about our species.

THE CHESS CON-GAME

For want of a better example, I call this global game, "chess." As children, we learn the chess rules and strategy of this particular family, neighborhood, school, society, ethos, religion, government, and so on. The better we get at playing chess, the more favors, advantages, and prizes we win.

If we're not so adept at playing chess, we can learn to "game" the system and play a hidden, backwards, and negative chess game within the game. In this "nothing succeeds like failure" sort of way, we convert defeats into even larger negative or backwards types of victories. This "secret victory of self-defeat" was the paradoxical theme of my first book.

In time, we learn a few positive or negative chess tricks and become outstanding positive or negative successes, at least in our own minds. Whether we limp along as low achievers or become wildly successful, we all think that we're really something special, or outstandingly inferior. Sadly, this self-aggrandizement, or egotism, is a necessary phase along the normal course of human psychological development. In fact, positive and negative self-aggrandizement or inflation are essentially the same, but I'll get to that later. The point is that each of us must build up an inflated self-image, so that we can later deflate and transcend it.

> *No delusion, no awakening.*
> Zen saying

RUG-PULLINGS

During our "terrible twenties" and "thrashing thirties," we go out into the real world and test drive our openly or surreptitiously inflated little self-esteems. Unfortunately, however, no matter how astutely or badly we play chess, the universe inevitably, persistently, and randomly pulls the rug out from under us. It's nothing personal. That's its job, to pierce and deflate these over-sized self-images and bring us down a notch or two.

> *The true way goes over a rope which is not stretched at any great height, but just above the ground. It seems designed more to make men stumble than to be walked upon.*
> F. Kafka

With each painful rug-pulling, the pieces and board go flying and get chipped and cracked. We bump our heads; we bleed; and we wallow in self-pity. We even show off our injuries and losses in a backward sort of way, by complaining about them. We think these existential insults earn us special sympathy and status. We manage to convince a fair portion of similarly duped fellow chess players to take pity on us and grant us special compensations, perks, and free rides.

We take these rug-pullings quite personally. We cry out in anguish to whatever gods may be about the terrible injustice of it all. "Why me? Unfair! Why can't the world just go the way I design it?" We blame others, fate, circumstances, and even gods. We then clean, stitch, and bandage our heads; clean up the blood stains; mend the damaged pieces and board; and dust ourselves off. Then, we retell and replay the highlights, continue to blame the outside and others, and try to manipulate others to shelter us from having to face, solve, and manage life's requisite riddles, failures, adversities, losses, pains, and tragedies. After all, our eyes are designed to look out there for solutions, not within.

> *One dog barks at a shadow, and a thousand dogs take it for reality.*
>
> Chinese proverb

> *We swim ... on a river of delusions and are effectually amused with houses and towns in the air, of which the men about us are dupes. 'Let there be an entrance opened for me into realities; I have worn the fool's cap too long.' ... Give us the cipher ...*
>
> Ralph Waldo Emerson

> *The real voyage of discovery consists not in seeking new landscapes, but in having new eyes.*
>
> Marcel Proust

> *Reality as ordinarily perceived is indeed a distortion and ... human suffering is the consequence of believing in that distorted view.*
>
> Arthur J. Deikman

We often consult with seemingly more ultimate, credentialed, and learned chess teachers and gurus, in order to further reinforce and sharpen our chess strategies and knowledge, so that this will not happen to us again, by God. Thereby, we manage to improve our win-loss records a bit. We tell ourselves that this is working. Sooner or later, however, the cosmos inevitably, randomly, and repeatedly continues to pull the rug out from under us, no matter how much we improve our games. That's its job.

CATCHING ON TO THE COSMIC CON-GAME: THE PUNCH LINE

If the head-bangings are harsh, intense, prolonged, repeated, and painful enough, they just might derail and block our chess game endeavors long enough to get our attention. Thereby, they might bang some uncommon sense into our foolish, stubborn, and swelled little heads. It's then that we might do something which is quite atypical among humans. We might be one of the ten percent who stop and notice that *we* may be wrong. What a concept! It dawns on us that no matter how well we play positive or negative chess, the universe pulls the rug out from under our tidy little games, every time. It's a sure-fire "no-win" "lose-lose."

When this finally dawns on us, we're ready to start to comprehend, appreciate, and accept the sacred gift that the universe has been trying to offer, all along. This comes in the form of an entirely new, surprising, and revolutionary insight or awakening. This is when we catch on to the cosmic con-game. As you may have already guessed, the punch line is that while we're so proud of our fancy chess sets, knowledge, and skills; the universe is, in fact, playing on the same board, ... but it's playing CHECKERS! ... CHECKERS! This is unbelievable! It's a game changer!

No wonder our moves didn't work. They couldn't have worked. We were playing the wrong game. What a grievously prolonged, disastrous, and catastrophic folly! We're all so completely hoodwinked! Of course! It couldn't have been otherwise. It turns out that our only real job on this planet is not to win or "game" the standard chess game at all, but rather to catch on to the cosmic con-game, to get the cosmic practical joke, to find out what kind of fools we are, and to switch games entirely, to the unapparent game, ... the simpler game that was right in front of our noses, all along. Now we can see with newly opened eyes.

This awakening, epiphany, or satori is totally unexpected and counterintuitive, ... a new "blind/vision." The merely two dimensional chess picture now expands into a totally unanticipated, exponentially expanded, and multidimensional hologram.

> *... in seeing the whole trick we have played on ourselves, we are free to awaken from the spell.*
> Ken Wilbur

> *[We] discover the ... reality we have ourselves created and put there to be sought.*
> Allen Wheelis

> *Shut your eyes in order to see.*
> Paul Gaugin

> *The best place to hide something, is in plain view.*
> Anonymous

> *The truth is the safest lie.*
> Anonymous

God hides things by putting them near us.
R. Emerson

There's absolutely no reason for being rushed along with the rush. Everyone should be free to go very slow.
... What you want, what you're hanging around in the world for, is for something to occur to you.
R. Frost

A GAME CHANGER

The real solution, then, is not to heroically persist in fighting the good-or-bad, win-or-lose, right-or-wrong fight. We miss the point by either complying with or gaming this standard and dualistic chess game. Either way, we're all mistakenly attached, thereby, to the very same useless, mistaken, and futile set of either-or rules. It's this very dualism which constitutes our fatal flaw. We fight between illusory and opposing distinctions until we realize that there is no fight in the first place, ... that we make the whole thing up.

Rather, the real solution is to become enlightened quitters. We must detach from and abandon the entire original and antagonistic chess game, itself. We must change out the whole paradigm and launch into an entirely new, simple, and expanded game. Checkers! This changes everything. This full appreciation and acceptance of the essentially absurd, backwards, and deceitful con-game of reality is, indeed, a reluctantly acquired taste. It's also essential.

Said another way, we must take our eyes off of the illusion of dualistic, win-or-lose, this-or-that goals; in order to notice that our spectacles, themselves, are the problem. They have flawed lenses which are prisms and which split up unified realities into the mirages of apparently opposite extremes. Our supposedly clarifying lenses thus distort the very reality that we thought we were seeing so clearly. Further, we realize that we must throw these self-deceiving "splitting-up-of-reality" glasses away entirely, and fix our gaze, instead, upon our prodigious internal and ever-renewing folly.

> *Zen is like looking for the spectacles that are sitting on your nose.*
> Zen saying

Now we can tend to the real job, that of realizing our own original errors of logic. That's when we can alter them and begin to recover from our immense self-deceit and self-conceit. After all, it's called a "confidence" game. We're too confident in our distorted illusions. Now we can start the humbling process of awakening and redeeming ourselves.

"CALAMORTUNITIES"

When we manage to decipher the cosmic con-game, we can see that existential and painful rug-pullings are actually the non-personified universe's sadistically/benevolent method of opening our eyes. These necessary rug pullings are really disguised lessons, opportunities, and treasures. I call them "calamortunities." These are the universe's gifts, the proverbial and enlightening whacks on the head, ice cold slaps of the face, or lightening bolts in the dark night, which can show us the way out of our dualistic blindness or quandary. The universe hurts our feelings, because we need them to be hurt, in order to open our minds and invite us to take the "road less traveled," that is, the road towards *inner* and paradoxical realms.

SELF-DECEIVING MACHINES

Typically, however, we stubborn little humans are blinded by our externally-oriented eyes and preconceived misconceptions. Instead of awakening to deeper and centered paradoxes within, we stubbornly continue to grasp for the dualistic rewards of the illusory "win-lose" goals out *there*. Thereby, we fail to comprehend these painful, and yet indispensable, insights. We wouldn't notice a paradox if it stood on its head in front of us, which is, in fact, what it does.

We're irrational, self-deceiving, and self-justifying machines, confirming the pseudo-veracity of our hopelessly futile and merely two-dimensional chess strategies to ourselves, even in the face of repeated, mounting, and obvious evidence to the contrary. We just argue our misguided little cases all the more.

> *If the law is on your side, argue the law. If the facts are on your side, argue the facts. If neither is on your side, argue loudly.*
>
> legal adage

Instead of taking a new and hard look at ourselves, finding out what kind of fools we are, and changing our own erroneous strategies and misassumptions, which, incidentally, comprises the real work of psychotherapy; we usually press on blindly for a lifetime with the same old doomed strategy of making excuses and blaming the outside. We even compound our folly by taking increasingly advanced chess lessons with our similarly mistaken friends and at the knees of enthusiastic but similarly misguided chess masters. Misery loves company.

> *Who looks outside dreams; who looks within awakens.*
>
> Carl Gustav Jung

It took me all my life to learn what not to play.
                                     Dizzy Gillespie

Man is like a swimmer who is fully dressed and hampered ... by his clinging clothes. ... To have the impression that he is swimming properly; ... may make him feel better and [yet it drowns] him ...
                                     Latif Ahmad

Men's value judgments are guided absolutely by their desire for happiness, and are therefore merely an attempt to bolster up their illusions by arguments.
                                     Sigmund Freud

DRAGGED INTO WISDOM

Don't get me wrong, here. We humans are constitutionally incapable of grasping the fullness of paradoxical wisdom without these repeated and painful rug pulling lessons. There are no pre-emptive, fast lane, and pain-free detours around life's enlightening adversities and failures. The cosmos must force us into wisdom at gunpoint, against our will. It has to drag us into the fire, while we resist, kick, and scream at every small and illuminating step along the way. No one in their right mind would actually volunteer to seek out such a seemingly backwards, painful, weird, paradoxical, and foolish wisdom. Unfortunately, we all must learn each lesson the hard way, repeatedly, and over an entire lifespan.

HOODWINKED

Think of it! We're all so inevitably and totally hoodwinked by the cosmic con-game. We're all initially duped by the universe into playing the catastrophically wrong game, the game that most around us solemnly and authoritatively certify as the correct game. We must find a way to forgive, accept, and reconcile ourselves to the fact that we're so terribly and tragically mistaken about almost everything that really matters in life. Everything! It's a thorough and fundamental hoodwinking. No one escapes. We all must lose face and find out what kind of fools we are, and then we must find our way "back to the garden," so to speak; that is, to the abundant, healing, and sacred garden of integrated paradoxical wisdom, within.

Central metaphors from earliest antiquity depict different versions of this same basic cosmic hoodwinking theme. I've mentioned Plato's Cave Allegory from the fifth century, B.C. In the Old Testament, as well, humanity is described as falling for the serpent's con-game, eating "the forbidden fruit," and thereby acquiring the dualistic "knowledge of good and evil." We sell our souls to the Faustian devil in exchange for the short-sighted and dubious privilege of chasing after the smoke and mirrors of mere illusion. The price for such seductive and imaginary treasures is far too dear. The cosmic con-game basically dupes us into being contradictory, perfectionistic, and extremist; instead of harmonious, reconciled, and centered.

Once this vastly and wildly distorted dualistic perspective is installed in the hard drives of our minds, we're lost. This is our collective tragic flaw. Thereafter, we're doomed to dance to the futile missteps of our computer's mis-programmed illogic. We're expelled, thereby, not from the Garden of Eden out there, but from the Garden of Eden within, with its already non-dualistic, balanced, centered, integrative, harmonious, "both-and," and paradoxical wisdom. Our "fall" is from this centered, unified, and sacred inner grace. It usually takes those few of us who awaken decades to retrieve it.

This mistaken dualistic logic is our "original sin," our collective originally mistaken pathway. It sets the stage for so many years and even entire lifetimes of playing the wrong and contradictory game, of being so thoroughly hoodwinked, of being expelled and lost. At the end of the day, we all must repeatedly and patiently redeem and forgive ourselves, somehow.

> *The secret of life is to appreciate the pleasure of being terribly deceived.*
> O. Wilde

> *[None] can be worth anything until they have discovered that they are fools.*
> Melbourne

> *To be conscious that you are ignorant is a great step to knowledge.*
> Benjamin Disraeli

> *The aim of a joke is not to degrade the human being but to remind him that he is already degraded.*
> George Orwell

CHAPTER 1

THE COSMIC CON-GAME

PART TWO

NATURE'S USE OF DECEPTION

The enormous trickery of the cosmic con-game is nothing personal. In fact, nature relies heavily on deception. It's everywhere, from the reciprocal dances of predator and prey; to the difference between what we see and what is too immense or microscopic for us to perceive; to the contrast between what we know and what we don't know about ourselves; and even to the balance between visible and dark matter. In nature, practically nothing is totally as it appears to be.

> *Trickery has always been a part of the healing process.*
> *By no means need it be sinister.*
> Sheldon Kopp

I know. Before my own small measure of awakening, I didn't like this universal and deceptive rug pulling, either. I wanted the universe to just be forthright, transparent, honest, and fair. Much about the design of the universe wasn't to my personal taste, but then, I wasn't consulted.

I wouldn't have had the wisdom, creativity, or practical joke kindness and cruelty to create such a baffling, deceptive, counter-intuitive, and painful hoodwinking scheme, wherein everyone is so profoundly fooled, usually for an entire lifetime. I wouldn't have had the paradoxical genius to create an enigma which disguises itself as an external treasure hunt; whose solution eludes all but the most unconventional, insightful, discerning, self-reliant, courageous, and resilient; and whose inner solution is freely given from the start, and yet must be repeatedly overlooked and then rediscovered as a result of our regrettably long, well-intended, misguided, mistaken, thwarted, seductive, required, and external endeavors.

We could theorize that those who are terribly afflicted right up front during their childhoods or teens might actually be the lucky ones on this weird and backwards planet. Their chess ambitions are dashed in a benevolently/cruel way from the very start, so that they theoretically have the opportunity to step back, escape the hubbub, look within, and expose the cosmic con-game at an earlier age. Sometimes this takes place. Unfortunately, however, many of these paradoxically blessed individuals merely learn to game the system and play a negative and victimized version of the same old chess game.

We might consider parents to be another such un/lucky group. Although children grant us vast and loving rewards, fulfillments, and lessons, indeed; they also demolish our idealistic agendas, notions, schedules, ambitions, funds, and possessions. Like the cosmic con-game, they nurture, redeem, and break our hearts. That's their job.

Thereby and unknowingly, children teach us far more than we teach them. They serve as our ultimate, beloved, and rug pulling little mentors, opening our eyes, and forcing us to stop and reevaluate our idealistic, but hopelessly mistaken chess game priorities. They expose us as the children grown tall that we are. They unknowingly and instinctively act in concert with the sadistically/benevolent and rug-pulling universe to enlighten us, to help us to catch on to the cosmic con-game, and to invite us to change games, entirely. They invite us, thereby, to redeem and discover our larger selves. What an unexpected and paradoxical blessing. Unfortunately, most parents, too, fail to awaken. So much, then, for our brash and idealistic theories.

EGO DEFLATION

The mortifying shame that our folly is so very exposed, that we've been so profoundly and chronically "had" by the universe; ... this is a necessary and deflating blow to our inflated little self-esteems. This required lesson is essential for our awakening. The universe must hurt our feelings. It must embarrass and humble us. It's good for us.

Like Icarus, we ignore the warning signs about our pursuit of needlessly risky, foolhardy, and larger-than-life ambitions. We fly too high and close to the sun, every time, only to singe our wings and plummet back to earth. After all, the deadliest sin is the sin of pride, grandiosity, or inflated self-esteem. None of us can take even the first step towards anything even remotely approaching redemption, wisdom, or awakening, until we do something very unusual among humans and exercise the humility to admit that *we* are wrong. We must shrink and deflate, in order to expand. We must surrender to reality. This is not what we had in mind.

We are always wrong in some essential way. ... We are never living out ... the story we think we are.

J. Carse

We inevitably spend our terrible twenties, thrashing thirties, and frantic forties trying to build ourselves up, according to conventional, contrary, dualistic, and "this-or-that" chess rules. This takes us in precisely the wrong direction, yet we must do this. It's a mandatory introductory course in the universe's circular, hoodwinking, provocative, and paradoxical curriculum. In fact, we all must freely consent to this initial hoodwinking, to this being strapped with our backs to the entrance to Plato's cave. We must choose to interpret reality according to mere shadows on the back walls. We must eat the proverbial forbidden fruit and volunteer to banish ourselves, as a result, from the garden.

It usually takes those few of us who even begin to awaken four or five decades to chop these compulsively re-aggrandizing and re-inflating self-images, these seven headed hydras, down to merely human size. Each time we think we've achieved a curative and stable humility, the inflated/small self reappears in one disguised form after another. Only when can we become persistently, authentically, thoroughly, and astutely small and humble can we begin to re-enter the garden of our paradoxically wise self within. He or she was waiting for us, all along.

LEARNING TO APPRECIATE AND FORGIVE BEING SO MISTAKEN

Maybe it's some consolation that we're not alone. All of us are fooled, ... no exceptions. I can assure you that I, too, have been and will be duped by almost every possible foolish and self-aggrandizing illusion. Ask those who knew me then, ... and now. I'm still learning the hard way. I have a lot to learn.

Maybe being thoroughly mistaken can be regarded as not being so unbearably embarrassing and humiliating, after all. In fact, we might come to see such humbling and healing revelations as helpful, precious, and even sacred passages. Maybe, we can get over our grandiose demand to know it all right from the start, without the benefit of those painful rug-pulling life lessons which we call "experience." We all must learn the hard way. Maybe we can forgive ourselves that our well designed and yet hopelessly idealistic end runs around life's adversities fizzle so badly and result in such terrible, redemptive, and instructive pain and loss.

> *If I had to live my life again, I'd make the same mistakes, only sooner.*
> Tallulah Bankhead

Maybe we can emerge from our phobia or prejudice against fully realizing just what kind of fools we are. We so resist the clarity of realizing that we're such awkward and life-long beginners. Maybe we can learn to even look forward to rug-pulling revelations to come, so that we can relish the inevitably hit-and-miss process of learning and growing. Maybe then we can really mean it when we ask others to critique us. We all need a collaboratively and compassionately critical helping hand. This helps us to move on and improve. Without it, we remain mired in the sticky self-deception of our own self-congratulation. We have so much to learn, and there's so little time within one puny little lifespan.

> *The necessity to ward off any self-accusation stunts the capacity for constructive self-criticism and therefore mars the possibility of learning from mistakes.*
> K. Horney

In fact, if we're not embarrassed when we review past errors, then we haven't really learned from them. Failures teach us to face our folly, so that we can let go of mistaken assumptions; so that we can stop beating our heads against reality; so that we can become open to the life-long process of change; and so that we can better learn to accept and harmonize with what is.

A self-appointed know-it-all has to be so right from the very start that he or she can't be open to any further learning or transforming experience. He stunts his growth and fixates himself at lower levels of understanding. He unknowingly places a ceiling on just how much unreasonably pleasurable insight and wisdom he can attain. He sentences himself to a lifetime of playing the foolish, futile, miserable, and self-limiting "know-it-all-already" chess game.

Thus seen, it's more than just permissible to admit to being wrong. Such humility is what makes us fully and gloriously human. It completes us. Failure and mistakenness are essential to our awakening, to the cultivation of the fullness of our very soul. They're good for us.

It's crucial to learn to forgive our inevitably foolish youth and early adulthood. Mistakes are just part of the training. We were destined to play the wrong game, all of us. If we can be humble enough to admit to and forgive our own essential mistakenness, we can then concentrate on the challenging enough task of learning and relearning the ropes of our new, improved, paradoxical, and more realistic clarity.

As a result, our limited and two-dimensional vision of reality transforms into a vastly expanded, multidimensional, and awakened perspective. It's only then that we can begin to see the fullness of reality clearly and for the first time. Let others stunt their own growth and waste their energies disputing past right-or-wrong, good-or-bad calls and injustices. We don't have time for such replays. We need to graduate, altogether, from this needlessly split-up and win-lose consciousness. We have our hands full with the difficult and boots-on-the-ground job of growing into more ultimate paradoxical wisdom, each day.

CON-GAME HUMOR

Some may understandably object to my explanation of something as serious and even crucial as enlightenment by using the metaphor of a con-game or practical joke. This seems to demean and belittle the whole and profound process of awakening. It sounds too trivial, deceitful, superficial, and paternalistic. Believe me, this realization of *The Divine Comedy* was not my first choice. I was a serious, dedicated, preoccupied, proficient, and chess-playing know-it-all. The universe, however, had to beat me bloody, bang some sense into my thick head, tickle my funny bone, and, thereby, open my eyes. It had to show me what kind of fool I was. It still does. The joke's on us all.

Now I echo many others, such as Dante, the laughing Buddha, and the Dalai Lama. I place gentle, kindly, self-effacing, and paradoxical humor among the highest of virtues. The basis of all integrated consciousness and wisdom is paradox, and paradox just happens to also be the basis of gentle and kindly humor. Who knew?

A truth is transforming, and a joke is funny, both for the same reason; because of the sudden and unexpected juxtaposition and integration of opposites. It's a magnificent and catch-you-off-guard spasm of fusion or alchemy, so to speak. Awakening to the humor of paradoxical wisdom is a sneak wisdom attack. It's a pleasurable and instantaneous induction of integrated paradoxical consciousness. It's the premier antidote to the dualistic cosmic con-game. If we catch on to the con, we then approach life with an ironic, kindly, sweet, and gentle sense of humor.

> *Man is most nearly himself when he achieves the seriousness of a child at play.*
> Heraclitus

Life does not cease to be funny when people die, any more than it ceases to be serious when people laugh.
George Bernard Shaw

You cannot deal with the most serious things in the world unless you also understand the most amusing.
Winston Churchill

Nothing in man is more serious than his sense of humor; it is the sign that he wants all the truth.
Mark Van Doren

So a sense of humor ... involves seeing the basic irony of the juxtaposition of extremes, so that one is not caught taking them seriously, so that one does not [earnestly] ... play their game of hope and fear.
Chogyam Trungpa

A serious and good philosophical work could be written consisting entirely of jokes.
L. Wittgenstein

The celebration of life and of joy is the only thing finally that brings healing. Understanding gets us only so far.
Joseph Campbell

We should tackle reality in a slightly jokey way, otherwise we miss its point.
Lawrence Durrell

Pleasure is the only thing to live for. Nothing ages like happiness.
O. Wilde

Imagination was given to man to compensate him for what he is not, and a sense of humor was provided to console him for what he is.
Robert Walpole

Laughter is a tranquilizer with no side effects.
Anonymous

Learning to laugh at yourself is the surest sign of maturity.
Anonymous

Laughter is carbonated holiness.
Anne Lamott

Think of your problems as a challenge in a game you enjoy playing.
Anonymous

What Is Success. To laugh often and love much.
R. Emerson

To know is not as good as to love. To love is not as good as to enjoy.
Confucius

Humor is an affirmation of dignity, a declaration of our superiority to all that befalls us.
Romaine Gary

The sound of laughter has always seemed to me the most civilized music in the universe.
Peter Ustinov

> *The joyfulness of infinite play, its laughter, lies in learning to start something we cannot finish.*
> James P. Carse

> *What is Buddha nature. To laugh.*
> The Buddha

THE ILLUSION OF SMOOTH-SAILING "WOMB-SERVICE"

Awakening doesn't produce an endlessly smooth sea of pain-free serenity. That's the siren song of yet another hoodwinking illusion, this time the illusion of "smooth-sailing," or "womb-service." It's our attempt to redesign the world according to our overly-idealistic, perfectionistic, self-aggrandizing, and self-centered specifications. We stamp our feet. We want what we want, and when we want it. Paradoxical humor doesn't deny or belittle life's considerable and even un/bearable pain, grief, and sorrow, all of which continue, whether we awaken or not. No mortal is immune. Such is life. As Buddhists say, "There is suffering." That's just a given.

> *There is praise and blame, gain and loss, fame and disrepute. Did you think this would not happen to you?*
> The Buddha

When awakened, we simply learn to stop adding to life's normal and requisite pain and suffering. After all, the most skillful art of living is embodied by how well we keep our sense of humor amidst the never ending frustrations, adversities, failures, tragedies, and calamities of life. Anyone can handle the good times.

Do not assume that he who seeks to comfort you now, lives untroubled ... His life may also have much sadness and difficulty that remains far beyond yours. Were it otherwise, he would never have been able to find these words.

R. M. Rilke

Amidst the distracting commotion of grasping-and-avoiding, praising-and-blaming; celebrating and grieving; ... we fail to notice that it's not the outer deprivations, losses, pains, ailments, tragedies, and setbacks of life that cause our pain. Rather, we cause our pain by the very pursuit of this inner demand for an endlessly comfortable, pain-free, and serene state of smooth-sailing. This is what inevitably dashes us into the shoreline rocks. Those seductive siren songs out there really spring from within. The universe cons us, because we want to be conned, ... by the mere and ever-receding mirages of our own impossible and extremist illusions.

Like Odysseus, we must strap ourselves to the mast and resist the folly of our own most urgent and self-destructive ambitions. If we don't, we fail to notice that such illusory prizes are mere consolation or booby-prizes. They're mere distractions and decoys from the search for authentic and abundant riches within. They're just part of nature's un/conscious hoodwinking con-game.

Complaining, whining, and being negative about life's rug-pullings are easy. These compound the folly by justifying and thus imprisoning ourselves in it. Achieving a sense of reconciliation, understanding, forgiveness, love, humor, and hope amidst life's most painful paradoxes, ... now that's hard. Such uncanny, compromised, integrated, and murky clarity leads to a centered coming together, to love. Isn't that the point, ... coming together? Any unawakened fool can split and tear apart.

THE AMUSEMENT OF THE GODS

Why does the universe reveal its deepest answers in the form of such baffling and painful riddles and enigmas? Why does it rely so heavily on secrecy, deception, seduction, and trickery? Why are the answers so silent, invisible, humble, ordinary, whispered, unimpressive, and seemingly inaccessible?

Perhaps whatever gods may be find it amusing to wind us up, imbue us with instinctive, archetypal, and impossible illusions; and then sit back and see who among us can decipher their con-game, find our way through their intricate maze, and rise, thereby, above our normal, wired-in, and foolish human nature. Maybe such gods place celestial bets. Maybe they really are lovingly/malevolent, as others have described.

Maybe the gods are only interested in those few who catch on to the cosmic con-game and who harmonize with their celestial, enigmatic, symphonic, and practical joking paradoxical wisdom. Maybe they just want acknowledgment, company, and a few laughs. Maybe these redemptive and come-from-behind harmonies produce magnificent and endless celestial laughter or even intergalactic orgasms. Who knows?

On the other hand, maybe all this is nothing more than a colossal, random, and impersonal cosmic accident. We tend to conjure up faces in the clouds and god-like intention amidst nature's care/less and uncanny forces. The possibility of infinite and impersonal randomness doesn't actually detract from the imponderable and innate genius, beauty, meaning, splendor, and wonder of the whole hoodwinking cosmos, at any rate. Maybe the point is to harmonize with the perfectly-balanced and paradoxical rhythms and secrecy of the universe's essence, be it gravity, dark matter, God, paradox, or whatever. Maybe the innate and non-personified paradox of the universe moves us in the same way that it attracts two chemical strands of DNA to mindlessly combine into those vastly mysterious states that we call life and consciousness. Maybe such musings are beyond us.

CHAPTER 1

THE COSMIC CON-GAME

PART THREE

The cosmic con-game metaphor contains a few additional lessons.

PROFOUND TRUTH AS SIMPLE, NON-DRAMATIC

First, the new and transformative checkers game is a simpler game. This runs counter to our compulsively self-aggrandizing chess-playing mind, which loves to make everything so impressively complex. We mistakenly think that if we're to awaken to profound and life-changing insights, these must be intricate, complex, convoluted, ingenious, and indecipherable. This makes us feel so very special, superior, unique, and grand. It makes the process of awakening needlessly complicated, however. We're such "drama-mamas," indeed. This is why Kurt Vonnegut referred to our self-aggrandizing chess-playing brains as "these tumors at the end of our spines which cause so much trouble."

In all things, the supreme excellence is simplicity.
Henry Wadsworth Longfellow

Simplicity is the most difficult thing to secure in this world; it is the last limit of experience and the last effort of genius.

George Sand

The truth is too simple: one must always get there by a complicated route.

G. Sand

Wisdom consists in not knowing; he who thinks that by widening his knowledge he is getting nearer to wisdom is merely destroying wisdom. ... knowledge, despite its obvious benefits, does sometimes have the unfortunate effect of only removing us from that which is of primal importance.

Shen Tao

this in-seeing ... is tragically easy to under-value, even dismiss offhand as quite trivial. In actual fact, its immense depth and spiritual power are nearly always overlooked ... this least expensive of realizations comes to us backed by no mystical credentials, endorsed by no burst of cosmic consciousness, no ecstasy. Quite the contrary, it's an all-time low rather than a high, a valley rather than one of those famous peak experiences.

D. E. Harding

We complicate the matter of inner growth by seeking out only the most brilliant and charismatic interpreters, lecturers, philosophers, and gurus, who speak in the most fashionable, impressive, obscure, and foreign-accented jargon. They must wear the right costumes, write the best books, and take the right drugs, all of which we, too, can wear, read, and use. We pride ourselves on being the first to teach about their books, whether we've read and understood them or not. "*We're* the in-crowd, and you're not."

Nature, on the other hand, prefers plain, simple, subtle, silent, non-dramatic, casual, unimpressive, easy, effortless, and elegant solutions. There's no sound track, drum-roll, fanfare, melodrama, or adrenalin rush. The answers seem so trite and readily available, right in front of our noses. We tell ourselves that there's got to be more to it than that. The cosmos is an understated and consummate trickster. It often even poses as folly.

> *A proverb distills the wisdom of the ages, and only a fool is scornful of the commonplace.*
> W. Somerset Maugham

> *The aspects of things that are most important for us are hidden because of their simplicity and familiarity.*
> L. Wittgenstein

> *The purloined letter, in Edgar Allan Poe's story, escaped observation by being excessively obvious.*
> D.E. Harding

NO ONE IS "SPECIAL"

Second, the playing pieces in checkers are all basically the same. This contrasts with the well-delineated hierarchy of chess pieces, each with its own special, unique, and exclusive power and status. We humans love the illusions of status, uniqueness, separateness, right-wrong, and superiority-inferiority. We seize on any pretext to distinguish ourselves from the pack. We love the sound and feel of looking down on others. It's one of our favorite pastimes. In fact, we routinely harm and kill each other over such illusory differences. I call this the "terminally-unique conceit."

In checkers, there's no such thing as specialness. Anyone can be "kinged." We're equal brothers and sisters. In fact, at a deeper level and beneath all these unimportant, artificial, and distracting external distinctions and roles, we're uniquely/identical twins.

We are all more the same than different.
Harry Stack Sullivan

Every person bears the whole stamp of the human condition.
M. Montaigne

Once the game is over, the king and the pawn go back into the same box.
Italian saying

Why set up a Group or Faction - which ... splits up humanity into us enlightened insiders and those endarkened outsiders ...
D. E. Harding

Whatever our souls are made of, yours and mine are the same.
Evelyn Bronte

The brotherhood of man is not a mere poet's dream; it is a most depressing and humiliating reality.
O. Wilde

The illusion of superiority is a seductive and self-aggrandizing siren song. When it comes to life's most important and authentic task of awakening to the hidden treasures within, we're all on a level playing field. No one has an enlightenment advantage. Each individual is the only person in all of history who can awaken to his or her paradoxically wise self. No one else can do this for us. In fact, apparent advantages, such as wealth, power, status, success, possessions, fame, ease, health, intellect, talent, beauty, and so on, ... these often serve to further obscure and block any significant degree of authentic inner awakening.

> *I have yet to meet an ignorant man whose roots are not embedded in my soul.*
> K. Gibran

> *It is the greatest of advantages to enjoy no advantage at all.*
> H. Thoreau

> *New York City is filled with the same kind of people I left New Jersey to get away from.*
> Fran Liebowitz

> *Anyone can be polite to a king, but it takes a civilized person to be polite to a beggar.*
> Anonymous

ONE MOUNTAIN PEAK, MANY PATHWAYS

Third, in both games, the specific pathway we choose is of no real importance. The quiet and plain truth is that ultimate answers are free, totally exposed, and readily available to everyone, each moment, and along any of life's pathways. There's no need to change jobs, professions, spouses, friends, crowds, locations, clubs, religions, libraries, wardrobes, or such. The indispensable, illuminating, and painful rug-pullings along any path can lead to the very same simple, profound, paradoxical, and generic truths. Efforts to get ahead and distinguish our special and separate selves miss the point. Toxic, deprived, abusive, inhumane, addictive, or traumatic settings and paths do matter, to be sure, but I'll get to that, later.

Within my limited knowledge of humanity's great religions, philosophies, psychologies, arts, literatures, theaters, meditations, and such; I find that all these seemingly disparate disciplines arrive at the exact same generic and core-curriculum wisdom. "One mountain peak, many pathways." Nevertheless, most in any culture or era miss the point and fail to decipher the cosmic con-game. Most are like the proverbial blindfolded wise men, who feel different parts of the same elephant and come to vastly different conclusions.

The truth is a mirror which God lets fall to earth. It shatters into pieces. Each human picks up a piece and thinks he possesses [all] the truth.
Meister Eckhart

This is counterintuitive. No matter which route in life we choose, we can't miss out on ultimate wisdom. It's as simple as that. Once we decipher the cosmic con-game, we discover the same generic wisdom on open display literally everywhere, each moment. It's hidden in plain sight. If a teacher can't say it simply, he or she doesn't know what he's talking about. We need no special credentials.

You may follow one stream. Realize that it leads to the Ocean. Do not mistake the stream for the ocean.
The Naqshbandi Order

God made Truth with many doors to welcome every believer who knocks …
K. Gibran

All religious presentations are varieties of one truth, more or less distorted.
Khwaja Salahudin
of Bokhara

The ultimate unity of the various religions of the world ... like the spokes of a wheel ... emanate from a common center.
Jacob Needleman

... a single stream of meaning and intent beyond the diversity of religious forms.
Claudio Naranjo

The ways are as many as the breaths in a man.
Sufi saying

You do not need to leave your room. Remain sitting at your table and listen. Do not even listen, simply wait. Do not even wait, be quiet, still, and solitary. The world will freely offer itself to you to be unmasked, it has no choice, it will roll in ecstasy at your feet.
F. Kafka

To believe your own thought is to believe that what is true for you ... is true for all men, - that is genius.
R. Emerson

The adventure the hero is ready for is the one he gets.
Joseph Campbel

"GETTING OVER" *OURSELVES*

Fourth, one skillful way of advancing a checkers piece is by jumping over the opponent's pieces. We can take equally skillful jumps over our own pieces, as well. We must, indeed, surmount significant external adversities, losses, tragedies, and competitions in life. More importantly, however, we must overcome, transcend, or "jump over," our own inner and unperceived obstacles, as well. These are far more formidable. We must "get over ourselves;" that is, our own self-created, self-limiting, self-sabotaging, self-blinding, and self-aggrandizing misassumptions, or "karma."

WE AND OUR "OPPONENT" DANCE AS ONE

Fifth, when we change games, we discover that the most profound objective of any game is to enjoy playing the game, to relish the moment-by-moment process and comradery. The objective has little to do with winning or gaming the specific contest. In addition, we discover that we and our designated opponent are not so much in competition or combat as we are in a highly cooperative, collaborative, and exquisite dance. As we play, we cooperate with each other in order to enjoy the movement, itself.

When competition pushes us to our finest performance, we discover what athletes, politicians, and others find, ... that, in the end, they need each other in order to discover, evoke, embrace, and display their finest selves. We discover that we and our designated adversaries are one.

INSIGHT: CROWNED ONLY WITH OUR DISCARDED OTHER HALF

Sixth, in checkers, when we finally make our way to the end of the board, we're "crowned," indeed, but only with the other half of ourselves, our discarded and unconscious selves. It turns out that the only accomplishment or arrival that really matters is that of discovering, embracing, and reconciling as much as we can with this other half of ourselves, which includes our paradoxically wise selves, as well. That's it. It's that simple. This is called insight.

The heroes and heroines in legends all around the globe realized at the end of their long odysseys that there was nothing all that important "out there" to see, experience, learn, acquire, or accomplish, in the first place. There's actually nowhere to go and nothing to prove. All the most crucial answers are within, where they've been, all along, waiting for us to discover them. External achievements, adventures, and crusades are predominantly self-created projects and decoys, ... mere distractions. They serve as material for our self-aggrandizing story lines or narratives. We think these make us more interesting, accomplished, secure, attractive, and unique.

These miraculous built-in movie cameras, our eyes, are designed to look out there, not within, where the most valuable treasures reside. We're thus endlessly duped by our own eyes. What a giant, distracting, and ever-receding mirage. We actually need nothing and no one out there to teach, fulfill, and complete us; and yet, paradoxically, we also do. More about that, later.

At the end of the day, the most challenging obstacle to our awakening is merely our own mind. This insight constitutes perhaps the most important contribution of meditation, philosophy, and psychology.

We have met the enemy, and the enemy is ourselves.
             Pogo

Sooner or later each of us must take the step that separates him from his ... mentors; each of us must have some cruelly lonely experience - even if most people cannot take much of this and soon crawl back. ... Each man has only one vocation - to find the way to himself.
Herman Hesse

No single event can awaken within us a stranger totally unknown to us. To live is to be slowly born.
Antoine Saint-Exupery

*Insight ... isn't simply learning something mildly interesting about yourself. It is **becoming** yourself.*
Janed Malcolm

The final mystery is oneself.
O. Wilde

The most important victory is the victory over one's self.
Oriental saying

The ideal we embrace is our better self.
Anonymous

REPRESSION AND PROJECTION

In fact, the checkers pieces we're crowned with turn out to be precisely the ones which we scorn and try to disown. We don't want these "disreputable" or less than ideal aspects, ... our anger, rage, cruelty, sloth, greed, lust, self-centeredness, inconsiderateness, jealousy, envy, treachery, fear, and so on.

We hide these so-called defects from ourselves by using two favorite defense mechanisms. First we stash or "repress" them into the unperceived depths of our unconscious minds. Presto! We're no longer even aware of their existence. Gone! What a relief! Second, we export or "project" these unwanted aspects onto others. By using our projective, or "projectoscopic," eyes, we convince ourselves that *other* people possess all the bad stuff, not us. We can further distract ourselves from the realization of our own negative aspects by becoming dedicated, thereafter, to the preposterous fool's errand of saving those others from their inner demons. That way, there's no need to waste our time looking within. What astonishing, arrogant, distracting, and destructive blindness!

> *I am firm. You are obstinate. He is a pig-headed fool.*
> Katherine Whitehorn

ALREADY IN PARADISE

When we catch on to the cosmic con, we're astonished to find out that we were already in paradise, or paradox, all along … we just didn't know it. Like the protagonists in *The Iliad and the Odyssey* and other similar stories all over the world, … at the end of our long and epic journeys, battles, and contests, we arrive precisely where we started. We realize that we were already where we needed to be all along, but our vision was blocked by our own preconceived, externalizing, self-important, and ambitious notions.

> *Marvelous! Marvelous! All beings are already enlightened! It is only because of their delusions that they don't realize this.*
> The Buddha

> *What a miserable thing life is: you're living in clover, only the clover isn't good enough.*
> Bertold Brecht

Man is unhappy because he doesn't know he's happy. It's only that. That's all! That's all! If anyone finds out he'll become happy at once, that minute... It's all good.
       F. Dostoevsky

There are questions that we wouldn't be able to get over if we weren't by our very nature [already] set free from them.
       F. Kafka

You can't get there from here ... For the place I really have to reach is where I must already be.
       L. Wittgenstein

...What we really want is what we [already] have, and not realizing this we crave different things we lack.
       C. Naranjo

...we make a journey to the 'promised land,' the other shore, and we have arrived when we realize that we were there all along.
       C. Trungpa

Man is born free, and everywhere he is in chains.
       J. Rousseau

Enlightenment can never be gained because it is ... already present.
       K. Wilber

We are all perfectly enlightened already. ... Everything one's heart could possibly desire is freely given from the very start.
       D. E. Harding

> *[The] wisdom that exists, exists in what you already have.*
> Pema Chodron

PATHWAY VERSUS THE GOAL

So, the present moment pathway turns out to be what's important, not specific externals or goals. All our external pursuits merely set the stage for our most important and sacred task of retrieving and engaging our inner and paradoxical wisdom, which was there, all along. Tell that to the children. They won't believe us any more than we believed our elders. Just like us, they think they must launch into unprecedented, innovative, award-winning, exclusive, and amazing outer adventures, crusades, causes, and quests; only to later find, with experience and upon reflection, that they, too, simply reinvented the same old wheel. It couldn't have been otherwise.

It turns out that the secret treasures reside within the very process of the striving, itself, not at the ever-receding rainbow's end. This here-and-now pathway is what's important. What's even more astonishing is that any pathway will lead to the same crucial and enriching insights. Further, we must enthusiastically choose to take these external excursions in order to realize their basic futility and arrive where we started.

> *The essence of life ... is in striving, not in achievement.*
> *No basic problems are ever really solved.*
> Arthur M. Schlesinger

> *Make living itself an art.*
> Anonymous

CHAPTER 2

PARADOX

PART ONE

The seventh major cosmic con-game lesson has to do with paradox. In checkers, after we're crowned with the other half of ourselves, we become a much more enhanced, powerful, and maneuverable game piece. We attain the ability to think, see, and move in all directions. We've graduated into the quietly ecstatic and expanded realm of paradox.

Viewing the world through this new, centered, and integrative lens allows us to synchronize with the ever contradictory and enigmatic essence of life, instead of struggling against it. In effect, we've graduated from two dimensional and two directional folly, blindness, and sickness … to multi-dimensional and multi-directional wisdom, insight, and health. Like the Phoenix, we've been reborn, at least to some extent.

As yet unawakened chess players look at such ultimate and healing insight, wisdom, and agility with understandable skepticism and derision. To them, paradoxical moves seem so backwards and incomprehensible. They take their immature and flat-earth dualism all the way to the bank; ... to the bank, that is, of the flimsy and vulnerable pleasures within their meticulously self-induced misery. Any extremism is so much louder and more charismatic than quiet and unimpressive centeredness. As a result, madness and folly often hold sway in the realm of human endeavors.

The majority is always wrong.
                                         H. Ibsen

PARADOX DEFINED

A paradox is composed of two principles, each of which contradicts and excludes the other, ... and yet both of which are true. A paradox is a poetic way of expressing, integrating, and balancing identical/opposites. A paradox thus sounds illogical and backwards to fixated this-or-that minds, since it talks out of both sides of its mouth. It's an ultra-logical/absurdity, which assumes that the opposite is also true.

A paradox is only a truth standing on its head.
                                         Alan Watts

The opposite of a profound truth may well be another profound truth.
                                         Neils Bohr

Opposition brings things together, and from discord comes ... harmony.
                                         Heraclitus

[A paradox is] the alliance of the necessary and the impossible.
                                         Vladimir Jankelevitch

Right words appear to reverse themselves.
Lao Tzu

One can ... read something said by a wise man in two totally opposite manners.
El-Arabi

The best questions have more than one answer.
Anonymous

Insight is precisely the timeless and non-dual mode of knowing.
K. Wilbur

There is nothing either good or bad, but thinking makes it so.
Shakespeare

Nature does not distinguish between good and evil.
Anonymous

The bait hides the hook.
Anonymous

Example paradoxes include:

The situation is hopeless, but not serious.
Play with earnest/indifference.
Success is important; failure is even more so.
It's vital to be a genuine fake.
Get off my back! I can only do two things at a time.
Enlightenment is free, but it costs us everything.
Work long and hard to discover that which is openly revealed from the very start.

Any attempt to escape entraps us all the more.
Travel widely to realize that there's no place to go.
Trust everyone completely, ... and watch your back.
Change others through total acceptance.
Just be kind, ... and kick ass.

Paradoxical logic utilizes the healing jujitsu or alchemy of compromise, reconciliation, fusion, and integration. This "both-and," centered, and embracing logic brings everything together. Ultimate answers lie in the harmonious, unified, and quiet center, not at the confusing, impressive, split-apart, partitioned, purified, and apparently opposing extremes.

Paradox creates an exponentially enhanced awareness of the unity and harmony which underlie the seemingly disparate shards of apparently irreconcilable contradictions. It's the cipher. It decodes the enigma of our dilemma-laden reality and allows us to awaken and dance in harmony with an enlarged and enriched reality. This goes far beyond the mere healing of our inner schism. It allows us to harmonize with the universe, ... with what is. It allows us to become our more profoundly wise selves.

LINEAR, DUALISTIC LOGIC

In contrast to paradoxical logic, our "normal" and limited chess-playing logic is linear, dualistic, exclusive, contradictory, argumentative, antagonistic, "either-or," "cause-and-effect," "win-lose," "right-wrong," and "all-or-nothing." It's the logic of contrasting, exclusive, and competitive "this-or-that" extremes. This splits everything apart. It creates illness, conflict, and war; not health, conciliation, and peace.

Indeed, linear or dualistic logic attempts to resolve life's contradictions. Unfortunately, however, it creates, instead, an illusory sense of certainty or pseudo-clarity by trying to keep in mind only one of side of any dilemma, which is only half of reality. It shallows us out and dumbs us down. It rejects the other half of reality and either represses or projects it. It thus re-invents reality according to its own one-sided, idealistic, perfectionistic, extremist, and mistaken rules. This amounts to a massive instance of wishful thinking.

In effect, our attachment to this over-simplified and childish logic sentences us to play the game of life in a half-blinded fashion. It's our fatal flaw. As a result, we spend our lives chasing after the mere smoke and mirrors of extremist and one-sided illusions. We're unable to reconcile and heal our illness-inducing, self-deceptive, and split-up linear consciousness.

There are no polarities in this 'ultimate reconciliation of opposites.'
J. Pearce

Linear logic is the basis of the normal speech and prose of any language. The embracing and unifying logic of paradoxical wisdom, on the other hand, is best expressed within the rhythmic and musical language of poems, lyrics, music, art, riddles, and jokes. It's the language of our most profound and paradoxically wise selves.

REALITY AS A PARADOX

Reality is served up only in packages of dilemma or paradox. The fullness of truth lies in the seemingly still, condensed, pinpoint, and yet expanded center of paradox. It's an enigmatic and ambiguous/clarity. Paradox expands the standard, limited, artificially split-up, and two-dimensional picture into a vast and multi-dimensional hologram.

Like astronomical black holes, the center of paradox is the whirlpool vortex around which everything revolves. It's the powerhouse of the cosmos and of the mind. It's the alpha and omega, the creative and destructive center of everything. As such, it translates, integrates, balances, reconciles, and deciphers the sea of contradictions that we call life.

The poetry of paradox is thus the ultimate decoding cipher or "enigma machine."

> *The real world is beyond our thoughts and ideas; we see it through the net of our desires, divided into pleasure and pain, right and wrong, inner and outer. To see the universe as it is, you must step beyond the net ..., for the net is full of holes.*
>
> Sri Nisargadatta

> *... attain the state before division, when ... opposites are seen still undivided, as totally, and at the same time, both ... the experience of non-duality.*
>
> Irmgard Schloegl

> *Paradox is the ultimate that reason can apprehend. Standing with one foot on each side of the paradox, one may be able to get his head beyond it.*
>
> C. Naranjo

> *... in genuine teaching the teacher cannot say what is being taught nor can the student say what is being learned.*
>
> J. Carse

> *To accept an orthodoxy is always to inherit unresolved contradictions.*
>
> G. Orwell

Mysticism ... the study of those propositions which are equivalent to their own negations.
Raymond Smullyan

All know that the drop merges into the ocean, but few know that the ocean merges into the drop.
Kabir

The road uphill and the road downhill are one and the same.
Heraclitus

I had to fall ill to see the hollowness and deformity of my most basic beliefs. ... had I turned all my conscious thoughts inside out, ... I would have been closer to the ... truth than by taking them, naively, at face value.
words of a patient,
quoted by Paul J. Stern

a ... Zen koan ... [is] designed to force the mind out of the trap of assertion and denial and into that quantum jump to the next higher logical level called satori.
P. Watzlawick

Infinite play is inherently paradoxical, just as finite play is inherently contradictory.
J. Carse

NATURE'S INHERENT INTEGRATION OF OPPOSITES

Paradox depicts what scientists have long known, that all forces and states in nature are rhythmic blends of balanced and opposing components, such as particle and wave, positive and negative, mass and energy, visible and dark matter, attraction-repulsion, centrifugal-centripetal, creation-destruction, life-death, predator-prey, and so on. Each seemingly stable, resting, and opposing component or state remains in ever-dynamic and exquisite balance with its paired opposite. In fact, each needs the other for its very existence. Inhale, exhale. Contraction, expansion. Win, lose. Appear, disappear. Birth, death. At the ultimate center of paradox, pairs of opposites intermingle, fuse, and dance together as one. Jung called this "alchemy." It's also called integration.

Furthermore, it's long been known by psychoanalysts that the unconscious part of the mind is in ultimate synchrony with this rhythmic, paradoxical, unifying, and non-contradictory essence of reality. After all, the mind is inextricably and merely a small piece of nature, itself. The unconscious, too, pays no attention to negatives, nor does it even distinguish between opposites. It sees them as identical or fused. Hypnotists have long used this principle. "Stop is "go;" "no" is "yes;" "evil" is "virtue;" "hate" is "love;" and so on.

Go beyond logic - the world functions in divine order.
                                              Anonymous

Stop acting so small. You are the universe in ecstatic motion.
                                              R.M. Rilke

Yes and no are not mutually exclusive ... our perspective may be limited through having become identified with one side or another of various pairs of opposites.
                                              J. Goldstein & J. Kornfield

... that which differs with itself is in agreement: harmony consists of opposing tension, like that of the lyre and the bow.
                                              Heraclitus

The best we can do ... is to settle for something in between.
J. Carse

THE RESOLUTION OF A PARADOX REMAINS A PARADOX

Any ultimate resolution of a paradox remains a paradox. The most profound resolutions are, themselves, only temporary and preliminary reconciliations, integrations, and compromises. They stir even more profound, illuminating, and worthy inquiry. Ultimate truths remain in the center, always in the center. Their essential contradictions can't be reduced to what linear thinkers really want, which is a single-pointed, either-or, static, and final answer. In fact, the enigmatic nature of paradox defies all manner of merely linear inquiry.

We can never finally arrive at the imaginary point of pure, black-and-white, definitive, universal, and permanent answers. Ultimate answers remain as non-linear, "both-and" enigmas, or mysteries. They reside more in the wordless realms of emotion and sensation than in the cognitive arena.

THE CENTER OF THE WHEEL

Picture a giant galaxy-sized spinning wheel, with a central axis and radiating spokes. Of course, the axis represents the black hole center of paradox, the integration of all those opposites which reside on opposite sides of the speeding outer rim.

Imagine the enormous and nearly irresistible centrifugal force of this huge spinning wheel or gyroscope. It naturally throws us towards its outer edges. This represents our normal attraction to foolish, split-up, and dualistic consciousness, our human nature. We're naturally prone to think in extremes and opposites. We cling to one or the other opposite, as we spin so fast at the vast outer edges.

In fact, this imaginary wheel is so immense that we can't even see or hear along the spokes and across the huge expanse to the opposing other side or principle. We perceive life, therefore, as a series of single, imbalanced, extremist, and all-or-nothing points along that small portion of the wheel's arc which our half-blind logic is able to perceive. This represents split up, partitioned, fragmented, pre-abstract, pre-integrated, and pre-paradoxical thinking.

The redemptive and healing journey towards the centered, integrated, and mature vision and logic of paradox is the journey which runs counter to this enormous centrifugal force. It pulls us along the spokes and towards the central axis of the wheel. This journey is accomplished only as a result of enormous effort, as we doggedly struggle against the compelling, seductive, and centrifugal pull back towards the outer rim. It's like fighting against gravity.

To make it towards the centered, integrated, and expanded vision and logic of paradox, we have to pull ourselves with great force along the spokes of this spinning wheel, painstakingly making small bits of progress, amidst inevitable and pleasurable setbacks, as we persevere, bit by bit, towards the center. The preference for this challenging, strenuous, and failure-ridden effort is a thoroughly acquired and seemingly unnatural taste. It also goes against the well-meaning and earnest advice of most around us, who enjoy the ease, exhilaration, speed, wind, thunder, self-aggrandizement, and self-confirmation of the outer edges. They love the sound of their own voices.

When we arrive at the stable and integrative center, we embrace the other half of ourselves. It's an ultimate healing of our split-up selves. We become our humble, larger, integrated, reconciled, and unified selves. Before that, and while we're so enjoying the wind in our hair on the speeding outer rim, we and our dualistic friends suffer from the highly pleasurable illusion of our separate, unique, special, grandiose, imbalanced, and split apart selves.

Notice that as we straddle the central abyss, we're no longer pulled in one direction or the other towards the outer rim. The opposing centrifugal forces are in perfect harmony and balance, here. We've reached that coveted central point of equanimity. This is the still and inner peace, serenity, acceptance, and trust we all want. This is paradoxical wisdom.

EARNEST/INDIFFERENCE

One example of this expanded paradoxical reasoning is the earnest/indifference paradox. In order to master any worthy and challenging skill, we must make dedicated efforts to learn and practice with great and meticulous effort, over a number of years. Such prolonged, dogged, and methodical practice creates a body of experience, the end point of which is an instantaneously functioning brain and muscle memory coordination.

Gradually, we're able to perform instantly and paradoxically; that is, with both focused and mindless effort. We dis/regard the goal, with earnest/indifference. We come to enjoy the pathway, itself. Such uncanny harmony becomes automatic, word/less, un/thinking, and spontaneously/premeditated. Long years of practice, preparation, and training are buried within the neurons of our unconscious brains, so that we're aware only of the present moment spontaneity, ease, freedom, harmony, and intention. We become the skill, so to speak. Too much thought interferes with spontaneous and instantaneous execution. In the final analysis, we can't achieve peak performance by using either extreme of earnestness or indifference, alone.

We must engage with supreme preparation, effort, concentration, seriousness, and intention, to be sure; but we must also participate in a spontaneous, effortless, distracted, playful, non-intentional, and letting go sort of way. It's not one or the other, but a blend. It's both/and, less/more. We can't solve the enigma with any efficiency or elegance by wholeheartedly and single-mindedly choosing one polarity or the other.

This earnest/indifference is what athletes call "the zone." Others call it "the flow." This is when we function nearly effortlessly and mindlessly at peak levels. It's when our cosmic, silent, and greatly enhanced coordination takes over. Time seems to slow down. Maybe this is that other dimension of time, or present moment/eternity.

THE ILLUSION OF UTOPIA, OF WOMB-SERVICE

We humans are naturally and initially motivated to one-sidedly win, solve, enjoy, capture, and keep it all, now and forever. These are idealistic "Utopias," wherein all needs are perfectly supplied; all mysteries are solved; all explanations are certain; all anxieties are soothed; all defects are remedied; all people and governments become enlightened; and everything is finished, settled, ordered, and under perfect control. In a utopia, there are no pains, fears, injustices, inequities, inadequacies, immaturities, illnesses, birth defects, and so on. "Nothing but blue skies, from now on."

On the way to the "someday" of such utopias, we fail to stop and notice that the term was coined by Thomas Moor to mean "Nowhere." It never existed! It's a figment of humanity's collective imagination. This illusion has existed from the very beginning of humankind. It's an essential and universal self-deception. Unfortunately, the longer we dwell in a such perfectionistic and mistaken duality, the more painful our lives become. This is where our psychological afflictions arise.

> *Those who hide from the pains of paradox and ...*
> *reduce anxiety by ... subordinating one pole to the other,*
> *will find themselves visited by neurosis and nightmare.*
> — Charles Hampden-Turner

> *The Utopian condition of which we all dream is that*
> *in which all people finally see the error of their ways*
> *and agree with us.*
> — S. I. Hayakawa

> *Nothing important gets resolved finally and forever.*
> — S. Kopp

An ancient oriental symbol for purity and symmetry is the white lotus flower. It thrives best atop the dankest of waters. This reflects the paradoxical im/purity of reality. Humanity has a long history of idealistic, foolish, and futile efforts to try to create such lotus-like, pure, pristine, perfect, special, exclusive, and permanent monuments, icons, celebrities, religions, societies, or governments. Human nature needs to revere, exalt, worship, and wall off an idealized, pure, and eternal god, principle, or individual.

In essence, we humans have the audacity to think that we can improve on reality and give it a white-washing make-over, in accordance with our own concocted, idealistic, and one-sided specifications. In each generation, we paint perfect castles in the sky. We then attempt to reside in them, and we invite others to join us. This is our collective hubris. It causes no end of self-created misery.

Such utopian efforts to establish purity and heaven on earth result in well-meaning, destructive, disastrous, and delusional catastrophe, every time. I know of not one exception! Witness the genocidal atrocities today and throughout history, when one group reinvents the utopian wheel and makes the preposterous effort to rid itself of all impurity by eliminating another group or by retreating into some isolated, idealized, pure, and pristine configuration. This is the essence of insanity. Ironically, the most horrid actions of humanity result from the most pure, well-meaning, and yet corruptive of utopian intentions.

> *The contradiction inherent in ... evil is that it originates in the desire to eliminate evil.*
> J. Carse

> *Evil begins in absolutes.*
> Anonymous

> *Lower your expectations of earth. This isn't heaven.*
> Max Lucado

Unfortunately, all groups, cultures, and governments base their most charismatic, moving, and self-justifying explanations, creeds, narratives, and anthems on this hopelessly flawed, linear, dualistic, perfectionistic, and idealistic logic. It's what we all long to believe. It incites mob rule. In fact, most humans remain permanently fixated in this over-simplified, naive, pre-abstract, and adolescent conceptual model.

It's our very attachment to this built-in linear logic, itself, which initiates many mental disorders. If we keep crawling out onto these ill-chosen, rotten, and purist utopian tree limbs while we chase the mere smoke and mirrors of extremist illusions; the limbs must break; we must fall; and we must have injuries and symptoms. It's the law. It's the provocative and harsh way the universe teaches us.

HOLOGRAPHIC, ALL-AT-ONCE, AND CENTERED BALANCE

In contrast, paradoxical logic harmonizes with reality. It's "both-and," inclusive, centered, integrative, and healthy. Mental health, itself, is often said to be balanced. Mature thinking brings together, embraces, and integrates opposites. It's centered, convergent, holographic, and all-at-once. It leads to peace, harmony, reconciliation, coming together, love, and mutual understanding.

In contrast, immaturity gives in to the centrifugal force of the gyroscope or spinning wheel. It's characterized by a splitting up of reality into seemingly purified opposites. It results in a one-sided and half-blinded view of reality. It inevitably produces prejudice, contradiction, divergence, conflict, war, psychosis, and horror. Anyone can split up, destroy, and cause conflict. It takes a truly wise and mature mind to foster tolerant/discernment, compromised/perfection, and collaborative/individualism.

Ultimate and paradoxical wisdom runs counter to our natural and primitive leanings. About one in ten of us are fortunate enough to overcome human nature by gradually and painstakingly overcoming and healing our split-up and extremist minds. At first, we can't stay in this integrated peace of the center. It takes extensive training, failure, and experience to do this. Many times along the way, and even at the end, we still succumb at times to the enormous and pleasurable pull of centrifugal force. We're only/and gloriously human.

Resolution means bringing opposites together to form a new unity.

Strephon Kaplan Williams

There is a point beyond the conflicts of illusion and truth by which lives can be put back together.

Joseph Campbell

CHAPTER 2

PARADOX

PART TWO

THE CRUCIBLE OF FIERCE TEACHERS

Life's most supreme and nearly unbearable challenges involve pain, loss, illness, disability, failure, tragedy, death, and so on. These extreme calamortunities are called fierce teachers. They abruptly and benevolently confront, frustrate, and derail our customary, utopian, split-up, either-or, dualistic, and "happily-ever-after" illusions and solutions. They efficiently and cruelly force us to consider paradoxical integrations, instead. At the center of paradox, we're forced to wrestle with these seemingly unresolvable enigmas. This is analogous to that happens chemically when two metals are super-heated in a crucible, in order to form an alloy.

When the non-personified universe forces us to face these fierce teachers, it provokes and invites us to enter into a beautifully/terrible and creatively/destructive white-hot crucible. There, our usual either-or and split-up illusions simply can't work to resolve our painful dilemma. In this predicament, we're forced to forge and melt opposing principles together into an alloy, instead of splitting them apart. What emerges is the sudden, surprising, indescribable, poetic, expanded, multidimensional, and pleasurable integration or alloy of opposites that we call an awakening or epiphany. This is not magic. It's just the routine/miracle of the everyday, integrative, and healing paradox of the universe.

In the midst of grappling with these painful fierce teachers, our integrated and amalgamated consciousness is thus born, like the Phoenix, from the ashes of our dualistic, split-up, and right-or-wrong illusions. Instead of taking sides, we can now embrace and integrate them. Such is the ingenious trickery and deception of the paradoxically wise and provocative universe.

PARADOX: AN INVOLUNTARILY ACQUIRED TASTE

This realization is not welcomed, at first. In fact, paradoxical logic is inherently confusing, incomprehensible, alien, and obnoxious. We're innately terrified of anything even remotely approaching the notion of dying to our previous this-or-that selves, in order to become more fully, intensely, and paradoxically alive. Practically no one volunteers during the good times for such a profoundly confusing process. We usually consider such a life-changing awakening only during the bad times.

This is why the most painful and obnoxious of fierce teachers are so necessary. They forcibly invite us to overcome our fear of such wholesale and seemingly self-destructive change by getting our attention, kidnapping us, and dragging us all against our wills, kicking and screaming all the way towards such a seemingly backwards, but vastly enhanced, transformed, painfully/pleasurable, creatively/destructive, and enlightened mode of thinking. This is a slowly, reluctantly, and painfully acquired taste. It's not for everyone, indeed. Most humans get through such supreme calamortunities by clinging all the more to their dualistic concepts. In the midst of their self-created misery, they tell themselves that it's working. This is understandable.

After some of us catch on to the cosmic con-game, we do what humans normally do. We consent to try to play the new and enhanced paradoxical game, but still within our habitual dualistic rules, in a certain either-or, resigned, "holding-our-nose," and "eating-our-greens," sort of way. We agree to learn this new and apparently backwards dance, but we insist on retaining our customary, out-dated, and dualistic choreography.

The compromised middle way of this new and paradoxical dance step seems so quiet, mundane, ordinary, and uninteresting compared to the thunder, grandeur, magic, and glitter of our usual and extremist dance of illusion. We're very reluctant, indeed, to forsake our familiar, comfortable, precious, fancy, pleasurable, and magical misassumptions. We'd rather shiver in our cold tent than go out into the cold night, get even colder, gather kindling and wood, and light an illuminating and warming fire.

This is natural. It is possible, however, to break free of our Platonic chains, get out of our chairs, go against our instincts, face discomfort and fear, and force ourselves to stumble towards the distant opening of the cave, where we can gradually get used to the bright light of reality. We can, indeed, choose to push ourselves further into this transformative dis/comfort zone, as we awaken and gather more ultimate, accurate, centered, and profound perspectives and insights.

In the midst of such a prolonged and failure-ridden process, we can grow to accept, tolerate, prefer, embrace, and even celebrate the indescribable centeredness, integration, and expansiveness of the new paradoxical mode. Once we come to reluctantly accept that the enigmatic/clarity of paradox cannot be reduced to a dualistic, pinpoint, and singular certainty, and that any paradox inevitably remains as an irreducible paradox; we can then even learn to appreciate and celebrate the never-ending and enigmatic con-game of life, with its enduring and confusing dilemmas. We learn to want what is. *WE LEARN TO ENJOY DILEMMA.*

This is an all-inclusive, stable, "center-of-the-cosmic-spinning-wheel," and gyroscopic type of perspective. There, we can straddle the abyss, the central point of paradox, in exquisite balance and serenity between the opposing, deceptive, and seductive pulls of apparent extremes. We can now see the distant, opposing, and dualistic pairs of principles on the outer rim of the spinning wheel, and yet we have no need to abandon the paradoxical center and seek an illusory sense of certainty by flinging ourselves desperately, frantically, and violently towards one extreme or the other. This new serene center of paradox remains an enlightening "CON/FUSION."

NOT ONE/NOT TWO

Perhaps one of the most enigmatic and central of the Zen paradoxes is illustrated by the "not one, not two" koan. It explains, for example, how the newly amalgamated alloy of paradoxical insight which is forged by the crucible of adversity both *is* and is *not* composed of its separate and contrasting components. This is one of the finest discourses on just how to conceptualize this weird jujitsu, integration, reconciliation, and fusion of opposites. It's said that once we grasp this koan, we master the entirety of zen. Although I don't fully understand it, I grasp what little I can of its basic principle.

> *To set up what you like against what you dislike*
> *Is the disease of the mind ...*
> *Do not remain in a dualistic state; ...*
> *As long as you remain attached to one extreme or another*
> *You will never know oneness.*
> Seng-ts'an

Mu: literally 'no' or 'not' ... - it transcends the illusory distinction between positive and negative, and is sometimes translated as 'not two.'
John Winokur

Our body and mind are not two and not one ... are both two and one ... Each one of us is both
S. Suzuki

Meditation practice is based on dropping dualistic fixation, dropping the struggle of good against bad. ... Technique is a way of imitating the style of non-duality.
C. Trungpa

Perhaps faithful, optimal, and committed love could serve as an apt illustration of this "not one/not two" koan. When we come together in love and sex, this initiates the emergence not only of our offspring and of all the complex tasks and projects inherent within the complex enterprise of committed love; but it also initiates and stimulates the simultaneous emergence of our individual, profound, and paradoxically wise part-selves. The sexual instinct is nature's way of seducing us in an ecstatic way into the alchemy or full catastrophe of this creatively/destructively and paradoxical fusion.

When individuals commit to each other, they agree to become "not one, not two." Optimally, each remains a fully independent and highly complex individual; and yet each chooses to compromise and dance together in harmony as one. The couple literally and enthusiastically "comes together." This is a natural drive. Although they share common views, values, and goals, they remain forever separated and individuated in fundamental ways, as well. They choose to love and work in concert, despite such profound and sometimes aggravating differences amidst their unity that they sometimes feel that they hale from entirely different planets. They enrich and fulfill each other with these seemingly irreconcilable differences. "Vive la difference." Each becomes so much more ... and less.

At first, we're able dwell in this "not one/not two" paradoxical center of love only briefly or episodically. After all, the very act of intercourse is an ecstatic rhythm of coming together and moving apart, until both partners melt and merge in spasmed and post-spasmed pleasure. In a way, orgasm is a temporary, glorious, and ecstatic fusion of our separate selves. Those that manage to merge for increasingly prolonged periods in this destructively/creative and pleasurable crucible enjoy a complex, enigmatic, and rapturous love dance that few around them can even contemplate, let alone appreciate or emulate. Most indulge in this incomprehensible and nearly ineffable closeness to only a small or occasional extent. Many settle for merely perverse, self-absorbed, and solitary imitations of such gloriously interpersonal and enigmatic unions.

Another metaphor for this "not one/not two" koan is the ancient yin-yang symbol. It's a circular and rotating two dimensional figure, in which the light underlies the dark, and the dark the light. This integration is further represented by the contrasting and smaller circles within each larger field. This reflects the exquisite balances and integrations which occur throughout all of nature.

> *Buddha ... came upon a master musician, teaching a student, and advising him that he must pull the string not too tightly, lest it lose its ability to make a note, and not too loosely, for the same reason ... but at just the right tightness. The Buddha was enlightened at that moment as to 'The Middle Way.'*
>
> Buddhist story

ILLUSION IS LOUD AND PROUD; ENLIGHTENMENT IS QUIET AND HUMBLE

Paradoxically wise compromise, integration, and diplomacy lead to enduring peace in a quiet, humble, polite, unimpressive, slow, non-dramatic, routine, subtle, methodical, unexciting, ordinary, modest, trite, harmonious, and non-magical sort of way. It's quietly, subtly, and compliantly revolutionary. It's not "special."

Adolescents, young adults, and societies, on the other hand, are drawn to all that's loud, grand, impressive, flamboyant, rushed, melodramatic, novel, exciting, extraordinary, showy, insolent, oppositional, combative, magical, and extremist. Such is the linear, inflated, and split-apart folly of normal human nature.

> *Monotony is the law of nature. Look at the monotonous manner in which the sun rises. The monotony of necessary occupation is exhilarating and life-giving.*
> Gandhi

> *Raise your words, not your voice. It is rain that grows flowers, not thunder.*
> Rumi

UN/LIMITED COMPROMISE

Centered, integrated, and reconciled compromise is the ordinary/miracle of paradoxical wisdom. Compromise means that we can settle, accept limits, and take the sacred and expanded middle way. By accepting compromise, we can know when enough is enough. Acceptance of limits is the real infinity. Limits are what set us free. It's through the embracing of our ordinariness that we realize our specialness. True freedom embraces and celebrates strict discipline.

Illusory pursuits, on the other hand, are ever intense and addictive, because by their very nature, they embrace only one extreme of the fullness of integrated reality. Like mirages, they recede forever into the distance. Such mirages can never be approached, reached, or satisfied, so they must be repeated, accelerated, intensified, and exaggerated endlessly and desperately, as if in so doing we could scream and will them into existence. They seduce us to remain fixated as proverbial, adolescent, demanding, and never-satisfied "hungry ghosts," with tiny mouths and huge bellies, grasping in vain for mere and unsatisfying smoke and mirrors.

EXTREMIST ILLUSORY QUESTS AS THE REAL HELL

This insatiable and addictive grasp for limitless illusion is, itself, the real and most hellacious of entrapments for those who remain fixated in adolescent and dualistic mentalities. It's their self-created hell. It's not that they choose this; they're simply not yet awakened enough to do otherwise. It's a natural result of their mistaken commitment to the pursuit of one-sided and extremist illusions. They haven't yet done their paradoxical homework. At the end of the day, astuteness, choice, discipline, renunciation, and self-deprivation turn out to be the most bountiful indulgences.

Poor is not the person who has too little, but the person who craves more.
           Lucius Seneca

Strengthen yourself with contentment, for it is an impregnable fortress.
           Epictetus

Enjoy what you have; let the fool hunt for more.
           Anonymous

Half an orange tastes as sweet as a whole one.
           Anonymous

Riches are not from an abundance of worldly goods, but from a contented mind.
           Mohammad

There is no greater misfortune,
Than not knowing what is enough.
There is no greater fault
Than desiring to acquire.

Lao Tzu

ALWAYS A PRICE: 52-48 CHOICES

For example, the normal and infantile wishes to be totally and permanently protected, safe, satisfied, comfortable, and indulged are mere and extremist womb-service illusions. All things pass. Everything comes with a price. To be profoundly and authentically happy, we must be among the few who cultivate the capacity to settle, to detach, to compromise, to have enough, and to accept limits. Thereby, we're able to embrace and straddle a realistically disappointed/satisfaction (dis/satisfaction), a dis/comfort, a limited/abundance, and a disciplined/freedom.

The great inner force that tends to pull us down is the principle of ease. It is 'anything to keep the baby quiet' for the moment.'

Earl Bond

While we pursue the unattainable we make impossible the realizable.

Robert Ardrey

Every joy has its sorrow.

Anonymous

All advantages have their price.

Anonymous

*To men, some things are good and some are bad.
But to God, all things are good and beautiful and just.*
                                             Heraclitis

Everything comes with a price, ... even paradoxical wisdom. When we awaken, we gain so much, indeed, but we lose our customary, highly prized, and extremist illusions. Paradoxical wisdom is thus a destructive/creativity and a failure-ridden/triumph. Everything is a blessing and a curse, with risks and rewards, progress and setbacks. All choices embrace enduring conflicts and negative consequences, ... even positive, optimal, and enlightened ones. The most meaningful, difficult, and challenging choices are close calls, with 52% of the factors in favor, and 48% against. There are always regrettable casualties. We're always right where we should be, balancing on a tightrope between the devil and the deep blue sea, between slightly larger and lesser goods and evils.

Thus, we must make real and compromised decisions. We must make do with reality's 52-48/total commitments. Furthermore, we must actually choose to embrace and celebrate our unavoidable and enduring state of conflict, ambivalence, dilemma, and con/fusion. It's where we live. It's always a messy/clarity.

LESS IS MORE: "PARADOXESE"

The real trick is to learn to embrace and even prefer the more profound game or logic of paradox, or "Paradoxese," of always straddling, embracing, and integrating with the multidimensional center. Notice that the very word "center" contains the word, "enter."

Just when we seem to "settle" for merely limited reality; and just when we compromise and apparently "eat our greens" and tame our childlike, extravagant, extreme, naive, impossible, and illusory demands; ... we're dumfounded to learn that such an initially depressing and seemingly smaller and deprived reality turns out to be far more expanded and satisfying than were the frenzied, desperate, empty, impossible, unreachable, childish, useless, and "extreme sports" types of outer quests. Compromise allows us to "enter" into the centered and expanded realm of paradox. Less/is more. Missing the party/is the real celebration. Who knew?

In fact, one of the most enduring and defining aspects of paradoxical wisdom is the capacity to settle. It's the capacity to accept "no" for an answer. This seems so backwards. It's a painstakingly acquired taste. It'll never be popular.

CHAPTER 2

PARADOX

PART THREE

**UNREASONABLE HAPPINESS:
GRATITUDE FOR WHAT IS**

When we reach the small measure of paradoxical wisdom which humans can attain, we enter into what I call unreasonable or unconditional happiness. This is when we're able to dance in harmony with the paradox of the universe; when we can accept, enjoy, cherish, and even celebrate simply what is. This stable, quiet, and grateful happiness endures and prevails, because it demands no artificially dualistic or extreme conditions. It transcends the transient, fleeting, reverberating, projective, and illusory stops between success and failure, hope and fear, pleasure-pain, good-evil, right-wrong, satiety-hunger, and so forth. Unreasonably happy individuals gratefully accept whatever comes their way. They can even manage to EMBRACE PLEASURE AND PAIN EQUALLY, at least at times. Imagine!

Any significant degree of unreasonable and unconditional happiness is an unusual achievement, indeed. Nevertheless, we can do this, at least some of the time. It's merely a matter of paradoxical detachment, awakening, persistence, and training. It allows us to be predominantly, enduringly, and optimistically grateful, … rather than one-sidedly negative, pessimistic, and resentful. It allows us to be fully accommodating/agents of change. One-sided, "glass-half-empty," and never-enough complaints, demands, resentment, dread, and pessimism are easy. Paradoxical, "glass-half-full," and satisfiable gratitude, accommodation, enthusiasm, and optimism are hard-earned.

Those who graduate into paradoxical realms can achieve the wonders of an expanded dis/satisfaction. They transcend their one-sided grief about what's missing or lost. They can appreciate and enjoy the previously unapparent, multidimensional, expanded, and abundant deprivation that they have. They reach, thereby, a level of unreasonable happiness that most can embrace only during the uncanny acceptance that can emerge during the effort to consciously experience and learn from one's own terminal illness. Those who are dying can get beyond endless and misery-inducing win-lose and loss-gain reverberations. They realize, moreover, that at a more profound level, there's actually nothing to gain or lose. Those who are unreasonably happy realize that they have all they need within. Not one, not two. Paradoxically, a settling for what actually exists is not a settling at all. It's a super-abundant and deprived indulgence.

An unreasonably and quietly happy state of cynical/optimism abides in those who expose and decipher the cosmic con-game; change games entirely; and proceed to embrace and live within the fully beautiful and terrible enigma of paradoxical wisdom for as small a percentage of time and depth as we humans can manage. These are the lucky/hard working sorts who integrate the artificial polarities of worry and bliss into a care/free state of mind. Therein, they can tend to difficult and risky chores and challenges with reasonable concern and effort, on the one hand; but also without undue fear, anxiety, worry, or angst, on the other. They can even do all this with an abiding, gentle, playful, and forgiving sense of humor, as they fumble along with the lifetime task of learning just what kind of fools they are.

HAPPINESS AS A CHOICE

Seen in this way, and like any other feeling state, unreasonable happiness is ultimately a matter of choice. It's a decision. Most fall short of this baffling, enigmatic, crucial, and seemingly nonsensical realization. This new unreasonable happiness doesn't come easily. "Fake it, 'til you make it." Previously embraced illusions and the negative feelings they produce don't just fade away. Nothing about the self goes away. Negativity can be embraced and integrated within the larger accommodations and reconciliations of paradoxical wisdom.

> *Life is a spell so exquisite that everything conspires to break it.*
> Emily Dickinson

> *There is no way to happiness; happiness is the way.*
> Anonymous

> *To every man is given the key to the gates of heaven; the same key opens the gates of hell.*
> Richard Feynman

> *Life consists not in holding good cards, but in playing well those you do hold.*
> Josh Billing

An optimist is a person who sees a green light everywhere, while the pessimist sees only the red ...light ... But the truly wise person is color-blind.
Albert Schweitzer

The most certain sign of wisdom over the age of fifty is a positive outlook.
Anonymous

ACTIVE AND PASSIVE; EARNEST/INDIFFERENCE

Paradoxical wisdom also integrates the active with the passive. As with all paradoxes, either extreme, alone, won't get us there. We need an integrated form of passive/activity, which is able to engage in a wise mix of astute action and inaction, or in/action. Not one/not two.

Idleness is the beginning of all vices, the crown of all virtues.
F. Kafka

Many concentrate on the passive and safe side. They avoid all difficult, risky, and enriching challenges, altogether. Others are drawn to the oppositely/identical extreme of the spinning wheel and fill their time with distracting and exacting "busy-ness,"... with compulsive, perfectionistic, tedious, never-ending, strenuous, competitive, and record-setting accomplishments and tasks. They spend so much time accumulating a never-ending C.V. of superiority, safety, and invulnerability-certifying triumphs, plaques, merit badges, and trophies... that they miss out on the actual living, being, and experiencing of their lives. Like many tourists, they're so busy enshrining themselves in the illusory permanency and credentials of photographs and "selfies" that they miss out on the enriching present moment being, altogether. They mistake a human doing, keeping, and collecting ... for a human being.

Either identical/extreme is a linear, all-or-nothing trap. It's not a matter of compulsive leisure or hard work. It's best to pursue life with the integration of earnest/indifference. We pursue goals with great enthusiasm, determination, energy, and commitment, to be sure, and we also maintain a serene indifference to the outcome.

Do your duty, always; but without attachment.
That is how a man reaches the ultimate Truth; by
working without anxiety about the results.
　　　　　　　　　　　　　　Bhagavad-Gita

It is ... the desire for the result that brings suffering.
Therefore, the doer is asked to relinquish all attachment
to the result.
　　　　　　　　　　　　　　A. Deikman

Besides the noble art of getting things done, there is the
noble art of leaving things undone.
　　　　　　　　　　　　　　Lin Yutang

You will never plough a field if you only turn it over
in your mind.
　　　　　　　　　　　　　　Irish Proverb

You miss 100 percent of the shots you never take.
　　　　　　　　　　　　　　Wayne Gretzky

To know, you must do.
　　　　　　　　　　　　　　Anonymous

Idleness is never enjoyable unless there is plenty to do.
　　　　　　　　　　　　　　Anonymous

A life spent in making mistakes is not only more honorable but more useful than a life spent in doing nothing.

        G. B. Shaw

If I had to live my life again, I'd make the same mistakes, only sooner.

        T. Bankhead

It's not the pursuit of happiness; ... it's the happiness of pursuit.

        Denis Waitley

SUCCESSFUL/FAILURE

Success is important, indeed, but failure is even more so. Successes show us what we did right. We already know that. Failures, on the other hand, help us to move the bar forward. They open our eyes by showing us what we don't know. If we remain within our customary realms of success, we're not pushing ourselves far enough. To keep learning, we must risk and even seek failures along the way. This taste for the illumination of failure is vital. Seen in this light, failure is the royal road to enlightenment. It's good for us.

If an experiment fails ninety-nine times, then I know ninety-nine things that don't work.

        T. A. Edison

In the search for truth, human beings take two steps forward and one step back ... who knows? Perhaps they will reach truth at last.

        Anton Chekhov

If you are irritated at every rub, how will you be polished?

Rumi

"MAYBE"

The same exquisite balance integrates good with evil, advantage with disadvantage. This calls to mind the classic teaching tale about a wise farmer. He was getting his mail at the road, when a neighbor came by and asked about how things were going. The farmer answered that his horse broke down the corral's gate in the night and ran away. The neighbor said, "Too bad." "Maybe," the farmer answered.

The next month at the mailbox, the farmer mentioned that the horse returned to the repaired and open corral with six wild horses. The neighbor said, "Good!", ... to which the farmer replied, "Maybe." The next month, the neighbor heard that the farmer's son broke his leg while trying to break in one of the new wild horses. He said, "Too bad," to which the farmer replied, again, "Maybe." The next month, the neighbor heard that the farmer's son was passed over when the army came through to seize all the local young men for the war, and he exclaimed, "Wonderful!," to which the farmer replied, "Maybe."

IN/JUSTICE

Each life has its measure of injustice, at least as we perceive and define it. After all, who are we to whine and demand a utopia wherein we're treated fairly at all times? When treated unfairly, unkindly, and even abusively, can we, nevertheless, straddle the center, with a detached and ironic sense of gratitude? Can we see in/justice as both a curse and a blessing, a calamortunity?

Many times along the way, hard-earned and deserved success is snatched away, suddenly and unfairly. Can we see this as an opportunity? After all, the acceptance of irretrievable loss is integral to anyone striving to reach a profound measure of paradoxical wisdom. In addition, we can often recover from loss to such an extent that we can use the experience to accommodate to and find even better life adjustments.

We see so many examples of this. A new and vastly improved building and enterprise springs from the ashes of the previously burned down building. The unfairly rejected lover finds his or her way to a soul-mate with a heart of gold, or to an enriching and illuminating life of solitude. The physician immigrant who's unjustly denied a medical license in his new country goes back into training and finds his or her way to a much more enjoyable and interesting medical or other career. The dancer or athlete suffers a career-ending injury and then finds his or her way to a satisfying alternative endeavor. These resilient, accepting, settling, and transcending transformations happen every day.

IF WE CATCH ON, IT'S BEST TO NOT LET ON; PLAY BOTH GAMES

Let's go back to the chess-to-checkers analogy. We've come to its eighth major cosmic con-game lesson. Even after we catch on to the cosmic con-game and convert to the unapparent game which is right in front of our noses, and even after we can now maneuver so paradoxically in multiple directions and dimensions, it's wise to keep all this integrated insight, perspective, and agility to ourselves.

It's astute to continue to at least appear to participate genuinely, seriously, and wholeheartedly in any society's foolish, adolescent, and linear chess game, as well. All societies are organized within that limited, half-blind framework. It's the best that human civilization can manage. We still have to pay our bills and taxes, stop at red lights, win and lose battles, make a living, acquire and maintain living quarters, take care of the children, and so on.

To get along, therefore, it's best to play both chess and checkers, simultaneously. Honesty *and* dishonesty are the best policy, often wrapped in astute doses of hypocrisy. True to paradox, each extreme complements the other. Not one/not two. It's a matter of straightforward/deviousness.

This caginess with others synchronizes with the crucial requirement that we must, on the other hand, be stringently honest with ourselves, if we're to reverse our normal and half-blinding repressive tendency to hide from unwanted inner aspects. This needed self-honesty does not imply, however, that we're required to also be totally and openly honest with all others, especially those with whom we're not so close, and/or with those who are not yet ready for full, frank, disillusioning, and paradoxical truths.

HYPOCRISY: GENUINE/FAKES

Hypocrisy has gotten a bad name. It's often not only shrewd and crafty to be deceitful, it's even required, ... at least if we choose to live with some degree of harmony and peace in such a deceptively/forthright universe and in the midst of such complex, unfathomable, unpredictable, and treacherously/cooperative mammals as humans. This is because standard chess players won't take it well if they sense that our insights penetrate further into life's murky enigmas than do theirs, and that we're not taking them so very seriously. Their resulting self-righteous, vengeful, obstructive, and damaging outrage will make things very difficult, I promise you.

It's best to be wily. It's best not to write such an audaciously revealing book such as this. An element of deceit is more skillful and astute than dogged and rigid forthrightness. In fact, one-sided and automatic honesty is for rookies.

> *Be happy about your growth, ... you can't take anyone with you, and be gentle with those who stay behind; be confident and calm in front of them and don't torment them with your doubts and don't frighten them with your faith or joy, which they wouldn't be able to comprehend. ... and don't expect any understanding...*
>
> R. Rilke

We must become "genuine fakes," as Paul Watzlawick said. We can like people, to be sure, but we must realize that others can be un/intentionally hazardous to our health. We trust people, but we must also watch our back. We must think for ourselves and seek advice. Besides, such astute deceptiveness harmonizes with reality's intrinsically dis/honest cosmic con-game.

> *Trickery has always been a part of the healing process. By no means need it be sinister.*
>
> Sheldon Kopp

While we attempt to awaken, and while we're still vulnerable to reflexively resorting to the projective extremism of our old, dualistic, all-or-nothing, and wholly honorable style; we naturally resist the task of adopting such a deceitful and wily strategy, at least at first. Maybe our naive attachment to such idealism is another reason why it takes so long to predominantly awaken and decifer the cosmic con-game.

It's best to go through life astutely and strategically, playing our cards close to the vest, like master psychotherapists. Therapists listen intensely and acceptingly, to be sure; but we also perceive what is said and omitted in a detached and multilayered way; while we consider hundreds of possible and more or less profound interpretations and interventions; while we simultaneously maintain a poker face; and while we listen to our own inner, deeper, and paradoxical wisdom. Otherwise, we get swept along with patients' distortions and illusions.

This takes energy! A therapist must be comfortable with being fully engaged with others while being simultaneously and utterly alone amidst his huge number of interventional choices. He or she must listen to patients and to his integrated self, within. He must be trustingly/suspicious, transparently/secretive, collaboratively/independent, relatedly/detached; and honestly/devious.

Another example of this dis/honesty jujitsu occurs in sports. It's not enough, for example, for a young and talented baseball pitcher to have the gift of an "in-your-face" and overpowering fast ball. Such overwhelming brute force is enormously successful for him at lower levels of competition, against opponents with merely normal nervous systems. To become a truly and consummately successful professional, however, and to be effective against similarly world class and unreasonably well-endowed, coordinated, and eagle-eyed big league hitters; ... a real pro must add trickery, deceit, and unpredictability to his bag of skills. In fact, all sports endeavors harmonize with the universe by routinely using trickery, decoys, and, of course, an ever-popular measure of outright and even systematic cheating.

THE DIS/TRUST PARADOX

I also know, again from experience, that we can always count on humans to tell the truth, unless it comes to certain urgent and unusual matters, like ... money, power, sex, status, success, glory, freedom, safety, survival, religion, family ... or anything else that really matters. There is, after all, no utopian land of perfect virtue and honesty. In nature, nearly nothing is as it appears to be.

In harmony with the universe, we all lie some of the time, especially and predominantly to ourselves. Remember, humans are consummate projection machines. Some are so consciously skillful, effective, and specialized at lying and projection that they're nearly undetectable. Since I know that we're all fooled at first about life, and since I understand that most others mean well when they promote various idealistic and disastrous illusions; I listen patiently, carefully, and compassionately. I hold them in my heart. I've been there. Nevertheless, and at the same time, I trust only my inner, deeper, balanced, and paradoxical wisdom. I accept help, and I also pack my own parachute.

I know that highly expert and professional manipulators and con-artists of all types love to create a loud, rushed, melodramatic, frenzied, and distracted atmosphere, so as to better distract their marks and ply their trade. To counteract this, I quietly and methodically maintain my own slow and seemingly boring pace and rhythm. I think quickly and talk slowly. I pass up all those "today-only," "too-good-to-be-true," and "only-for-you" offers. These rushed scams are deceptive techniques designed to exploit impulsive, self-aggrandizing, and wishful thinking. Flattery will often get you everywhere.

I settle for merely hitting the ball squarely. I let self-inflating fools strike out while swinging for the fences every time. The best crystal ball is the independent knowledge of past and present performance, so I observe behaviors, get several bids, and ask for references. In the end, however, I must take full responsibility for my merely human and fallible judgments and decisions, amidst my inevitably limited perspective and knowledge. No whining. If they fool me, it's my responsibility. I've been "had" many times before. Likely, there's more of this to come. I'm only human.

Neither one-sided and naive trust, nor extremist and cynical suspiciousness can be accurate, applicable, and astute at all times on this straightforwardly/deceptive planet. To be realistically strategic, and to accept our place in this ever-treacherous and enigmatic universe, we must embrace both extremes of this dis/trust paradox.

COMPASSION ABOUT BEING PREDOMINANTLY MISPERCEIVED

It's best to be patient, compassionate, indifferent, and even grateful about others' continuing misconceptions, criticisms, and illusions about us. We go through life amidst a sea of such misperception. Good company is preferable, indeed, but bad company may well teach us even more. In fact, if nine out of ten around us agree with us, then we'd better beware. What we say and do should step on most people's illusions about life to some extent, no matter how diplomatically skillful we may be. We should stir their disagreement, resistance, disdain, and objections. If most applaud, it may well signal that we're headed on a one-sided, dualistic, projective, and thus self-deluded pathway.

> *When a true genius appears, ... all dunces are in a confederacy against him.*
> Johathan Swift

Those who misunderstand us now are fellow identical twin travelers. Their same inner paradoxically wise selves are waiting to be fully realized/or ignored. They're simply at another point on the spiral staircase. We know how they feel. We, too, once wholeheartedly believed these very same inflated, one-sided, and imprisoning illusions. "They" are us.

> *To your mind, I am mad.*
> *To my mind, you are all sane...*
> *My 'madness' is from the power of Love;*
> *Your sanity is from the strength of unawareness.*
> Khidr

That which is generally considered to be the highest or noblest attainment of humankind is in reality the lowest of the high ranges possible to humankind.
Khidr

A fool's paradise is a wise man's hell.
Thomas Fuller

This is the path of sages, ... who are so wise you can't even spot it. They fit in, and go about their business.
K. Wilber

I took the road less travelled by, and that made all the difference.
R. Frost

The soul knows ... that if the Divine were to appear, the ego would not recognize it. The heavens cannot open for the soul; they are already open.
J. Carse

Education should teach us to play the wise fool rather than turn us into the solemn ass.
Kenneth E. Eble

... we often find something quite different from what we were looking for, and often on a path quite different from the one we had first taken in our vain search for it. ... we are like the alchemists who, while looking only for gold, discovered gunpowder, china, medicines, and even the laws of nature.
Schopenhauer

CHAPTER 3

RESISTANCE TO CHANGE, TO AWAKENING

PART ONE

All humans are redeemable. We all have the capacity to awaken at any moment from our normal, mistaken, projective, contradictory, and split-up consciousness. Most don't, however. Most of us utilize our one-sided misperceptions to try to validate our factory-installed misassumptions, all the more. We unknowingly sentence ourselves, thereby, to a lifetime of pursuing these self-concocted, purified, and ever-receding mirages.

THE BRENNER RULE OF NINE OUT OF TEN

We unconsciously write the entire melodrama of our lives, while we think that we're just reacting to novel, situation-specific, and justifiable external circumstances. It's not our fault, we say. We do this in spite of all the enlightening hints of reality's painful rug-pullings. Paul Watzlawick mentioned that the difference between the behavior of humans and experimental rats in a maze is that rats learn from experience.

The majority of people ... prefer opinion to fact.
                                C. Rosset

"You don't know what you don't know." Undaunted, ever self-justified, and fixated chess playing adults act like headstrong, domineering, and imperial five-year-olds. They bark out urgent and yet vastly mistaken complaints, criticisms, rants, instructions, and commands, ... especially to the truly wiser paradoxical individuals around them, whom they perceive as "obviously" deficient, backwards, and even bizarre.

> *It is the tragedy of the world that no one knows what he doesn't know; and the less a man knows, the more sure he is that he knows everything.*
>   Joyce Cary

> *Every mind must know the whole lesson for itself - must go over the whole ground. What it does not see, what it does not live, it will not know.*
>   R. Emerson

> *The value of an idea has nothing whatever to do with the sincerity of the man who expresses it.*
>   O. Wilde

> *You can fool too many of the people too much of the time.*
>   James Thurber

> *The truth can be spoken only by someone who already lives inside it; not by someone who still lives in untruth and only sometimes reaches out from untruth toward it.*
>   L. Wittgenstein

There are many who have grave scruples about deceiving others, but think it nothing to deceive themselves. Still, it is doubtful whether the self-deceivers can ever really tell the truth.
E. Hoffer

Most advocates of realism ... are hopelessly unrealistic.
Nehru

What concerns me is not the way things are, but rather the way people think things are.
Epictetus

This brings us to "The Brenner Rule of Nine Out of Ten:" Nine out of ten people on this tiny and insignificant planet have not only missed the boat; they've travelled inland, and they'll never see the water, again. This applies to all settings, groups, and times. It doesn't matter whether we're pampered or neglected, privileged or deprived, educated or ignorant, healthy or challenged, gifted or impaired, successful or defeated. Specific externals and childhoods don't actually have anything to do with this wired-in mistakenness of human nature. It couldn't have been otherwise.

Ninety percent of everything is crap.
Sturgeon's Law

Nine-tenths of all existing books are nonsense.
Benjamin Disraeli

Eighty-seven percent of all people in all professions are incompetent.
Gardner's Law

There are more horses' asses than horses.
John Peers, "Soderquist's Paradox"

The majority is always wrong.
Henrik Ibsen

There are well turned-out follies, just as there are smartly-dressed fools.
Chamfort

The conventional view serves to protect us from the painful job of thinking.
John Kenneth Galbraith

Most people would sooner die than think; in fact, they do so.
Bertrand Russel

What luck for rulers that men do not think.
Adolf Hitler

Most men live lives of quiet desperation.
Henry David Thoreau

In harmony with the cosmic con-game, we're all predestined to be essentially mistaken about almost everything that really matters in life. We're all set up and duped. It's nothing personal. It's an equal, confusing, and rug-pulling calamortunity.

WISDOM AND FOLLY

To make matters even more confusing, great wisdom and great folly are often nearly indistinguishable, at least at first. Sometimes only an awakened and highly discerning mind can detect the difference. As we've discussed, loud, certain, foolish, melodramatic, extremist, projective, and dualistic opinions are inherently more impressive and persuasive than are quiet, wise, doubtful, centered, insightful, and paradoxical views. Folly often carries the day. Moreover, it tends to win elections.

> *The partition between the sage and the fool is more slender than the spider web.*
> K. Gibran

> *Only mature minds can grasp the simple truth in all its nakedness.*
> Ramana Maharshi

Although wisdom and folly lead to realities that are miles apart, they often begin merely one millimeter apart. Ah, but that first millimeter of mistaken dualistic logic makes all the difference. It leads to starkly contrasting universes.

Both wisdom and folly are backed by well-thought-out, referenced, sanctioned, authoritative, and persuasive arguments. Both require single-minded and even stubborn commitment in the face of teeming external "evidence" to the contrary. The wise and the foolish are equally praised by their respective supporters for their uncommon truth, strength, decisiveness, commitment, perseverance, judgment, independence, and creativity. Both are equally vilified by their reciprocally identical detractors.

UNWILLING TO PAY THE PRICE

In order to decipher and transcend the cosmic con-game and thus reach towards our small share of paradoxical wisdom, we must literally abandon all the assumptions that we imagine to be true. We must have the courage to venture into entirely new, independent, and unsanctioned realms of thinking. This is a very lonely trip, indeed. We must be willing and even drawn to "go for broke," in order to achieve uncommon and over-arching insight, wisdom, love, or innovation.

> *My aim is to teach you to pass from a position of disguised nonsense to something that is patent nonsense.*
> Ludwig Wittgenstein

> *To gain that which is worth having, it may be necessary to lose everything else.*
> Bernadette Devlin

> *You cannot discover new oceans unless you have the courage to lose sight of the shore.*
> Anonymous

> *What is the price of experience? It is bought with the price. Of all that a man hath, his house, his wife, his children. Wisdom is sold in the desolate market where none come to buy, ...*
> William Blake

And the end of all our exploring
Will be to arrive where we started
And know the place for the first time.
Through the unknown, remembered gate
When the last of earth left to discover
Is that which was the beginning;
At the source of the longest river
The voice of the hidden waterfall ...

Not known, because not looked for,
But heard, half-heard, in the stillness
Between two waves of the sea.
Quick now, here, now, always -
A condition of complete simplicity
(Costing not less than everything)
T. S. Eliot

Happiness is itself poisoned if the measure of suffering has not been fulfilled.
C. Jung

Beyond a certain point there is no return. This point has to be reached.
F. Kafka

Such adversities and risks along the journey towards insightful and paradoxical wisdom are understandably daunting. Who wants to volunteer to take such a prolonged, lonely, and painful odyssey towards something so seemingly weird as paradox, ... something that most well-meaning and even learned others agree is utter nonsense, ... and something which we can never wholly grasp, conceptualize, or share.

WE VOLUNTEER AT GUN-POINT

It's likely that we'll have the courage to launch into such a seemingly foolhardy and enigmatic endeavor as paradoxical wisdom only if we're forced, if we have no choice. We must "hit bottom," as they say in twelve-step programs. When we're pinned against the wall, and when we really have no other choice; that's when we're likely to "elect" to let go of our precious misassumptions and attempt to acquire such uncommon and counterintuitive insight.

> *It seldom happens that a man changes his life through his habitual reasoning. ... He continues to plod along in old paths until his life becomes frustrating and unbearable - he finally makes the change only when his usual life can no longer be tolerated.*
> Leo Tolstoy

> *I never let go of anything without leaving claw marks.*
> Anonymous

After such a desperate and enlightening disillusionment takes us hostage at gunpoint, we're actually amazed that we survived at all. We're dumb-founded that, in addition, we involuntarily and accidentally broke into such a rare, unanticipated, and expanded region of insight and unreasonable happiness. How did that happen? When we grasp the full magnitude of this new, pleasant, and weird wisdom, we want more. We're like involuntary hostages who not only survive captivity, but even become enthusiastic converts. We may even become willing to tentatively and tenderly try this strange new full catastrophe living, again.

If we fail at our next attempt at paradoxical wisdom, we often skitter back to the seeming safety of our habitual, comfortable, and linear illusions.

Whew! This feels better. It feels like I'm home, again. That was exciting, different, eye-opening, challenging, and even life-changing, but it must have been a fluke. I must have been high. I'll never have to see or feel that, again, thank goodness! It makes a good story, though. I'm glad I've finally come to my senses. I'm back on track, now.

The prospect of the awakened state ... we prefer to run back to our prison ...
                                    C. Trungpa

If we manage to stumble upon and actually succeed at this backwards and paradoxical happiness thing another time or two, even for brief moments, then we can really start to catch on to the cosmic con-game in an expanded and consistent way. This new way starts to grow on us. That's when the fun really starts. That's when life has "initiated" us, against our wills, kicking and screaming at each step, into this weird, elusive, and predominantly paradoxical wisdom. Now we begin to get it. Now we've come to even develop a taste and preference for it.

Being merely human, however, we often forget how we got there. Further, we're reluctant to admit to having been so terribly and completely mistaken in the first place, just like everyone else. We often spin the whole experience, so as to put ourselves in a better light and preserve our falsely inflated sense of self-respect.

At this point, we often make the preposterous claim that we actually knew what we were doing all along. We only seemed to fall for life's cosmic con-game. We weren't forced, we tell ourselves. We were the brave ones who had the singular and courageous wisdom and foresight to voluntarily enter into that terrible and creatively/destructive crucible. That sounds better. We're loathe to admit that we, too, had to be dragged into paradoxical wisdom, kicking and screaming at every painful, humiliating, disillusioning, vulnerable, and eerie step.

CAN'T DECIPHER THE CON FOR OTHERS

Sadly, we can't catch on to the cosmic con-game for others, not even for our own most beloved spouses, children, parents, or friends. A word to the wise is sufficient. To others, the entirety of Proust will not suffice. "We're all in this alone," as Jane Wagner and Lilly Tomlin said.

Wise men don't need advice. Fools don't take it.
                                    Benjamin Franklin

For him who has perception, a mere sign is enough.
For him who does not ..., a thousand explanations are not enough.
                                    Haji Bektash

Each of us must decipher life's ultimate solutions for ourselves. This means that we must pay the exorbitant price of admission; we must contradict our own most cherished and celebrated misassumptions; and we must persevere against the well-meaning advice of most around us. In the end, this profound inner awakening is achieved only within the starkest and most unconfirmed solitude. Incidentally, we can say the same thing about delusion.

Believe nothing, no matter where you read it, or who said it, no matter if I have said it, unless it agrees with your own reason and your own common sense.
                                    Buddha

Teachers open the door, but you must enter by yourself.
                                    Chinese proverb

We do not receive wisdom, we must discover it for ourselves, after a journey through the wilderness which no-one else can make for us, [and from] which no-one can spare us, ...

M. Proust

The universe teaches primarily through each individual's painful and desperate head-bangings. No exceptions. Short-cut, extremist, and pleasurable pathways to wisdom are usually mere mirages or outright cons. These easy, instant, and non-painful solutions are often depicted in novels, sitcoms, plays, and films. That's why we call them "fiction." Real or "non-reel" life epiphanies don't come so easily.

Once again, this principle applies impartially and universally, even to our own children. In my humble experience, there's no way to preemptively endow them by age sixteen or eighteen with this profound, weird, astute, and paradoxical wisdom. They're just not ready to relinquish their natural, age-appropriate, and healthy measure of dualistic, self-aggrandizing, and "know-it-all" narcissism.

No amount of well-meaning, loving, profound, and even enlightened parental instruction and guidance will render our children immune to the universal hoodwinking of the cosmic con-game. Being so tragically and totally mistaken is a required part of the gig. Sadly, during their terrible twenties, thrashing thirties, and fitful forties, our children, too, must learn the hard way from life's painful calamortunities. They have to face the fiercest of teachers, just as we did. We can't protect them from this existential, dangerous, and even sacred passage, responsibility, and privilege. They must have the courage to strive for and face the abyss, themselves; and we must have even more courage to stand back as ex-parents and not interfere. In truth, we have no choice in the matter. They won't listen, anyway.

"NO DELUSION, NO AWAKENING"
Zen saying

I know. At first, I didn't like this existential predicament any better than you do. I wouldn't have had the wisdom, genius, and practical joke cruelty to create such a baffling, counter-intuitive, and painful hoodwinking con-game; whose solution eludes all but the most courageous, insightful, curious, persistent, independent, and afflicted; wherein everyone is fooled about nearly everything that really matters in life; where we can't shelter and protect even our own beloved children, who must learn these things the hard way for themselves; where the gap between madness and wisdom is hair thin and often undetectable; wherein we have to be dragged kicking and screaming against our wills towards an inevitably small measure of wisdom and authentic happiness, only to fall back hundreds of times along the way; where we can shout the naked and paradoxical truth from the roof tops, and yet nearly no one will hear or believe us; and where we must have the courage to realize that if most around us agree with us, we're likely going in precisely the wrong direction.

But then, I wasn't consulted. I'd have created a reality where literally everyone would have caught on to the cosmic con-game right away, permanently, and thoroughly as an automatic and enjoyable endowment of normal maturation. The con would have been only a temporary rite of passage, which would have ceased by late adolescence. I wouldn't have put everyone through such terrible and life-long pain, loss, and mistakenness, in order to learn life's most fundamental and profound lessons. I wouldn't have left the masses out. All truths would have been universally accepted and confirmed, and everyone would have been awakened. My way seems more humane, egalitarian, and kindly, doesn't it. Ah, but that's how all utopian illusions seem to be; that is, too good to be true; ... something for nothing.

As I've described, most of us resist these desperate opportunities to learn the backwards secrets about life. Instead, we argue our futile and mistaken cases all the louder. Thus, the greatest and most ultimate wisdom is predominantly disregarded, contradicted, and ridiculed by most well-intentioned and even learned others.

Unlike folly, our inevitably small measure of paradoxical wisdom is tired, pained, exhausted, relieved, tentative, grateful, and rather uncharismatic. When necessary or expedient, wisdom even poses as folly. Those of us who strive to grasp a small portion of the enigma of paradox have our hands full with simply moving on; looking within; deciphering further and unending instances of just what kind of fools we are; and discovering, thereby, further universal secrets, amidst inevitable setbacks and losses, and all within merely one lifetime.

The growingly and imperfectly wise have little time or energy to spare for stopping to complain and seek reparations. After all, our primary task on this tiny little planet is to find out just what kind of fools we are, not to enjoy the illusion of being "made whole" to our original, illusory, inflated, impossible, and idealistic demands. Our most sacred task is to simply and humbly let go, wake up, and settle, ... as much as we can. We have our hands full, indeed.

It took me all my life to learn what not to play.
                                               Dizzy Gillespie

CHAPTER 3

RESISTANCE TO CHANGE, TO AWAKENING

PART TWO

BEGINNER'S MIND

Nothing remains the same. All things pass. For instance, we can never experience the same stream or cloud from one moment to the next. The individual we relate to today isn't the same person as he or she was yesterday. Our seemingly stable body, itself, replaces cells constantly, in every tissue. We literally start anew each moment, as we wrestle with novel realities and enduring paradoxes.

Even past the age of eighty, we're happiest and most fulfilled if we continue to play the game of life as if we were mere beginners. Life continues to come at us at the speed of life. Each year, we must manage even more crucial and puzzling enigmas. The ante keeps going up! We never actually reach anything approaching our nirvana fantasy of smooth-sailing, of having it made. Our tiny lifetimes are so short, and we have so much to learn. If we keep our eyes open and our curiosity alive, life forever remains a humbling experience of ever-deepening and illuminating discovery.

We barely have enough time to recapitulate eons of evolutionary developmental changes in the womb; learn thousands of bits of complex realities and procedures as children; make endless rookie and ego-inflated mistakes during early adult life; fall for the cosmic con-game many times thereafter; have numerous calamortunity-induced awakening and endarkening cycles of therapeutic disillusionments and regressions; begin to decipher the cosmic con; fall for and re-decipher the con again and again; graduate to predominant, unreasonably happy, and astute paradoxical wisdom; stumble and learn even more about what kind of fools we are; and finally continue to learn, while we try to maintain a reasonable level of this messy, unstable, and unpopular insight and balance for as long as possible, even during a short or lengthy time of terminal mental and/or physical deterioration.

We must keep moving and stay fast on our feet during the entire unpredictable course of our tiny, in/significant, and sacred little lifetimes. Our life trajectories almost never conform to our well-intentioned plans. Moreover, paradoxical wisdom, itself, is certainly not what we expected.

> *It is in change that things find rest.*
> Heraclitus

> *The great God in the white coat ... is unfortunately always moving the cheese, ...*
> Guy Claxton

> *The heart of the confusion is that man has a sense of self which seems to him to be continuous and solid.*
> C. Trungpa

A good man is always a beginner.
                                    Martial

Be willing to be a beginner every single morning.
                                    M. Eckhart

The wisest mind has something yet to learn.
                                    Anonymous

In the beginner's mind there are many possibilities; in the expert's mind there are few.
                                    Shunryu Suzuki

Minds are like parachutes. They only function when they are open.
                                    James Dewar

A visitor arrived inquiring about Zen. Master Nan-in ... silently poured him a cup of tea and continued pouring until the cup overflowed. "Stop! Why do you continue to pour?" asked the visitor. "To show you," replied Nan-in, "that you are like this cup: so full of your own preconceptions that nothing can go in. I can't tell you about Zen until you have emptied your cup."
                                    Zen tale

You too must not count overmuch on your reality as you feel it today, since, like that of yesterday, it may prove an illusion for you tomorrow.
                                    Luigi Pirandello

Even if you're on the right track, you'll get run over if you just sit there.

Will Rogers

... the patient is finally and at last faced with the one, single, ultimate choice: will he choose growth or will he refuse it?

Esther Menaker

... Life ... entails change and suffering, and ... there can be no creative progress except by defeat of the preceding stage.

Anonymous

If in the last few years you haven't discarded a major opinion or acquired a new one, check your pulse. You may be dead.

Gelett Burgess

Only a fool never changes his mind.

Anonymous

Many men die at twenty-five and aren't buried until they are seventy-five.

B. Franklin

RESISTANCE TO CHANGE

Most of us endlessly resist such radical and lifelong inner change. Change seems so odd, so unwelcome. We would rather pretend to ourselves that we're right, than stumble along, find our way by losing our way, realize what kind of fools we are, and finally become predominantly awakened and happy, ... all while learning even more about what kind of compulsively self-confirming and self-aggrandizing fools we are.

This reminds me of a particularly headstrong and resistant patient. Many years ago, I was trying to interrupt her endlessly self-absorbed, reality-distorting, projective, and self-justifying complaints in order to make a therapeutic interpretation, when she said, "Would you shut up? I want you to just nod and agree with everything I say!" So I did.

> *The truth knocks on the door and you say, 'Go away,*
> *I'm looking for the truth,' and so it goes away. Puzzling.*
> Robert Pirsig

> *We would rather be ruined than changed.*
> *We would rather die in our dread than*
> *Climb the cross of the moment*
> *And see our illusions die.*
> W. H. Auden

> *Humankind, Cannot bear very much reality.*
> T. S. Eliot

> *... we would rather be ruined by praise than saved*
> *by criticism.*
> Norman Vincent Peale

> *As a matter of self-preservation, a man needs good*
> *friends or ardent enemies, for the former instruct*
> *him and the latter take him to task.*
> Diogenes

> *Every neurotic ... is averse to checking with evidence*
> *when it comes to his particular illusions about himself.*
> Karen Horney

Men and nations behave wisely once they have exhausted all the other alternatives.
Abba Eban

Everybody wants to be somebody; nobody wants to grow.
Goethe

... Change is always in the nature of a discontinuity or a logical jump ... [it] appear[s] as illogical and paradoxical.
P. Watzlawick

That popular notion that 'of course, a person who suffers wants to be helped if only someone is able to help him' is not really so ... there is the humiliation of simply having to yield to another person, of giving up being himself as long as he is seeking help ... Once he would gladly have given everything to be rid of this agony, but he was kept waiting; now it is too late, now he would rather rage against everything and be the wronged victim of the whole world and of all life, [he] has his torment on hand ... no one takes it away from him for then he would not be able to demonstrate and prove to himself that he is right. ... The person in despair believes that he himself is the evidence ... and therefore he wants to be himself, ... in order to protest against all existence with this torment.
Soren Kierkegaard

SELF-DECEIVING & SELF-CONFIRMING MACHINES

This all-too-common and inexhaustible capacity for the wholesale denial of an ever-changing and enigmatic reality is truly ingenious. Sadly, it may well be humanity's most proficient skill. We're really good at fooling ourselves. The folly of denial seems to set us free and clarify everything, if only in our small-minded, dualistic, and misguided imaginations. This hidden pay-off of self-confirmation enables us to happily disregard the shackles of mere and distasteful reality, altogether; and, thereby, to cheerfully proceed to the all-too-puny measure of frenzied, desperate, and illusory enjoyment which is imbedded within the teeming immensity of our intricately self-engineered misery and destruction.

In fact, armed with sufficient and efficient measures of self-blinding denial, we humans are consummate self-deceiving and self-confirming machines, ... confirming, that is, of our own immense folly. We're such spin doctors. We instantaneously and unconsciously manipulate any available data as "evidence" that we were right, all along. In fact, I've come to question the validity of the terms "honest truth" or "non-fiction," altogether. We doggedly climb further out on that rapidly deteriorating tree limb of illusion. We must fall. It's actually good for us.

It is in the ability to deceive oneself that one shows the greatest talent.
          Anatole France

Ego's intelligence is tremendously talented. It can distort anything.
          C. Trungpa

The world wants to be deceived.
          Sebastian Brant

We lie loudest when we lie to ourselves.
                                        E. Hoffer

Nothing is so difficult as not deceiving oneself.
                                        L. Wittgenstein

During a carnival men put masks over their masks.
                                        Xavier Forneret

Beware lest you lose the substance by grasping at the shadow.
                                        Aesop

The basic psychological problem is trying to be what we are not.
                                        Schaeffer

Man ... is ready to distort the truth intentionally, he is ready to deny the evidence of his senses only to justify his logic.
                                        F. Dostoevsky

The drunkard searched for his lost wallet beneath the lamp post because the light was better.
                                        Abraham Kaplan

RATIONALIZATIONS

We skillfully distort what we see by using "rationalizations." These are the ever-ready fictitious explanations or self-justifications that we give ourselves each moment for what we think, say, and do. Often, they comprise the bulk of our inner and outer conversations. In fact, I doubt we could do without them for longer than a moment.

These "reasons" actually have little to do with the real and often deeply unconscious sources of our behaviors and attitudes. Rationalizations serve to convince ourselves, primarily, and others secondarily. The persuasive deception and damage our folly inflicts upon others is merely collateral damage, compared to the enormous and grievous injury it inflicts upon us.

Rationalizations shield us from having to consider any objective data or insight which could possibly challenge our either-or, clear-cut, self-congratulating, and self-aggrandizing misassumptions. Rationalizations thus throw us even deeper into self-imposed prisons. In effect, we serve as our own most dreaded jail-keepers.

> *[The neurotic's] capacity for ... unconscious reversal of values is perfectly amazing.*
> K. Horney

> *We can easily forgive a child who is afraid of the dark; the real tragedy of life is when adults are afraid of the light.*
> Plato

> *Men take more pains to mask than to mend.*
> B. Franklin

> *All the faults of humanity are more pardonable than the means employed to conceal them.*
> La Rochefoucauld

> *A book must be an ... ax to break the frozen sea within us.*
> F. Kafka

Rationalization is one of our strongest defenses against looking at ourselves realistically, and, thereby, against having to take the trouble to realize that *we* are the ones who are mistaken. We engineer our own misfortune. We must change, not others, ... and not reality. It is we who must adapt, compromise, and surrender to objective realities. In effect, our actions reveal, while our self-justifying and projective words conceal.

We communicate through a veil of words.
C. T. Brenner

It's mortifying to realize that we're all basically mistaken, at first, about nearly everything that really matters in life. We've all been hoodwinked by the cosmic con-game. We've all been "had." Most of us can't tolerate this insight. We run away, crying and screaming.

Rationalizations help us to pretend to ourselves that we're on the right track; that we're not really so very frightened; and that we're truly enjoying ourselves. In reality, we're merely whistling in the dark. The truth is that we've sold our souls to the devil within, in exchange for the dubious privilege of chasing the ever-receding mirages of mere illusion. "Come on in and join the fun," we crow to others, but mostly to ourselves. We strive to convince ourselves that these merely empty and illusory booby-prizes are genuine, realistic, and satisfying.

THINK LIKE OUR PARADOXICALLY WISE PART-SELF: DOUBT OUR OWN THOUGHTS

It's vital, therefore, that we learn to doubt our own thoughts and conclusions. The ultimate test of the truth of our thoughts is whether they're paradoxical; that is, whether they're centered, and whether they embrace and integrate opposites. If our thoughts are polarized, extreme, and singular, they reflect only half of the truth. If they contradict themselves, then they're closer to the uncanny and nearly inexpressible paradox of truth.

In effect, we must train ourselves to think in an integrative way, like our paradoxically wise part-selves. This is how psychotherapists try to think. When we consult with patients, we listen in a unique way. We hear their long and earnest accounts of their pasts, replete with explanations of how their current behaviors developed. These are carefully and unconsciously designed arguments and apologies, meant to console, convince, and confirm patients' conscious adult minds. Patients sincerely believe these somewhat falsefied narratives.

Therapists listen, instead, to the echoes of patients' primitive and sneaky inner five-year-old part-selves, who peek out at us around the corners of their rationalizations, to see if we're really listening and discerning the truth between the lines. These five-year-olds seem to even want to be discovered and interpreted. We therapists know that these inner part-selves have been leading their conscious adult-selves around by the nose. We try to decipher these hidden and childish themes or repetition compulsions.

> *... the ... repressed word articulates itself in a coded, cyphered form. ... the symptom can not only be interpreted but is ... already formed with an eye to its interpretation: it is addressed to the Big Other presumed to contain its meaning.*
>
> Slaroj Zizek

Psychotherapists "listen with the third ear" to these hidden, internal, and unconscious con-games. Once we discern the inner five year-old's over-all agenda and psychodrama, then things become clear to us. Our job becomes one of gradually, kindly, and diplomatically "interpreting" these unconscious themes and messages, and informing the patient's conscious adult self about them, even over his or her strenuous objections. This intricately collaborative interpersonal endeavor empowers the patient to become aware of the previously unheard melodies and choreographies he's been dancing to. Then, he can choose whether he wants to put away childish illusions and "settle" for the much more immense abundance hidden within what appears to be "mere" and paltry reality.

> *When I was a child, I thought like a child, ...*
> *St. Paul*

> *Longer boats are coming to get us.*
> *Cat Stevens*

Patients consult with therapists in order to recover from symptoms, and in order to make what they imagine to be progress. We know, however, that patients' most meaningful and profound progress will be measured more by what they discard than by what they acquire and accomplish. Patients must learn to walk away from their many pleasurable, but limiting and self-imprisoning misassumptions.

To think like a psychotherapist, that is, like our paradoxically wise part-self, ... this boils down to the process of learning to look past our merely conscious and superficial explanations. These often contain merely self-deceptive and self-justifying rationalizations, which miss the point. They're the five-year-old's one-sided siren song decoys. Rationalizations fail to embrace the wholeness of the most profoundly paradoxical truth. We must transform the patient's earnest and well-meaning narratives into a life-changing realization that he or she's been acting from motives and drives about which he's largely unaware.

Anyone can train themselves to think with unquenchable and humble curiosity, like a detective or scientist, in this self-contradictory, psychotherapist-like, and paradoxically wise way. It's a necessary and un/usual skill.

CAUGHT IN THE MAELSTROM

The mistaken chess player is like an untethered mariner far at sea and alone on a ship's deck and on a moonless and stormy night, who's suddenly swept into the water by an immense, silent, unseen, and unanticipated wave. The power of the wave throws him so far from his ship that he finds himself suddenly alone in the cold and stormy sea, unable to rouse help from his distant, below-deck, and often still sleeping fellow crew members. Further, he finds himself caught up in a very, very fast current. He's traveling at speeds he's never experienced. Alone and in the midst of such utter darkness, he's unaware of the larger reality.

Picture that in reality, he or she's caught up in a miles-wide, oceanic, circular, and ever downward spiral or whirlpool. All he can perceive is the pleasure of being caught up in the exhilarating speed of what he perceives as a straight and linear current. He loves this feeling. He thinks he's really getting somewhere. His perceptual model is limited to two dimensions, to a flat earth idealism. What he can't perceive is that there's a depth dimension hidden within this pleasurable and speeding immensity. He doesn't realize that within this giant spiral, he's in grave danger of being sucked into the deadly depths of the huge vortex.

If I were to somehow magically appear on the nighttime scene, floating like a butterfly in the air above him, and if I were to explain that he's really in a giant and deadly three dimensional "suck-you-down-the-drain" trap, he or she'd call me a liar. He wouldn't be able to take a look at himself and consider that he might be so terribly and terminally mistaken. If I were to offer him an opportunity to escape and return to placid, calm, and safe waters away from the maelstrom, he'd turn me down flat! He'd likely say something like this:

Those slow-moving, calm, and peaceful currents over there are so boring and ordinary. Anyone can handle them. I've done that all my life! I'll never go back to that ship! I'm entering new and exciting territory, here, don't you see? I'm making history!

What good fortune that I was swept overboard. Now I can see clearly. This is where the fun, meaning, and action really are, and now you come along and ask me to leave it behind. You're just too scared to jump in and share this wildly and unprecedented intensity, meaning, and enjoyment with me. You refuse to enter into the future.

I can see right through you! You don't really want the best for me, do you? You really just want to hold me back, break the spell, hold back progress, and spoil my fun. You're stuck in some conventional, safe, and old-fashioned way of looking at things. I've moved so far beyond you. You're just blind, yourself. You're boring. Get out of my way, old man! Leave me alone!

In fact, if he or she were to eventually succumb and get sucked under, he'd be so thoroughly self-deceived and self-congratulatory that even if he could experience a final instant of insight into the larger and deadly reality, he'd rationalize that all this enhanced, fast-moving, and short-lived fun was well-worth it, anyhow. He'd gladly choose to go out with a bang. He'd even be singing that most popular, defiant, and horrid refrain of hell-bent self-defeaters, narcissists, extremists, and terrorists everywhere: "I did it my way!"

So it is with fixated and dualistic chess players. They go for the fast-moving, loud, exciting, and impressive aspects of mere this-or-that extremes. They're unaware of that crucial extra dimension. They go through life in a half-blinded manner.

If I can push this analogy a bit too far, as I usually do, we can imagine that if the trapped mariner-chess player moves his arms or legs in the slightest incorrect way amidst this huge, irrepressible, and pleasurable maelstrom, he or she thereby unintentionally creates a bit of dynamic drag. This takes him down much quicker, into even speedier, more exciting, and deadlier depths. If he remains perfectly still, he can manage to stay at much the same level for quite some time, perhaps until the giant maelstrom spends its energy and dissipates.

The skillful such mariner might realize that amidst this predicament or calamortunity, he or she can just relax and be in the present moment and learn to do his best to navigate amidst this immensity. He might maintain his curiosity and observe that if he moves his hands ever-so-slightly to just the right uplifting angle, he can carefully and slowly elevate his position closer to the safe upper edge of the whirlpool, … and beyond. But, then again, this astute, enlightening, and even life-saving maneuver would take him into those dreaded, safe, boring, and serene waters. He'll have none of that!

Amidst life's loud, distracting, and impressive maelstrom, the most crucial and profound answers are found when we stay very still and cease to join in with others who are permanently enthralled and transfixed by it's speedy currents. Thereby, they ultimately engineer and expedite their own doom. They're understandably caught up in the heady addiction of those intoxicating, seemingly unprecedented, and lethal speeds.

If we're able to steer towards paradoxical wisdom and away from the all-too-impressive maelstrom, we must choose to take "the road less travelled" and head for those horrid, dreaded, safe, boring, unpopular, and serene waters. It's then that the fog clears; we expose the con-game; we solve the riddle; we gain the courage to persevere and pay the price; and we find our way, not only to an abiding inner peace, but also to a much more abundant, expanded, exciting, ever-resilient, and multidimensional happiness! Unfortunately, when we crawl back into the cave or vortex to warn others about the con-game, as Plato depicted in his Cave Allegory, we're viewed with great skepticism and even outright rebukes and persecution. Such is life. It couldn't be otherwise.

CHAPTER 4

THE INNER CONGRESS

PART ONE

"I know my own mind." This is the sound of naive, short-sighted, all-or-nothing, superficial, and non-introspective humanity. We normally consider our conscious mind to be the totality of our awareness. We cling to the disastrous illusion that we live in a simplistic and straightforward universe, instead of the ultimately deceptive one we have.

> *Man has no individual 'I'. ... Each minute ... , man is saying or thinking 'I.' And each time his 'I' is different. ... Man is a plurality. Man's name is legion.*
> George Gurdjieff

> *Consciousness occurs simultaneously at different levels within any human mind.*
> John O. Beahrs

Every self is divided. Each includes contradictions ...
　　　　　　　　　　S. Kopp

The root of sin ... is the identification of my total self with the self of which I am aware.
　　　　　　　　　　H. A. Williams

People ... know, more or less consciously, that they are made up of rather separate aspects that can feel like separate people acting autonomously.
　　　　　　　　　　R. Stoller

Only the shallow know themselves.
　　　　　　　　　　O. Wilde

As is true in all fields of human endeavor, ... intelligent, learned, and dualistic minds disagree. Different schools of psychology describe the inherently split up mind in different ways. The part of the mind of which we're largely unaware has been called the unconscious or subconscious mind, the "lower self," the "inner child," the "id," the "it," the "other," the "shadow," and so on. To make things even more confusing, the complex architecture within this vast unconscious region is described in various ways, according to complex, competing, and well-established psychological schools. Such subdivisions of the unconscious mind have been called "part-selves," "introjects," "complexes," "personalities," "alter ego's," "archetypes," "fragments of the mind," "multimind" aspects, and so on.

THE BIRTH OF THE SPLIT UP MIND

We actually don't know why the mind is normally split up into various parts. If psychological development goes well, a massive burying or repression of primitive thoughts and impulses occurs by the time the child is seven or so. Before then, children's minds are predominantly unified and uninhibited. This is partly why they're so utterly charming. They freely say and do all those primitive, naive, aggressive, and sexual things we adults tend to keep under wraps and behind closed doors.

This massive sweeping-under-the-rug repression marks the separation of the unconscious mind from the conscious mind, or ego. This sets up a normal "repressive barrier" against an awareness of the more primitive and "dark" side of human nature. The growing child can thereby disown and put away confusing and "uncivilized" aspects of the self. He or she can be single-mindedly organized and focused on learning the many complex skills and concepts that are needed in any society. This is much more efficient.

DECEPTION

Repression accounts for the element of deception within the very make-up of our minds. It's a natural part of our cosmic nature. To some degree, we all deceive others and ourselves much of the time. This makes civilized society possible. It wouldn't do for us to just blurt out and act on the various negative or uncensored elements of our thoughts. After all, humans are compliant, positive, cooperative, and social beings. The alternative would be the all-too-common horror of random, impulsive, disorganized, dysfunctional, violent, murderous, and unworkable anarchy or terrorism.

Most importantly, we lie to ourselves. If we become unaware of our primitive and unbridled side, then we no longer have to be confused by so many conscious choices. We can simply and whole-heartedly proceed along more conventional and socially constructive lines.

He lies loudest who lies to himself.
                                                     E. Hoffer

DENIAL, REPRESSION, AND PROJECTION

The concrete, dualistic, black-and-white, pre-abstract and pre-paradoxical childhood mind thus attempts to disown the dark side of human nature. The child resorts to our favorite unconscious defense mechanisms of denial, repression, and projection. "I'm all good, I am, I am, ..." the child thinks to him or herself, thus *denying* the presence of the inner evil and sordid side of human nature.

The child's ego *represses* such aspects; that is, he or she sweeps them under the rug and banishes them to a secret and hidden domain, ... to the unknown and out-of-sight depths of his own unconscious mind. Presto! Now that's better. He's no longer confused or conflicted. The bad stuff disappears or gets explained away, ... poof! No more distracting, confusing, delaying, and cumbersome decisions about what to do with these upsetting, contradictory, and confusing feelings, thoughts, and impulses. This is quite a relief.

In addition, the child attempts to remain unaware of these upsetting inner aspects by detecting them only in others, and not in himself. This is *projection*. He or she becomes a veritable Rorschach projection machine, foisting the images of unwanted inner aspects onto others. While he views life through this distorting "projectoscope," it's doubtful whether he can perceive an even remotely accurate picture of himself or objective reality. Instead, he uses his "projectoscopic" lenses to focus on saving others from their dark sides.

The child hones these new and self-blinding skills of denial, repression, and projection during childhood and adolescence, so that by his adult years, he's a master of self-deception.

NOTHING ABOUT THE SELF JUST GOES AWAY

If this simplistic, black-or-white, "get-completely-rid-of-the-dark-side" denial, repression, and projection could possibly work, ... this would be a sweetheart deal, indeed. Nothing about the self goes away, however. Banished unconscious aspects wait and fester. From their perch within the deeply hidden and more or less unperceived recesses of the mind, they cause no end of mischief. Our every attempt to deny, disown, banish, project, or escape them only entraps us all the more. Thereby, we inadvertently become our own most dreaded jail-keepers.

> *The ... shadow ... represents all those personal characteristics that the conscious personality does not wish to acknowledge. ... there can be no self-realization without the experience of [inner] evil.*
>
> C. G. Jung

> *It is funny how mortals always picture us [devils] as putting things into their minds: in reality our best work is done by keeping things out.*
>
> C. S. Lewis

> *... only someone who is ready for everything ... will ... sound the depths of his own being.*
>
> M. Rilke

> *The willingness to go the individual way must inevitably lead to terrific [inner] conflict. ... it involves ... the pursuit of the opposites, which includes both dark and light within.*
>
> Elizabeth B. Howes

Amazingly, even those children whose repressive barriers are defective, and who are unable to desist from thinking, speaking, and acting on their negative, primitive, aggressive, and terrifying impulses and feelings; ... even those children engage in frank denials and lies. They make excuses and blame others for their own misbehavior. It wasn't their fault, they say. I'll have much more to say about this, later.

FIXATION OF THE REPRESSED

While the conscious mind, or ego, gradually matures with age, the repressed or unconscious parts of the self tend to remain "fixated" at the various psychological ages that they were when they were first banished or repressed. This creates the havoc of various-aged internal parts of the self, which exist more or less unknown to each other and to the conscious mind. Each of these thinks in rather childish and concrete ways, each at his or her own appropriate and limited level of psychological development. Each has his own agenda, in contrast to the conscious mind and/or to the other unconscious parts; and each is often immature and grandiose enough to think that he, alone, is the authentic and whole self.

This is the tragic flaw in the whole irrational and escapist process of "deny-and-get-rid-of-the-bad-parts" strategy. The young child's attempt at a repressive, sweeping-under-the-rug solution, itself, becomes the problem. Although it seems like a good idea at the time, it eventually results in the cacophony of competing, clashing, self-aggrandizing, ungovernable, center-of-the-universe, and confusing identities, complexes, or part-selves which are collectively known as the unconscious mind.

Woe to the nation in which each tribe claims to be a nation.

K. Gibran

*If the scissors are not used daily on the beard it will
not be long before the beard is ... pretending be the head.*
H. Jami

THE REPETITION COMPULSION: INTROJECTS LEARN TO RUN THE PRISON

These discarded and repressed unconscious infantile parts of the self continue to be "wired in" to the brain's eventually conscious circuits. This takes place at a deep and mostly unperceived level. Each of these "I-am-the-whole" introjects of the unconscious competes with the others and with the conscious mind.

Furthermore, while they're condemned to their hidden inner dungeons, it dawns on them that they can convert this very imprisoned obscurity into an advantage. They thus learn to capitalize on and utilize this invisibility to attain surprising degrees of stealthy power over their unaware and distracted conscious minds or jail-keepers. This allows the banished inner childlike part-selves to contribute to and exercise considerable and unnoticed influence on adult thoughts, feelings, attitudes, assumptions, energies, impulses, decisions, and actions. The inmates thus learn to at least partially run the prison. They become, thereby, irrepressible.

*Human nature ... can endure no restraint; if it binds
itself it soon begins to tear madly at its bonds, until it rends
everything asunder, the wall, the bonds, and its very self.*
F. Kafka

Perched within their secret and unsupervised unconscious domains, they're now able to move efficiently and decisively. They turn the tables and effectively direct the unwitting conscious mind to do their bidding; that is, to dance to the steps of their childish and impossible narratives or fantasies. They do this by installing secret and undetected hard drives, or malware, so to speak, with which they can commandeer the unaware conscious mind.

From their deeply hidden and unperceived perch, the unconscious parts of the mind can interfere with and even commandeer the conscious self's more logical, balanced, realistic, and mature intentions and objectives. They whisper unperceived, powerful, and sometimes irresistible feelings and commands. These hard drives of stories or siren songs are usually perceived at a conscious level as fantasies. There are instances, however, when the unconscious mind abandons all such stealthy packaging and resorts, instead, to issuing blatant and audible commands to the conscious mind. We call these "hallucinations."

Fantasies drive us over many years to repeat uncanny, illogical, impulsive, and even extravagantly self-defeating behavioral patterns. These are called "repetition compulsions." The unconscious mind uses these to trick the conscious mind into implementing such repetitive themes as "champion," "failure," "winner," "loser," "victim," "peacemaker," "provoker," "savior," "devil," "favorite," "unwanted," "unworthy," "lover," "hater," "abuser," "forgiver," "avenger," and so forth. Even worse, the unconscious inserts these themes into any life circumstance, regardless of fortunate or unfortunate specifics.

Unconscious part-selves enjoy this secret control over this conscious and know-it-all adult self, who understandably has his or her hands full with the task of managing life's normal deluge of distracting, challenging, and urgent external demands, and who's entrapped in the never-ending, linear, and illusory distinctions between victory and defeat, pleasure and pain, right and wrong, hope and fear. The conscious mind thinks he's acting or reacting in case-specific ways. He fails to notice that he's dancing in harmony with an unperceived, controlling, and stereotyped repetition compulsion. In a way, the conscious mind thus unknowingly becomes the unconscious part-selves' puppet or beast of burden.

The conscious mind is left to explain and justify his or her uncanny, repetitive, irrational, confusing, and self-defeating behaviors to himself, mostly, ... and also to others. He tries to explain and excuse his errors by using rationalizations. He claims, thereby, that he did these childish, backwards, inexplicable, and often contradictory things with good intentions; or that he didn't really do them, at all; or that he did them in reaction to this or that more or less imagined provocation or stimulus; or that the other guy did them; or that such disastrous repetitions are actually a good thing; and so on. The conscious self is a versatile, talented, and highly skilled spin doctor.

The conscious mind desperately tries to justify its one-sided misassumptions or illusions about himself, such as having total control, purity, rationality, authenticity, relevance, foresight, and virtue. By so doing, he or she inadvertently plays into the designs of the unconscious parts, who use these illusions to amp up the enjoyment of their secret, baffling, and sabotaging control over the distracted and know-it-all ego.

These unperceived inner child part-selves use our own mistaken and dualistic logic to trick us to dance, like marionettes, to the tunes of their unheard siren songs or repetition compulsions. Think about it. Our unconscious and child-like part-selves can impose their feelings, thoughts, and agendas in virtual protection and secrecy, hundreds of times a day, ... without resistance or argument from the distracted, busy, overwhelmed, and preoccupied conscious mind.

The unconscious child-selves can usually commandeer and hoodwink the adult self only as long as they're hidden. They can't pull this off in the light of day, because their agenda would sound as blatantly childish, immature, foolish, impulsive, short-sighted, ill-advised, fearful, thrill-seeking, self-aggrandizing, self-defeating, destructive, unethical, and irrational as it is. The civilized adult conscious mind would never fall for that, except in dire circumstances. I'll have a lot more to say about this unconscious repetition compulsion when we take up the secret victory of self-defeat. It reveals how we even unconsciously choose many of our psychological afflictions.

> *Our very life depends on everything's*
> *Recurring till we answer from within.*
> R. Frost

WE CAN'T HIDE OUR DARK SIDES

We humans instinctively put our best faces forward. We dress up and act in public as if we're totally logical, kindly, well-intended, harmless, and trustworthy. We pretend that we've got our acts together. Family members can attest otherwise, however. They see us at home, where we relax and let our defenses down.

Keen observers of human nature can read the unintended signs or "tells" of these unconscious and immature aspects of the self. These tells are the subtle hints, habits, tics, facial expressions, or slips of the tongue which reveal those often contradictory aspects of ourselves that lurk behind our public masks. To the truly discerning eye, we're each on open display. We may as well be frank, especially with ourselves. Our every phrase, gesture, pose, action, or inaction gives us away.

> *At the masquerade, we wear masks over our masks.*
> Anonymous

> *Society is a masked ball, where everyone hides his real character, and reveals it by hiding ... A man cannot utter two or three sentences without disclosing to intelligent ears precisely where he stands in life and thought ...*
> R. W. Emerson

NOTHING TO HIDE; IDENTICAL DARK SIDES

It turns out that we actually have nothing to hide in the first place. Our lower selves, or primitive "ids," are identical. We each possess the seeds of the same more or less repressed negative, dark, and forbidden set of thoughts and impulses. My dark side can beat up your dark side. There's no need to feel embarrassed.

The paradoxical trick is that we each must retrieve and re-own this other half of ourselves, if we're to unify and thus heal our split-up minds and come to the fullness and richness of integrated consciousness. We can then exercise astute judgment about how and if to manifest these aspects. In such a process, we can stop fooling ourselves with impossible and half-blind notions of perfection, purity, strength, and virtue. After all, the objective in checkers is to be crowned with the other half of ourselves. This process enriches us with much more energy, power, insight, happiness, and maneuverability. Thus, both repression and de-repression are needed in the midst of life's exquisitely balanced rhythms.

It is always a danger
To aspirants on the Path

When they begin
To believe and act

As if the ten thousand idiots
Who so long ruled and lived inside

Have all packed their bags
and skipped town
or
Died.
Hafez

CHAPTER 4

THE INNER CONGRESS

PART TWO

THE EXECUTIVE SELF OR "EGO"

The higher reasoning, conscious, and executive portion of our brain is located in our vast, newly enlarged, and sophisticated prefrontal cortex. This is what sets us apart from lower animals. We call this magnificent center of conscious reasoning the "ego." This is the part of our mind which can reason and multitask in profound, sophisticated, and situation-specific ways. It can simultaneously utilize judgment, insight, foresight, strategy, calculation, language, discernment, anticipation, abstraction, balance, compromise, organization, and integration. It masterfully manages and coordinates complex, simultaneous, and pressing external realities. As such, it problem-solves and makes possible much of what we do each day. Moreover, it can be trained to function in exquisitely complex and coordinated ways. It's the consummately instrumental part of our mind that we ordinarily consider to be the entirety of our mind.

Unfortunately, this intelligent, multitalented, sophisticated, trainable, and skillful ego remains vulnerable to the folly of its own self-aggrandizement. It's thus easily duped by the unheard, manipulative, and unconscious part-selves within. It falls for, justifies, and makes excuses for all those wired-in, dualistic, and childish illusions. Worse, it even makes these impossible and conflicting misassumptions sound reasonable, by using its instantaneous abilities to deny, repress, project, and rationalize. This isn't the ego's fault. It's designed to make sense of, interpret, and handle what it sees and hears out *there* in the dangerous, demanding, rushed, and confusing outer world. It's not designed to look critically at childish and irrational misassumptions which arise imperceptibly from within.

Different psychological systems demarcate various and complex subdivisions of the ego. I'll not get into this.

THE PROFOUND, INTEGRATED, OR PARADOXICALLY WISE PART-SELF

Many consider the ego and its various sub-parts to be our ultimate and deepest self. Others refer to an even more profound self, within, which I call the integrated or paradoxically wise part-self. This is our centered, uncanny, and "god-like" part, which perceives and even harmonizes with the universe's fundamental, balanced, non-deified, enigmatic, unified, and paradoxical wisdom. Thereby, and not incidentally, this integrated self harmonizes with the cosmic con-game.

This paradoxically wise part-self can't be adequately described by prose. I and others describe it as profound, objective, detached, serene, super-mature, imperturbable, unafraid, enduring, balanced, unemotional, and paradoxical reason. It straddles the center of paradox. It can be regarded as a tiny and all-inclusive personal shard of what some cosmologists theorize and even calculate as a universe comprised solely of pure consciousness, itself. We can picture it as

our inner, balanced, cosmic, and enlightened gyroscopic self which can orient us all our lives toward
deeper, universal, and paradoxical wisdom. This may be, therefore, our tiny personal speck of the collective and non-personified cosmic soul or consciousness.

> *All know that the drop merges into the ocean, but few know that the ocean merges into the drop.*
> Kabir

> *Stop acting so small. You are the universe in ecstatic motion.*
> R. M. Rilke

If we gain enough distance from our customary, frenzied, external, and illusory pursuits, we might just encounter a brief glimpse, taste, or experience of this paradoxically wise part of the self. We call this an awakening, epiphany, or satori. This happens during insight-oriented psychotherapy, as well as during various forms of meditation, prayer, contemplation, exploration, reverie, and wonder. The integrated self simply, indifferently, and non-critically waits for the busy and distracted conscious mind to perceive, appreciate, and eventually join with it, as it silently, independently, and dispassionately minds its own cosmic business and resonates with the universe, ... with what is. This is a profound, gyroscopic, and irresistible symphony.

Once we experience even a brief and ecstatic taste of such infinite and paradoxical harmony, which may well be the most we can ever experience it, we're swept off our feet. We can be hooked, thereafter, for life! This is the irresistible and compelling inspiration that can motivate and sustain us as we go through those inevitable, required, repetitive, painful, and prolonged dark nights and seasons of illusion-laced confusion, doubt, and denial. The same can be said, however, about the compelling false awakening of any average, self-deceiving, and extremist delusion.

Unlike the narcissistic, attention and approval-seeking conscious ego, this ever-humble and integrated part-self can easily "go it alone," against the endless dualistic clammer and criticism of any group or community's predominant beliefs, illusions, rules, and agendas. It refuses to stoop to such lower levels. It's simply not interested or impressed. It's like a super Mr. Spock. It's been exemplified by various gods, saints, prophets, philosophers, teachers, parents, religious leaders, and other wise men and women. These serve as our role models for paradoxical wisdom.

Perhaps we should call this our "transcendent self," "universal consciousness," or "enlightened self." Some have called it our soul, higher self, or "Inner Self Helper." Religious and philosophical types call it many things, such as the "Holy Spirit," Atman, the Tao, or Buddha nature.

This integrated part-self embraces all parts of the mind. Much of it resides out of our awareness in the unconscious. It's also part of the ego and its sub-parts. The inner paradoxically wise part-self is our soul or "uber"-self, our largest, finest, funniest, unifying, integrating, enlightening, and fusing self. It's the part of the self which pulls us towards the most profound center of ourselves and the universe.

The ideal we embrace is our better self.
Anonymous

God has placed in each soul an apostle to lead us upon the illumined path.
Yet many seek life from without, unaware that it is within them.
K. Gibran

We are star dust…
Joni Mitchel

NO LONGER TORN

The integrated self is profoundly patient, quiet, kind, loving, gentle, compassionate, tolerant, diplomatic, detached, non-critical, non-controlling, non-violent, and non-needy. It's not like the immature, demanding, Old Testament, and all-or-nothing god or super-ego of anger, punishment, and vengeance. It fully and light-heartedly comprehends, observes, and endures the mistaken notions, follies, antics, tactics, crimes, and even atrocities of the other parts of the self, all along. It's like the only balanced and sane child in the madhouse of the family, or, in this instance, the intrapsychic family of part-selves.

The integrated self can achieve this stable, centered, detached, indifferent, and kindly serenity, because it straddles the abyss. It straddles the center of paradox. It's not remotely tempted by the siren songs of the extremist outer rim of the cosmic wheel. As a result, it's no longer torn between dualistic, either-or extremes. This is the inner peace and serenity we so crave to approximate.

EVER ABIDING AND NON-INTERFERING

Incredibly, and in stark contrast to our well-intended, judgmental, meddlesome, serious, controlling, self-aggrandizing, lecturing, and interfering conscious mind; the integrated self refrains from judging or interfering. It avoids acting as a mere guide, referee, or authority. It doesn't take sides in our foolish, flat-earth, and dualistic game of win-or-lose, right-or-wrong, or superior-inferior. It transcends such artificial and superficial distinctions.

Can you imagine? It has all the ultimate answers, and yet it leaves the sacred project of our most profound and urgent awakening to the well-intended, but distracted, misguided, short-sighted, and not-yet-wise ego. In fact, the integrated self aligns with the universe and seems to be indifferent about whether the conscious mind ever deciphers the cosmic con-game, awakens to the unconscious, or embraces the fullness of paradoxical wisdom at all. This is Olympic quality detachment and objectivity! The Buddha would be proud.

This means, of course, that no matter how skillfully we fool ourselves at a conscious level, somewhere inside we know what we're really up to. Our integrated self watches and abides from within. At this level, we're actually "onto," "wise-to," and "over" the trickery of our self-aggrandizing little egos and unconscious part-selves, all along.

> *Freud's belief regarding psychotic people: "In some corner of their mind ... there was a normal person hidden, who, like a detached spectator, watched the hubbub of illness go past him."*
>
> R. Stoller

> *The progressive clarification and strengthening of the observing self is the special contribution of Western psychotherapy.*
>
> A. Deikman

> *He is thirsty, and is cut off from a spring by a mere clump of bushes. But he is divided against himself; one part overlooks the whole, sees that he is standing here and that the spring is just beside him; but another part notices nothing, has at most a devination [or inkling] that the first part sees all. But as he notices nothing he cannot drink.*
>
> F. Kafka

Accepting that the universe keeps its secrets, and integrating with cosmic and paradoxical consciousness or wisdom, the integrated self similarly refuses to reveal any short-cut hints about the true nature of its inner, profound, harmonious, and uncanny existence. It waits to see if we become interested and curious enough to catch on to the cosmic con-game, get the joke, and start to awaken to the profound symphony of cosmic consciousness.

> ... the ... repressed word articulates itself in a coded, cyphered form. ... the symptom can not only be interpreted but is ... already formed with an eye to its interpretation: it is addressed to the Big Other presumed to contain its meaning.
>
> Slaroj Zizek

The integrated self can be discovered only by a conscious self who's motivated to look within and change him or herself. It's all within. Knowledge about the integrated self's inner presence can/not be earned by virtue, knowledge, or performance. It is/not something we can accomplish, attain, acquire, or bequeath. Rather, it's more like something we can discover, "get," or awaken to each moment, temporarily, and one person at a time, in a stumbling and fumbling sort of way, like we do with the cosmic con-game, and, moreover, like we do in the midst of trying to master any other worthy arena of challenging human endeavor.

Yet, paradoxically, we must embark on our external odysseys and strive to attain, accomplish, or acquire, in an illusory way; so that we can encounter the endless adversities, failures, and losses which will gradually and eventually give us enough illuminating pain to get our attention and escort our focus towards vastly more meaningful inner regions. Only then can we begin to awaken. We must travel widely, in order to learn that there's essentially nowhere to go. We must cultivate and retain an ego, in order to transcend it.

Like the universe, the paradoxically wise and integrated self is compassionately/indifferent about life's intrinsic elements of inequity, injustice, pain, trauma, loss, and even death. "It's already broken," as some Buddhists say. It doesn't complain or whine. It fully accepts that all these experiences teach us what little we can comprehend about the most profound of life's truths.

The integrated self is amazingly accepting of reality in its full beauty and horror, mercy and harshness, glory and abomination. It fully embraces that all things, beings, and itself must pass; that most people miss the boat permanently; that difficult, painful, unfortunate, and even tragic compromises are the rule; that accidents, mistakes, adversities, losses, absurdities, injustices, illnesses, injuries, tragedies, and deterioration happen; and that it all couldn't have been otherwise. The integrated self is thus the enlightened part of the self that good-naturedly embraces the full, centered, beautiful, ecstatic, harmonious, horrible, catastrophic, ineffable, exquisite, and paradoxical enigma and genius of reality.

Life is a spell so exquisite that all else conspires to break it.
E. Dickinson

BALANCING ON THE DISC-TOPPED ORB

Picture this. Imagine that we're in a very special "enlightenment gymnasium." Its marble floor is level and polished. We're seated with legs crossed atop a specialized, two-part, and rickety gizmo. This starts with a marble sphere, which is about two feet in diameter. Placed and centered atop this sphere is a thin, rigid, sanded, and painted wooden disc, which is three feet in diameter. Our task is to sit cross-legged and balance on this disc, grasping its rounded edges, as it balances precariously atop the sphere.

At first it's quite a challenge to remain perched and balanced atop this non-attached and easily collapsable contraption for only a few seconds, before we tip over, and the whole thing falls apart with a resounding and echoing "bang." It takes months of training and practice to attain the skill of staying in balance for even short periods of time. During this time, we also master the skill of remounting after we fall, without even getting off of the disc or breaking out of our seated posture. Maybe after several years of diligent practice, we can master the knack of balancing for prolonged but limited periods, but only in the sanctuary of this quiet, placid, and non-stressful gym.

Picture that we're eventually required to leave the sanctuary of our meditative and contemplative gym and go out into the hubbub of reality all day, while still seated and balanced on this unstable disc-topped orb. We can master staying atop this now mobile balancing contraption only as long as is humanly possible, amidst the inevitably jolting commerce of life's demands, duties, movements, distractions, adversities, frustrations, rug-pullings, and all. By venturing outside the gym, we exponentially amp up the challenge of this already intricate enough and nearly impossible balancing act.

Reality's indifferent, existential, and provocative job is to stress us and to knock us off this finely balanced contraption. It's nothing personal. After causing endless falls, life is usually successful at permanently discouraging most of us. Most finally give up on this rickety and seemingly unreasonably heroic and irrelevant balancing project, altogether. Most of us forsake this essential and ambitious project; get off this gizmo for the last time; deny its pivotal and enlightening importance; and return to our preferred, seemingly more stable, and yet illusory pedestals of linear, unbalanced, extremist, illusion-laced, and either-or logic. That seems to be so much easier.

If we persist and strive to be one of the exceptional one-in-ten courageous and determined sorts who persevere with this unusual cosmic balancing act atop these disc-topped orbs, we can learn over many years of practice and experience, usually fifty years or more, to master this challenge, but only within an all-too-imperfect batting average. We try to remain balanced on this contraption, mostly by learning to remain optimistic and perched on the tipped-over disc after adversities knock us over, while we artfully lean over and regain our balance and position upon the ever-besieged orb. We even come to attain the ability to anticipate and lean into the next life blow, in order to maintain our balance and avert the tipping over. Nevertheless, we still topple many times each day. If we persist, we finally and acceptingly discard our useless illusion of smooth-sailing womb-service.

Unfortunately, no matter how much we swivel our gaze, we can perceive only so much of reality, since half of reality's tests and provocations come from behind. When we fall, we must shake it off and remount. At any rate, the central objective of the game, like life, is to enjoy the brief experiences we can achieve of this balanced and centered inner journey or pathway, itself, not to actually arrive somewhere or accomplish something out there. The most profound objective is to re-unite with our integrated and paradoxically wise part-self within, as often and fully as we can.

This is when it helps to have a face-to-face partner in life, who's also unusually motivated and ambitious enough to pay their own years of exorbitant dues in the sheltered gym to learn to balance upon their own disc-topped-orb contraption. We can serve as loving, compassionate, and collaborative partner-critics for each other. We can watch each other's backsides and warn each other of incoming blows.

The more we help each other, the more simultaneous, profound, harmonious, and pleasant "balance time," or paradoxical wisdom we're able to maintain together. This quietly and exponentially enhances our individual and combined enjoyment and fulfillment. Even so, we must be very forgiving of each other and ourselves. We do tip over at times; we occasionally fail to detect incoming blows for the other; we sometimes issue false alarms; and sometimes we inadvertently even cause our partner's imbalances, while we're trying to help. We're only human.

If we reach out to steady or protect our partner from an incoming blow, or if we try to lift him or her back onto their unstable gizmo after a fall; we lose our own center of balance, and we tip over. We're thus of no help. Our enabling and well-intentioned reaching out is really an unkind and even damaging hindrance to us both. That's the catch. We have to limit ourselves, therefore, to mere verbal coaching, because the primary aim is to remain in centered balance, ourselves, as much as possible. That's how we can be of the most help to ourselves and our partner.

It's best that we learn to stay balanced and recover on our own, as much as possible, and with a little help, no matter how tuned in and loving our partner may be. At the end of the day, no one else can do this for us. We must become ultimate and yet highly fallible self-balancers and self-soothers. We must become resilient and intrepid. This harmonizes with the amazingly detached and paradoxically wise part-self, within, as well as with the im/pure, im/personal, and paradoxical wisdom of the universe. More about this will follow in Chapter 7, which deals with insight.

No bird soars too high if he soars with his own wings.
William Blake

This paradoxical balance metaphor reflects many aspects of how optimal couples function together. The intricacies of such wondrous relatedness will be covered in chapters to come. Back to the integrated part-self, it remains aloof, detached, indifferent, objective, and balanced. It waits to be discovered by the conscious mind, yet it doesn't lift a finger to raise a ruckus and call attention to itself. Maybe that would distract it and throw it out of its perfectly balanced and gyroscopic paradoxical synchrony with the detached and indifferent cosmos. Maybe that's the wisest approach, all things considered.

IDENTICAL INTEGRATED SELVES

Your integrated self contains the same intrinsic, generic, and ultimate wisdom or cosmic spark as mine or anyone else's. In fact, it has the same uncanny perspectives as did the paradoxically wise and integrated selves of our wisest ancestors within any of the world's finest traditions or cultures. We're identical twins, remember? Jung's concept of the "collective unconscious" comes to mind. All we have to do in order to occasionally tap into our common and collective cosmic consciousness is to decipher the cosmic con-game, put down our prized and award-winning projectoscope, turn our gaze within, commit to paradox, and seek to resume the form of our integrated selves or souls, as much as we can. It's really that simple.

Who looks outside dreams, who looks inside awakens.
C.G. Jung

CHOOSING THE PARADOXICALLY WISE PART-SELF; I AM NOT MERELY MY THOUGHTS

The oriental, hackneyed, and yet applicable "namaste" greeting comes to mind. It's roughly translated as, "My higher self greets your same higher self." Implicit is the added request, "Let's not inflict our most horrid part-selves on each other, today, ... OK? Let's keep those infantile parts of ourselves under wraps." That's the realistic, humble, forgiving, mixed, and compromised sound of civilization, paradoxical wisdom, etiquette, consideration, and tolerance. It's the best we humans can do, given the reality of these fallible, half-blind, split-up, and projective conscious human minds. Bless the inner, outer, impure, and fallible peacemakers.

The brain's job, you see, is to produce a continuous flow of thoughts, even during significant portions of sleep. It has no obligation to insure that these thoughts are accurate, fair, realistic, sane, balanced, serene, insightful, kindly, wise, or profound. In fact, we usually prefer to upset, frighten, excite, and incite ourselves and others with the most base and extreme elements of our many thoughts. This is called "melodrama," or "catastrophizing."

My life has been filled with terrible misfortunes, most of which never happened.
                                            Michel de Montaigne

CHAPTER 5

INTEGRATION

INTEGRATION REMAINS FALLIBLE, CHANGING, AND UNSTABLE

Again, the ultimate resolution of a paradox remains a paradox. Its solutions can never be reduced to a simple, static, permanent, either-or, extremist, singular, and linear truth. Thus, enlightenment doesn't mean that we permanently transcend our congress of part selves and become transformed into wholly purified and "fully-realized" beings, as some claim. This amounts to yet another utopian illusion. The uncanny and un/compromising inner congress remains an uncanny and un/compromising inner congress. Paradox remains paradox.

The best we can manage is an ever-imperfect, humble, dynamic, forgiving, and uneasy truce, balance, cooperation, collaboration, reverberation, and coordination between our disparate parts, and amidst a non-deified, imponderable, and unpredictable universe that doesn't care in the least about our personal, naive, and idealistic notions. This is the essential, compromised, tentative, and messy nature of integration. It may well be awkward, cumbersome, challenging, delaying, limiting, aggravating, and even maddening at times; but it's also gloriously and ultimately enriching, expansive, authentic, intimate, pleasurable, and beautiful.

> *Every self is divided. ... the opposing aspects of our personalities remain in an uneasy state of tension.*
> S. Kopp

> *[Paradoxical wisdom] is expressed in a keen responsiveness to the great dilemmas, paradoxes, ambiguities, and uncertainties pervading human action and subjective experience.*
> Roy Schafer

A FOREVER TORN SORT OF INTEGRATION

We remain forever torn, fragmented, and conflicted amidst enduring inner contradictions and ambiguities. We inevitably have split minds, all our lives. It's our nature. We're never totally unified, "saved," and healed. The best we humans can manage is an on-again-off-again and ever-unstable reconciliation, as we pause and consult with our paradoxically wise and centered part-selves. In so doing, we can accept and supervise the rest of our dualistic and foolish part-selves.

Conflicts between our various inner parts can paralyze us with doubt, indecision, ambivalence, and fear as we waver between choices. It's like having a clumsy, argumentative, and unmanageable inner congress, which stops and tediously debates the pro's and con's of each and every step and issue, a congress which often outvotes the humble, quiet, and paradoxically wise part-self.

He is a free and secure citizen of the world, for he is fettered by a chain which is long enough to give him the freedom of all earthly space, and yet only so long that nothing can drag him past the frontiers of the world. But simultaneously he is a free and secure citizen of Heaven as well, for he is also fettered by a similarly designed heavenly chain. So that if he heads, say, for the earth, his heavenly collar throttles him, and if he heads for heaven, his earthly one does the same. And yet all the possibilities are his, and he feels it; more, he actually refuses to account for the deadlock by an error in the original tethering.
                    F. Kafka

Maturity of mind is the capacity to endure uncertainty.
                    John Finley

Doubt is not a very pleasant status, but certainty is a ridiculous one.
                    Voltaire

An image is a stop the mind makes between uncertainties.
                    Djuna Barnes

DOUBT AND UNCERTAINTY AS VIRTUES: 52/48 COMMITMENT

We must eventually choose to relinquish the naive and childish illusions of certainty, purity, and single-mindedness; forgive ourselves for continuing to be so terribly and completely hoodwinked by the cosmic con-game; and finally arrive at some small degree of acceptance, peace, humor, and reconciliation about our inescapably split-up, conflicted, argumentative, and foolish minds. We must pause and proceed in a humble and careful way, weighing the options of each issue, and remaining intricately balanced between and aware of our persistent, inner, and contradictory preferences, attitudes, agendas, and viewpoints.

Life is served up only in packages of enigmas or dilemmas, ... not in those tidy, easy, halcyon, and 100% certainties that we imagine. Life's most important, challenging, intriguing, and illuminating choices are, therefore, difficult, compromised, and 52-48 close calls, indeed. Often, we must fully commit to what we realize are imperfect, difficult, serviceable, and highly flawed compromises, whose advantages sometimes come with terrible casualties. We must embrace the multifaceted and paradoxical art of doubt-laden/full commitment. This is the messy and compromised nature of being human.

Seen in this light, reasonable degrees of doubt, hesitation, ambivalence, and compromise can be regarded as mature and realistic virtues, not vices. We can come to value that pregnant pause wherein we weigh, balance, and coordinate our internal differences and disagreements. It's more realistic to settle for the mere, murky, compromised, and paradoxical reality we can have, rather than to childishly stamp our feet and demand the impossibly perfect clarity of our favorite, dualistic, cost-free, and naive illusions.

To illustrate this impurity principle, even the oxygen which is so essential for life comprises only 20% of the air we breathe. We're not designed to breathe pure oxygen. Rather, we're designed to extract that precious 20% from the messy amalgamation. Isn't it beautiful and fitting that all these unnoticed breaths we take each moment reflect the principle of compromise which is so essential for ultimate and paradoxical enlightenment?

Keeping this in mind, our childish and one-sided "confidence" in our artificially split-up, purified, and immature view of reality can thus transform into a much more confidently/doubtful, un/perplexed, un/certain, and humble grasp of the true and nuanced fullness of impure, compromised, and paradoxical reality.

The stupid are cocksure and the intelligent are full of doubt.
                                                              B. Russel

The truly civilized man is always skeptical and tolerant ... based on "I am not too sure."
                                                              H. L. Mencken

Sometimes it proves the highest understanding not to understand.
                                                              Gracian

Such is the idea of a great and noble life - to endure ambiguity in the movement of truth and to make life shine though it; to stand fast in uncertainty, to be [thereby] capable of unlimited love and hope.
                                                              Karl Jaspers

When ordinary life is known as a profound mystery, then we are somewhere near to wisdom.
                                                              A. Watts

The only period in life that should give us cause for uncertainty is that brief stretch from the cradle to the grave.
                                                              Anonymous

Reality is nothing but a collective hunch.
                                                              Jane Wagner & Lily Tomlin

We are always wrong in some essential way. ...We are never living out exactly the story we think we are.
                                                              J. Carse

In the greatest confusion there is still an open channel to the soul.
        Saul Bellow

Friendship remains. Somehow, love remains - and the most precious gift, doubt.
        Jorge Luis Borges

Sixty years ago, I knew everything; now I know nothing; education is a progressive discovery of our own ignorance.
        Will Durant

The man of doubt lets everyone remain in peace, while the man of certainty never stops until he has rung everybody's doorbell.
        Clement Rosset

The most beautiful thing ... [you] can experience is the mysterious.
        A. Einstein

It is not the answer that enlightens, but the question.
        Eugene Ionesco

  This integrated, coordinated, and confusing/confluence becomes our most profoundly clarified enlightenment, our most paradoxical "CON/FUSION." In the end, we must accept our uncivilized, dualistic, and unconscious parts. Otherwise, we remain as mere and empty half-selves, so to speak, who can't accept and utilize the enriching depth and diversity of our own multifaceted, messy, and enriching fullness.

  This integration is a dynamic compromise. Perhaps even the most ambitious and profound among us will be able to attain a workable synchrony and unity with our collective paradoxically wise part-selves for only ten or twenty percent of the time. Then, we can embrace, abide, and resolve the schism of our "split-up-ness." In the center of paradox, the unconscious and conscious dance in balance and harmony with each other, with our paradoxical selves, and with the universe. I'll say more about this, later.

This awakening is a truly amazing, ever fallible, ever-renewing, and yet everyday transformation, metamorphosis, expansion, or re-birth, so to speak. It makes us much more fully and unfathomably human and infinite, within life's ever-present limits. Great discipline is a prerequisite for total freedom. Again, enlightenment is free, but it costs us everything, and it yields so much more. After all, that's what we're after.

> *The character of human life ... is 'ambiguity': the inseparable mixture of good and evil, the true and false, the creative and destructive forces. ... The awareness of the ambiguity of one's highest achievements (as well as one's deepest failures) is a ... symptom of maturity.*
> Paul Tillich

> *A philosophical truth ... procures no certainty, but it protects the mental organism against the whole family of germs which disseminate illusion and madness.*
> C. Rosset

> *It is easy enough to praise men for the courage of their convictions. I wish I could teach the ... young ... the courage of their confusions.*
> John Ciardi

METHODICALLY SIDING WITH OUR PARADOXICALLY WISE SIDE

The end result of a hard-earned, compromised, and optimally-awakening life is not nearly what we had in mind. We are not going to become perfectly serene and imperturbable demigods when we grow up. Paradoxical wisdom is more about doggedly applying a simple, useful, and fallible method during each present moment. Integrated consciousness is simply the meticulous, hit-and-miss, and moment-by-moment practice of kindness, centeredness, gentleness, and the middle way. When we manage to embrace our small percentage of light-hearted enlightenment, we simply learn to think, pause, balance, and consult with our paradoxically wise part-self, so that we can then speak and act in Paradoxese, as much as possible.

OWNING AND CHERISHING ALL OF OUR PARTS

In the end, we need all our aspects. Remember, the paradoxically wise part-self resides in, abides, and embraces all regions of our minds. For example, the dark side contains so much of our vital passion, emotion, energy, drive, aggression, sexuality, creativity, and spontaneity. Even its violence is needed, at times. The conscious, trainable, and problem-solving ego is needed all our lives to coordinate and carry out increasingly skillful elements of higher and abstract reason within the ever-changing complexities of reality and society.

In harmony with nature, paradoxical wisdom is not about getting rid of any of our aspects. Nothing about the self goes away. Like it or not, we must enthusiastically embrace the messy totality of our forever fragmented, conflicted, afflicted, foolish, and split-up brains. INDIVIDUAL LIFE IS A TEAM SPORT. It's a combatively/harmonious serenity. Sometimes, it's a desperate/serenity.

The art of living is more like wrestling than like dancing.
Marcus Aurelius

SPLIT CONSCIOUSNESS THROUGHOUT THE UNIVERSE

Most would agree that I've already gone too far in describing this principle of split consciousness. I should leave it at that. Nevertheless, and as usual, I'll push this inner congress line of thought even further, since, at my age, I'd like to pass on as many of the of paradoxical secrets that I think I know, as fast as I can. I have a theory or prediction which is safe enough to mention at this point in human history, since no one now or in the foreseeable future will be able to confirm or disprove it. That's pretty handy, don't you think?

The evidence is now overwhelming that in the unlikely possibility that we survive long enough as a species; that is, if we incurable little big-shots don't exterminate ourselves too soon; ... that we will eventually encounter one or two of the likely untold numbers of intelligent extraterrestrial life forms that still survive in this immense universe. Such alien life-forms may not be carbon or oxidation-based, as we are. They may be nitrogen, helium, or chelation-based, or whatever. They may take on gaseous, liquid, slimy, underground, or frozen appearances unlike anything we presently recognize as being alive. They may reside in another dimension of time.

Such beings have very likely evolved gradually, themselves, over millions of their planets' or moons' years, too, from their more primitive, ancestral aliens, just as we did. Due to the universe's requirement that any new and improved species be gradually evolved and merely jury-rigged around previous internal glitches; these aliens, too, likely possess, within their slime brain equivalents, the still wired-in and influential remnants of their own pre-slime ancestors. Thus, they, too will have conflicted and split brain equivalents. They, too, will have to wrestle with an unruly inner congress.

If it's any consolation, then, they're very likely to be just as hoodwinked, initially, by this same generic cosmic con-game in their own alien ways, as we are. They, too, will have to gradually awaken. Thus, they will likely be just as neurotic, ... and dangerous. Now this unimportant little con-game analogy of mine takes on truly cosmic, grandiose, and arguably delusional proportions.

CHAPTER 6

JUST B.E. K.I.N.D.

PART ONE

Integration in action is kindness.
Dan Siegel

This book's core curriculum or take-home message is the simple mantra: **B.E. K.I.N.D.** A mantra is a compact and practical way of reminding and guiding ourselves to return to and stay in a measure of centered, integrated, and paradoxical wisdom, as often and as long as we can. As you can see, **B.E. K.I.N.D.** serves as a mnemonic as well. This is my wildly audacious attempt to distill the small part of what I know about the wisdom of the ages into an even more useful, comprehensive, multidimensional, repeatable, and instructive mantra-mnemonic.

SIMPLE/COMPLEXITY

Some of the world's most ancient and worthy traditions go so far as to distill the essence of wisdom into a single word or principle, such as love, the present moment, the golden mean, insight, faith, gratitude, detachment, humility, devotion, acceptance, awakening, or such. All of these are worthy, indeed.

Like many others, however, I've found that the essence of paradoxical wisdom is simultaneously simple and complex, singular and multiple. It's a nearly ineffable, poetic, and ever-dynamic reconciliation and integration of seven essential factors, not just one.

The overt and literal meaning of my little mantra is important and central enough: "Be kind." In almost any situation, we can't go wrong if we start from a position of basic compassion and lovingkindness. Maybe I should stop there. Instead of the specific reminder of "What would Jesus, Muhammad, Buddha, Moses, or Rumi do?" we can pause and say, "What would my paradoxically wise part-self do. Can I train myself to pause and just be kind?"

In addition, the literal meaning of the first word, "**B.E.**," is similarly important to keep in mind. We must train ourselves to inculcate the separate elements of the mantra, so that they become nearly automatic and fused. We train ourselves, thereby, to not only practice, but also to "**B.E.**" the method.

SELF-CREATED "PROVOCATIONS"

Most of what we perceive as external provocations or aggravations are mere figments of our projective imaginations. We complain that others and/or reality have stepped on and violated one of our precious little illusions. Many of the nine out of ten unawakened types walk around with this unconscious and projective chip on their shoulders, ready to take unwarranted offense at the slightest imagined or real flicker of disrespect for their larger-than-life sense of self. They discern these flickers from mere shadows on the back walls of Plato's cave.

Anyone can escalate such self-concocted quandaries. It's all too easy to complain, destroy, oppose, fight, and split apart. In so doing, we forget that it takes two to fight, and we ignore our own hand in instigating and continuing conflicts. In contrast, calming the situation and escorting a cruel and negative scene into a reconciliation, kindness, collaboration, or even a mutual epiphany, ... now that takes skill, insight, and elegance. "Blessed are the peacemakers."

CALMING THE INNER BEAST

The habit of initial and prevalent kindness has far more important internal pay-offs, however. As we've discussed, outer aggression may well be satisfying, or "sadist-fying," but it only gratifies, justifies, and emboldens the inner and illusion-laden self-attacker, all the more. Each time he or she witnesses our self-serving, win-lose, and often mistaken conscious attacks on reality and others, he concludes that his childish, disastrously erroneous, and dualistic misassumptions are legitimate. As a result, he grows into an even more self-confirmed, arrogant, formidable, abusive, and emboldened self-attacker, indeed.

Like Pogo, "We have met the enemy, and the enemy is ourselves." An air of kindness thus calms, soothes, buffers, and disarms our inner attacker. Isn't that the point, ... to train ourselves to be consistently kind to ourselves? In the language of Paradoxese, we need to become gently, lovingly, compassionately, and collaboratively self-critical.

FORGIVENESS AND GRATITUDE

Most importantly, the habit of predominant kindness enables us to establish and maintain an enduring, nurturing, and healing internal environment of forgiveness. Rather than reflexively and harshly rebuking ourselves each time we stumble, we can gently and kindly forgive our inevitable and foolish shortcomings, errors, failures, and human nature. Forgiveness enables us to utilize mistakes as opportunities. This transforms us into open-minded, optimistic, patient, good-humored, empathic, and gentle beginners; instead of closed-minded, pessimistic, impatient, irritable, insensitive, and aggressive know-it-alls. In effect, we become our own best therapists.

As we get better at predominant patience and tolerance towards ourselves, we become more forgiving and kindly towards others, as well. We may even come to forgive the non-personified universe, itself, for thought/lessly placing us in this vast, enigmatic, and painful con-game, in the first place. If we decipher the cosmic con-game, we might come to even appreciate it for the ultimate, pleasurable, painful, and life-long learning opportunity that it really is. We might be able to settle, thereby, into a quiet, accepting, and good-natured enjoyment of all that's beautifully/terrible about the "full catastrophe," as Zorba the Greek says. John Kabot Zinn calls it *Full Catastrophe Living*. It couldn't be otherwise. It's always been this way.

When we accomplish this inner awakening, we actually go far beyond forgiveness. We even become grateful for the illuminating pain of each set-back, loss, tragedy, conflict, and defeat. We go beyond merely and brashly daring the cosmos to "hit me with your best shot." We arrive at the paradoxical realm of grateful and unreasonable happiness.

THE B.E. K.I.N.D. MNEMONIC, THE CIPHER

Each letter of the mnemonic stands for one or two of the seven basic elements of enlightenment that I'm able to discern. Maybe seven steps are simpler than traditional twelve step programs. Maybe they're not.

So here it is, the whole **B.E. K.I.N.D.** seven-step program for paradoxical wisdom, all spelled out:

B. = **BALANCE: PARADOXICAL CENTEREDNESS,** INTEGRATION, reconciliation, fusion, compromise, collaboration, convergence, coming together.

E. = **EMBRACE: EQUANIMITY** and **SERENITY** amidst **ACCEPTANCE** and celebration of ourselves and of what is: of the beautiful and the terrible, the positives and the negatives, the successes and the failures.

K. = **KINDNESS:** love, closeness, caressing, compassion, nurturance, collaboration, diplomacy, devotion, forgiveness, gratitude, optimism, humor, curiosity, and creativity.

I. = **INSIGHT:** self-reflection, self-reliance, self-solutions. It's an inside job. What about ourselves can we change? We instigate, create, and preserve our own happiness and unhappiness.

N. = **NOW:** Drop into the all-at-once and condensed/eternity of this present and only moment.

D. = **DISILLUSIONMENT** and **DEFLATION:** detaching from illusions, especially of self-aggrandizement. Deflation and humility: getting over ourselves; settling for and learning to want simply that which is. Perhaps **B.E. K.I.N.D.** should acknowledge and honor each of these "**D**'s" separately, by including two **D**'s: "**B.E. K.I.N.D.D.**"

ALL-AT-ONCE AWAKENING

I've contrived the letters of **B.E. K.I.N.D.** in order to form a memorable and useful sentence. I don't mean, thereby, to suggest a linear, rigid, and stepwise sequence to this all-at-once process of awakening. In harmony with the instantaneous nature of the universe, all seven elements, and even their integrated opposites, harmonize equally and simultaneously. In the midst of the infinite and instantaneous symphony of the universe, they lose their separateness and become fused. Each element is necessary, and yet no one of them is sufficient in and of itself.

Each human thought or fantasy exists in this all-at-once, multi-layered, balanced, integrated, and paradoxical way, in order to produce the ineffable grandeur and scope of present moment bits of miraculous, multidimensional, paradoxical, and merely ordinary human consciousness. What a privilege to synchronize so exquisitely with the hidden and enduring essence of the cosmos! Jung and others call this "numinous," by which they mean sacred, supernatural, holy, incomprehensible, spiritual, mysterious, or ecstatic. It's un/knowable, in/expressible, and in/comprehensible.

Stop acting so small. You are the universe in ecstatic motion.
          R. M. Rilke

BE KIND, BE BLIND, AND EMBRACE

Having said that the exact order of the letters is not important, I have to admit that this is not entirely correct. The opposite is also true. It turns out that the "**K.**," "**I.**," and "**E.**" letters of **B.E. K.I.N.D.** emerge as crucial and even emergency first steps in managing any intense, urgent, and risky conflict or dilemma. This is especially true for beginners, especially us life-long beginners.

The best strategy is to stop and use **KINDNESS**, **INSIGHT**, and **EMBRACING** right away. These block our usual, instantaneous, reflexive, and disastrous first impulses to be resentful, unkind, projective, and provocative when we handle adversity. It's best to **B.E. K.I.N.D.** and BE BLIND, ... blind, that is, to our habitual outer projections and distractions. It's best to first turn off our "projectoscopic" eyes and look within. The final emergency step is to stop and EMBRACE our inner five year-old. We must pause and let him or her have their say, right away, in the privacy of our minds, so that we can avoid making a bad outer situation worse. We can then implement the rest of the letters in any order.

B.E. K.I.N.D. DRILLS AND TRAININGS

Let's implement this relationship-saving, career-saving, and even life-saving mantra-mnemonic. It's really very simple. We can train ourselves to automatically consider and act on these seven elements of enlightenment spontaneously, simultaneously, accurately, and in real time.

First, we memorize the letters and meanings. We recite the expanded meanings of the letters to ourselves, until they become so etched into our minds that they become our default mode, our new instinct. Then, for years we methodically and silently pause and say, "**B.E. K.I.N.D.**" to ourselves, before we speak or act in our customary, dualistic, competitive, self-aggrandizing, and win-lose sort of way. We can even learn to consider multiple **B.E. K.I.N.D.** alternative responses, before we speak or act. This is the **B.E. K.I.N.D.** PAUSE. Such a delayed and thoughtful platform from which we can behave is like being in a constant meditative and mindful state of mind, while we perform with paradoxical wisdom. This ingenious and instantaneous pause enables us to act with predominant astuteness, diplomacy, balance, kindness, and humor.

At first this process is quite slow and awkward, like learning any new dance, sport, skill, language, or such. "One-two-three, one-two-three;" "square up, step in, and follow through; square up, step in, and follow through." As we face each situation, we pause and repeat, "**B.E. K.I.N.D.**"

GENERIC B.E. K.I.N.D. TIME

Here's a generic example of this **B.E. K.I.N.D.** maneuver or drill. More specific examples will follow in chapters to come:

1). **K: KINDNESS:** How can I pause and start with the over-all meaning of the mantra-mnemonic and just be **KIND**? That's always the first and most important priority. It's the cross-your-hands-over-your-heart "uber-message." Once I remind myself to be kind, compassionate, and forgiving to myself and others, I can proceed to the second emergency step, or letter.

2). **I: INSIGHT:** The next crucial step is the anti-projection step of **INSIGHT**. How can I end this all-too-human externalization impulse and just focus within? It's best to pause and say nothing for just a moment, while I consider my options. How can I make *myself* happy within this situation? What *inner* measure can I perform, regardless of and in concert with outer circumstances?

It's always an inside/outside job. I write the whole play. How can I change and be more self-reliant, motivated, creative, and resourceful; rather than waiting for some idealized other or reality to fix things for me and/or take the blame?

3). E: EMBRACE: The third emergency step is ACCEPTANCE. What painful part of myself and reality am I not **EMBRACING** and ACCEPTING? Where's my one-sided, half-blind, and perfectionistic illusion? It's high time for me to give up on the notion of single-pointed, one-sided, and pain-free answers. Acceptance, acceptance, acceptance. Once I've practiced these first three emergency steps, I can proceed to implement the rest of the **B.E. K.I.N.D.** letters in any order, or, even better, all at once:

4). B: BALANCE: How can I devise a **BALANCED** and *CENTERED* response and approach? It's the centered harmony, always the center. Where's the *PARADOX*? How can I listen to, embrace, honor, and integrate both sides of this argument or dilemma at the same time, instead of being polarized, extremist, and combative?

5). N: NOW: How can I stay in the present moment? How can I settle for here-and-**NOW** solutions, instead of distracting and justifying myself by blaming and editing the past or by trying to guide, improve, and control the future in some permanent and utopian way? Let it be, ... **NOW**.

6). D: DISILLUSIONMENT and **7). D: DEFLATION:** How can I achieve a healing **DISILLUSIONMENT**, a *detachment* from yet another grand and foolish illusion? How can I **DEFLATE** my big shot, center-of-the-universe, and king or queen baby self-image? Where am I mistaken? How am I trying to give reality and humanity a utopian makeover? Humility, humility, humility.

B.E.COMING THE B.E. K.I.N.D. METHOD

We actually have to slowly and awkwardly break down each dilemma or conflict into these seven overlapping factors. Later, like any trained skill, this process becomes automatic and integrated. This is when these seven steps come together, coordinate, harmonize, and fuse into a single, centered, non-verbal, and silent symphony. This is when we've arrived at being fully-trained in the paradoxical art of the **B.E. K.I.N.D.** method.

At this point, we're able to drop the systematic, orderly, and rote self-coaching, altogether. It's like the virtuoso card trickster, orator, dancer, gymnast, or diver, who, after years of practice, can expand the present moment; pause and think in mid-deal, mid-sentence, mid-step, or mid-air; respond to ever subtler changes in circumstances; and even change courses; ... all in the midst of amazingly rapid, seamless, fused, multifaceted, coordinated, and complex fingerings, phrases, steps, flips, and spins.

At this point, we stop the excessive and obsessive thinking and perform all this step-wise and intricately coordinated mental jujitsu mindfully and mind/lessly. We simply and effortlessly enjoy the experience of the doing and the **B.E.**ing. We can **B.E.** the **B.E. K.I.N.D.** method. We become enlightenment, like we become the trained dancer, down to our very bones.

Hard-won and methodical wisdom becomes our well-trained, reflexive, wordless, and mindless intuition. We're in the zone. We've become one with the paradoxical universe. This is when we really get rhythm. It's when unreasonable happiness really shines. It's that simple, but it takes time, training, and practice. In fact, it's doubtful that we can ever enter into such inexpressible and paradoxical wisdom without first entering into some sort of lengthy, disciplined, and rigorous training.

> *... The basic aim is always the same: by tirelessly practicing a given skill, the student finally sheds the ego with its fears, worldly ambitions, and reliance on objective scrutiny - sheds it so completely that he becomes the instrument of a deeper power, from which mastery falls instinctively, without further effort on his part, like a ripe fruit.*
>
> Karlfried Durkhiem

At this point, we can even express and embody the fullness of enlightenment within a simple gesture, expression, move, or posture. These are "short-hand" ways of simultaneously embodying these seven **B.E. K.I.N.D.** principles. For example, we can sit in a centered and balanced posture, or we can walk slowly in meditation. We can form our hands together, or cross them over our hearts. We can combine this with bowing or kneeling. We can do Tai Chi, for example. Any such centered, mindful, and humble posture, expression, gesture, or movement will do, as we harmonize with the exquisitely balanced and paradoxical universe.

PARADOXICAL WISDOM SEEMS FOOLISH TO MOST

This **B.E. K.I.N.D.** blueprint or template is only one of many throughout the disparate cultures of history. To most, such paradoxical wisdom seems silly, impractical, trite, mundane, over-simplified, pretentious, and foolish. "Not another platitude, please! Get your head out of the clouds. What drugs are you on?" It takes an unusual mind to discern and embrace such foolish/wisdom.

> *The truth is so simple that it is regarded as pretentious banality.*
>
> D. Hammarskjold

Wisdom is often disguised as foolishness.
Anonymous

None attains [any] degree of Truth until a thousand honest people have testified that he is a heretic.
Junaid

It takes a wise person to recognize another wise person.
Anonymous

CHAPTER 6

JUST B.E. K.I.N.D.

PART TWO

A PRESENT MOMENT INTEGRATION

B.E. K.I.N.D. serves as a quick, practical, "boots-on-the-ground," and moment-by-moment reminder, framework, or guide about thinking and acting in synchrony with our paradoxically wise part-self, as well as with the ultimate wisdom of the paradoxical universe, itself. In addition, paradoxical wisdom coordinates instantaneously with the entire congress of our unawakened part-selves.

Our complex, integrated, and multilayered brains are organized in these instantaneous, singular, and yet multifaceted narratives, which we call fantasies or scenes. We're all on stage each instant for these complex, elaborate, theatrical, integrated, symphonic, epic, and star-studded productions. This is the invisible and profound inner dance, collaboration, team sport, or "multimind," which comprises what we experience at a conscious level as individual and singular consciousness.

B.E. K.I.N.D. AS A GUIDE TO DECIPHER THE COSMIC CON-GAME

After we begin to awaken into paradoxical wisdom, the universe continues to come at us at the speed of life. It informs, tempts, provokes, hoodwinks, and enlightens us throughout our lives with its ever-versatile rug-pulling calamortunities. These continue to frustrate any remaining illusions we might have. Rug-pullings tempt us to break form from our balanced and straddled paradoxical "grace." They cause us to revert to our dualistic, conflicted, contradictory, argumentative, and extremist worries, fears, regrets, guilt, second-guessing, indecision, discouragement, negativity, projection, and resentment. This annoying disruption of our new, hard-won, centered, and integrated consciousness is the universe's gift. It's nothing personal. It forces us to enhance our paradoxical wisdom even more.

> *Life is a spell so exquisite that all else conspires to break it.*
> Emily Dickinson

B.E. K.I.N.D. gently supports us to reassume, continue, and enlarge our inevitably small measure of paradoxical wisdom and balance. Awakening to paradoxical wisdom is a crooked, partial, imperfect, painful, failure-ridden, and failure-utilizing process or pathway, ... always a work in progress. Defeats and failures transform into essential, necessary, and quietly ecstatic opportunities. Setbacks are meant to be relished, not dreaded. That's when we can push our paradoxical insights to even more profound levels.

It's unimportant whether we can speak and write in the most eloquent style of Paradoxese. The real test is whether we can quietly, humbly, and silently walk the walk on the present moment tightrope across reality's canyon, and without the net of illusion. Halfway across, words don't matter. What counts is whether we can manage the provocative wind gusts, just **B.E. K.I.N.D.**, and stay in paradoxical balance, ... amidst and even because of life's adversities. We can picture **B.E. K.I.N.D.** as the present-moment and silent balancing pole. It's the gyroscopic and compassionate guide. It helps us to arrive right here, right now.

B.E. K.I.N.D.: AN ANTI-CON AND ANTI-ILLUSION CIPHER OR TEMPLATE

A mantra-mnemonic acts like a highly condensed and encoded creed or anthem. Incidentally, this is also how our every unconscious and illusion-laden fantasy or delusion works. As we pause and repeat "**B.E. K.I.N.D.**" to deal with various and dynamic realities, it enables us to keep ourselves out of the momentary sling of the cosmic con-game rug-pullings. In addition, it enables us to keep our eyes on more profound, inner, paradoxical, and perhaps even universal goals. It can be musical, rhythmic, rhyming, or anything else that makes it simple, easy, memorable, available, applicable, versatile, repeatable, and teachable.

B.E. K.I.N.D. is essentially an "anti-con," "anti-projection," "anti-illusion," "anti-delusion," or "anti-wired-in-and-foolish-human-nature" cipher, template, guide, reminder, or framework. Each moment, before and after we stumble, it quietly reminds us to turn our gaze within and continue to seek out our balanced and compassionate center. As such, it's an ever-available, instantaneous, kindly, gentle, humorous, and paradoxical antidote to the constant, persistent, tempting, and distracting background noise of our dualistic, projective, conflicted, frightened, catastrophizing, lazy, greedy, resentful, angry, and predominantly negative five-year-old part-selves' chatter. It reframes these habitually self-aggrandizing and yet defeatist messages into more positive, realistic, centered, useful, healing, effective, insightful, and wise perspectives. The dissonant and upsetting inner cacophony transforms, thereby, into a harmonious and soothing symphony.

After we're trained, paradoxical wisdom must operate faster than we can think, at the present moment speed of life. We can ruin it, if we think too much. We can't lug around computers, reference books, or manuals; nor can we take a time out, while we huddle with teammates, consultants, coaches, supervisors, and therapists to debate the pros and cons about our next thought, word, or action. We're on stage each instant at life's improv.

Even after awakening, it usually takes further years of devoted and tedious self-training and practice to become so consummately simple, present, graceful, fluid, efficient, accurate, innovative, spontaneous, fresh, gentle, effortless, and understated. As we use **B.E. K.I.N.D.**, we eventually replace and expand our intuitive, customary, split-up, dualistic, and projective thinking. Paradox becomes our new and more coordinated intuition, ... our more comprehensive, versatile, and profound default mode. It's like building up wisdom's jujitsu-like neurological muscle memory.

We can learn to be distractedly/alert, methodically/spontaneous, single-mindedly/diverse, and steadfastly/revisable during each fleeting present moment, which is really the only time in all of eternity that we get to use it. Since life happens so fast, and since reality can be interpreted from so many competing, debatable, and more-or-less distorted perspectives; we must execute ultimate paradoxical and symphonic wisdom, words, and moves hundreds of present moments each day, regardless of external opinions. Keep it simple, and keep it now.

B.E. K.I.N.D. AS NON-MAGICAL AND NON-CEREMONIAL

B.E. K.I.N.D. is merely a useful, quiet, and ever-present echo-reminder from our paradoxically wise part-self. It's not magical or mysterious. It's just a humble and even mechanical method we can use to give ourselves a comforting and loving wisdom-reminder, each moment. What would our paradoxically wise part-self think, say, and do to talk us away from the painfully/exhilarating outer edges of the spinning wheel, and towards the sacred and centered wisdom and enjoyment of paradox?

We needn't be afraid of the concept of enlightenment. It's not some magical, unattainable, and permanent state of mind available only to those who study exotic and demanding disciplines for years; in ancient languages and terminologies; in uncomfortable positions; in exotic robes; at austere, exclusive, and inaccessible foreign retreats; in solemn and stilted manners; and at the knees of mysterious, uncanny, unfathomable, and foreign-accented saints and gurus. We can think and speak it in any plain and simple language. There's really nothing inherently foreign, magical, or ceremonial to it, at all. It's only a simple, applicable, deliberate, casual, ordinary, here-and-now, failure-ridden, and good-humored method. One step at a time. *Chop Wood, Carry Water.*

Moreover, a mantra-mnemonic isn't limited to times of formal, structured, ceremonial, or solemn study, prayer, contemplation, or meditation. In fact, it's designed to be used where life is really lived: on the improvised, casual, ordinary, and non-ceremonious run; under significant and insignificant instances of duress, distraction, duty, and criticism; and in the present moment. I do my own best **B.E. K.I.N.D.** meditations all day long, while walking, working, playing, interacting, and falling asleep. In fact, I try to be in a nearly constant state of insight or mindful meditation. I'm only human.

THIS EMINENTLY TRAINABLE CENTER, ALWAYS THE CENTER

We can do this. Enlightenment, or paradoxical wisdom, is merely a way of ending our self-defeating preference for the heady illusions on the outer and dualistic rim of the cosmic spinning wheel. Enlightenment enables us to spend as much time as we humans can, instead, at the ever-moving center of ourselves and the universe, at this very instant of eternity. If we seek the center and come from the simple integration of our hearts, we're golden. If we choose, instead, the false grandeur, complexity, and deception of outer and opposing extremes, where we come from our dualistic, split-up, imbalanced, conflicted, combative, and uncooperative mind, ... then we're toast.

Paradoxical wisdom is readily achievable at any present moment during our entire lifetime, and amidst any of life's paths. It can occur gradually, or all at once. It can be fleeting, episodic, or permanent. It's well worth the seemingly unreasonable price tag. After all, we have the luxury of being re-born in each present moment/infinity.

My simple mantra-mnemonic, **B.E. K.I.N.D.**, can't improve on the world's most ancient and traditional lovingkindness mantras, sutras, or creeds. Perhaps, however, my addition of simultaneous mnemonic elements, together with kindly humor, humility, and forgiveness, can add expanded dimensions. Like traditional metaphors, parables, and teaching tales throughout humanity's disparate disciplines; it can be fully utilized in the present moment, or it can be expanded and studied at length, when we have the luxury of time.

MULTIPLE IMBEDDED MESSAGES

The most elite therapists, hypnotists, and sages of all times have used this simultaneous and embedded layering of multiple, compelling, and ultimate messages. In fact, some skillful and experienced therapists prefer to distract and bypass the ever-resistant, contrary, argumentative, self-aggrandizing, and know-it-all conscious mind, altogether. They emulate the universe's practical joking con-game preference for the illuminating and provocative use of trickery and deceit. They know that a therapeutic suggestion can have an exponentially enhanced influence if it tacitly enlists and harmonizes with the more accessible, multifaceted, talented, and hidden resources of the unconscious mind. Such a profound synchrony from within can inspire a powerful conscious awakening which we call an epiphany, satori, or enlightenment.

Incidentally, con-men and -women of all kinds also prefer to bypass the conscious mind. The difference is that they want nothing to do with their or others' paradoxically wise selves. Their aim is to appeal to childish, foolish, illusion-driven, and corruptible human nature. After all, their goal isn't to be helpful, instructive, enlightening, or kind. Rather, their aim is to exploit and take candy from a baby, not to help it to catch on and grow up.

Once again, we see how the first steps of wisdom, enlightenment, helpfulness, and kindness can appear to be nearly identical with those of folly, mistakenness, treachery, and cruelty. These opposites can sound so equally enticing at the start, but they lead to strikingly contrasting universes.

PARADOX MEANS PARADOX

Each of these seven basic factors remains a paradox. Again, as we approach the ultimate and centered reconciliation of any truth, and as we magnify and expand it for further study; we find that it remains in the form of a nearly inexplicable paradox. It can't be collapsed and split apart into our preferred, illusory, single-pointed, utopian, and this-or-that answers.

The ever-elusive, centered, push/pull, and conflict/harmony among opposing, wrestling, balanced, and dynamic forces and principles, ... this is the only possible truth. Enlightenment is more like a contentious debate than a serene prayer. The only thing for sure is that nothing's for sure. After all, we're forced to build our foundation on shifting and self-contradictory sands, because that's simply the only place there is in this paradoxical universe. It's perfectly safe.

The art of living is more like wrestling than dancing.
Marcus Aurelius

Our brain, itself, is an intrinsic part of the inevitable and ineffable mystery and paradox of the universe. Our un/reliable and im/balanced perspective is formed by the haphazardly evolved, miraculous, in/accurate, and split-up human mind, which embraces multiple and deceptive conscious and unconscious parts; ... replete with obscure, conflicting, competing, changing, more or less illusory, and yet weirdly and wildly integrated agendas and alliances. This greatly complicates the task of deciphering the paradoxes of reality amidst the deceptive and artificial dualities of fiction.

This hazy and distorted lens of our minds confounds, contaminates, skews, and yet illuminates literally everything we think we see or know. We somehow manage to do all this in our own way, amidst our own culture, and within our own unique set of misassumptions, repetition-compulsions, ignorance, knowledge, and wisdom. We're left with the daunting tasks of feeling, discerning, communicating, and then even acting on these inexact, flawed, contradictory, changing, and yet profound and even inspired observations and conclusions. We're merely/and amazingly human.

B.E. K.I.N.D. PUT INTO PARADOXESE

Since integrated consciousness is paradoxical, I should attempt to put my little mantra-mnemonic into the language of Paradoxese. The simpler, shorter, and non-Paradoxese version of **B.E. K.I.N.D.** a few pages ago is a bit more useful, however, as a boots-on-the-ground, practical, and daily reminder and guide. Nevertheless, I include this "both-and" version for more academic and detailed discussions:

B. = IM/BALANCE: LINEAR/PARADOX, "CON/ FUSION," prosaic/poetry, extremist/centeredness, contradictory/convergence, contentious/collaboration, perfectionistic/compromise, multiple/singularity, expansive/fusion

E. = ALL-EMBRACING/ESCAPE: ALL-ACCEPTING/ DISCERNMENT; equal celebration of life's terrible/ beauty, painful/bliss, tearful/laughter, chaotic/equanimity, in/tolerance, in/attention, in/activity, earnest/indifference, 52-48/commitment, anxious/serenity, in/security, and inner congress

K. = KINDLY/KICK-ASS COMPASSION, tough/love, un/conditional love, autonomous/intimacy, indifferent/ concern, in/sincerity, cynical/optimism, complaining/ gratitude, un/reasonable and un/conditional happiness.

I. = EXTERNALIZING/INSIGHT: What can I change about circumstances? What can I change about me? It's an outside/inside job; reactive/internal authorship, in/ attentive self-reflection; imprisoned-limited-and-disciplined/freedom

N. = NOW: PINPOINT/INFINITY: present moment/ eternity, timeless/eternity, in/finity, dis/regard of the past and future, stable/change, here-and-now/planning

D. = DIS/ILLUSIONMENT: dis/satisfaction, constructive/ disappointment, mis/assumptions, idealistic/compromise, im/perfection, pristine/messiness

D. = DE/INFLATION: ordinary/specialness, identical/ uniqueness, foolish/wisdom, hoodwinked/awakening, deprived/indulgence, converging/expansivenes.

Much of the rest of this work applies each of the seven elements of this **B.E. K.I.N.D.** mantra-mnemonic to the daunting present-moment project of embracing and letting go of this life with as much paradoxical wisdom as we mere humans can muster. I've left out a specific chapter on the **K.**: KINDNESS element, since the practice of kindness is essential over-all, and is intrinsic within each of the others. Nevertheless, kindness is the central theme of Chapter 15, which deals with romantic love.

CHAPTER 7

INSIGHT

PART ONE

We've come to a consideration of the "I." letter of **B.E. K.I.N.D.**: INSIGHT. This is the anti-projection and "BE BLIND" letter. Insight-oriented psychotherapy directs our attention away from our day-to-day "projectoscopic" preoccupation with the veritable maelstrom of outer distractions, and towards the immense and profound riches within. Any deep awakening or recovery is essentially an inside job.

IT'S ALL A CHOICE

Insight amounts to a realization that whether we know it or not, we write and direct the entire melodrama or "karma" of our lives. Those of us who choose to strive for a growing measure of paradoxical wisdom come to realize that the control of both happiness and unhappiness is entirely in our own hands. At the most profound level, both are a matter of CHOICE.

Insight is the awareness that if we are as yet unawakened, or if we have momentarily fallen back into a dualistic and half-blinded unhappiness, *we* have become our own jail-keepers. It's the realization that we choose to make ourselves miserable by clinging to good-or-evil, win-or-lose illusions. Thereby, we choose our frantic, hopeless, and misery-inducing joys, … instead of engaging the more strenuous task of seeking more enduring, profound, paradoxical, and authentic happiness.

This is a revolutionary change in perspective. We don't have to rely on others and circumstances to change. We can learn to rely primarily on our own resources. The change we need is between our ears. After all, at the end of the cosmic con-game checkers board, we're crowned only with the other half of ourselves. The crucial and game-changing maneuver is always to pause, stand back, turn our gaze within, and question our own basic misassumptions.

This is the predominantly insightful solution, and yet, of course, outer solutions, responsibilities, and endeavors are also factors. Not one, not two.

The journey across the great ocean of existence is a journey inward, … the deeper you get … the more you meet truth.
Ram Dass

… "higher" always means … "more inner," … "deeper," … less visible…
E. F. Schumacher

What a man really has, is what is in him. What is outside of him, should be a matter of no importance.
O. Wilde

Our very life depends on everything's
Recurring till we answer from within.
R. Frost

God has placed in each soul an apostle to lead us upon the illumined path. Yet many seek life from without, unaware that it is within them.
K. Gibran

The well-bred contradict other people. The wise contradict themselves.
O. Wilde

It is our mind, and that alone, that chains us or sets us free.
Dilgo Khyentse Rinpoche

Those who know others are intelligent;
  Those who know themselves have insight.
Those who master others have force;
  Those who master themselves have strength;
Lao Tzu

What is necessary, after all, is only this: solitude, vast inner solitude.
M. R. Rilke

... no use plowing deeper than your own soil.
H. Thoreau

No one can drive us crazy unless we give them the keys.
Doug Horton

If someone throws you a ball, you don't have to catch it.
Anonymous

Nothing outside yourself can cause any trouble. You yourself make the waves in your mind.
S. Suzuki

Happiness ... is very difficult to find ... within, and it is impossible to find ... elsewhere.
C. Rosset

Your medicine is in you, and you do not observe it. Your ailment is from yourself...
Hazratr Ali

WE ALREADY HAVE IT ALL, WITHIN

It's so hard for us to cease our habitual focus on all this outer-directed striving. It's so hard to just **B.E.** our most profound inner selves. Thereby, a human doing can become a human **B.E.**ing. When we're still, quiet, and inner-directed, we discover that we already possess all the resources we need within.

This is an astonishing change! There's nothing essential out there to acquire or become. There's no place out there to go. We can turn off the shopping and travel channels. The most illuminating answers are within, along any pathway or set of circumstances. The answers are right here and right now.

The stillness, mindfulness, and enjoyment of meditation can take place wherever we are. There's no need to seek more nurturing and inspiring places or others. After all, we close our eyes in meditation in order to look within, in order to become utterly alone and detached from the distractions of surroundings, and in order to listen to the most ultimate and sacred inner answers that follow when we simply listen to the full mix of our own foolish and paradoxically wise insights. We can just as well do that at home alone. We can turn off the televisions and computers, altogether.

The inner show is far more enjoyable, illuminating, and astute. In fact, outer shows and attractions are worse than distractions; they're stark deprivations.

After we get the knack of this formal insight meditation process, we can take it on the road, so to speak. We can remain a human **B.E.**ing while we're **B.E.**ing a human doing. This is the beauty of striving for a nearly continuous state of mindful and insightful meditation.

The luxury of an awakened guide, mentor, teacher, or author can hasten and enrich our search, indeed, especially if he or she can teach us one of the many simple and portable methods, such as **B.E. K.I.N.D.** Nevertheless, it turns out that our paradoxically wise part-self is the most profound and fascinating teacher we could ever desire. It lies in wait for us to discover and reunite with it, as much as we can, and regardless of the specific method we use. All roads lead to this same inner self.

At the end of the day, the most ultimate and essential wisdom is self-taught, regardless of the level or quality of formal education, guidance, training, or methodology.

You don't have to go anywhere to get somewhere.
Anonymous

Traveling is a fool's paradise. We owe to our first journeys the discovery that place is nothing.
R. Emerson

Stay where you are, and all things shall come to you in time.
Kabir XL

You do not need to leave your room. Remain sitting at your table and listen. Do not even listen, simply wait. Do not even wait, be quite still and solitary. The world will freely offer itself to you to be unmasked, it has no choice, it will roll in ecstasy at your feet.
F. Kafka

There is no need to run outside
For better seeing, ...
... Rather abide
At the center of your being;
For the more you leave it, the less you learn.
Search your heart and see
... the way to do is to be.
Lao Tzu

Instead of going to Paris to attend lectures, go to the public library, and you won't come out for twenty years, if you really wish to learn.
L. Tolstoy

Human beings ... are always running after something: money, honor, pleasure. But if you had to die now, what would you want?
Taisen Deshimaru

Happiness belongs to those who are sufficient unto themselves. For all external sources of happiness and pleasure are, by their very nature, highly uncertain, precarious, ephemeral, and subject to chance.
Schopenhauer

Once again, the answers are paradoxical, both-and. It's not that we should withdraw completely from all forms of outer-directed responsibility, duty, ambition, striving, recreation, accomplishment, service, and education, ... all in order to retreat to the serenity of the mountainside, where we can forever content ourselves with contemplating our admittedly profound navels. There's room in life for a balance between getting somewhere out there and looking within. In fact, as we've discussed, we must enthusiastically take outer journeys in order to arrive where we began and realize that the greatest journey is within. We must see the world in order to gain great insight at home.

It's "both," "and," "neither," less," and "more." Along the pathway of any challenging outer endeavor or discipline, we literally stumble upon life's ultimate secrets, but only if this effort stimulates us to look within and rely on abundant inner resources.

I like what is in work - the chance to find yourself.
Joseph Conrad

PROJECTION: OUR FAVORITE AND PREDOMINANT SELF-DECEPTION

Our eyes are miraculous cameras. They're designed to look "out there." That's where the predominant dangers were, eons ago. This outer gaze was our illuminating protection, then. It's now our self-deceiving projection. Focusing through our "projectoscopic" eyes, we're such compulsive and consummate projection machines that we tend to distract ourselves all our lives from the vastly more immense, accurate, and fulfilling banquet of paradoxical wisdom within.

Using this externalizing and self-deceiving method, we export unconscious inner conflicts and perceive them only as we project them ... onto the distracting screen of the outside and others. Thereby, we create endless and needless outer crusades, battles, conflicts, and melodramas, without realizing that we actually create and provoke them, ourselves, in order to unknowingly act out inner, repetitive, and self-aggrandizing melodramas, as directed by our unconscious five year-old playwrights. This seduces us to fall for the inner con-artist's decoys, every time. This can lead us to entire lifetimes of confusion, folly, and wasted energy.

> *Let us not seek our disease out of ourselves; 'tis in us ...*
> Seneca

> *God made the senses turn outwards, man therefore looks outwards, not into himself. ... This ... confidence trick has taken in countless earnest seekers. The treasure of treasures they wore themselves out searching for is in fact the most accessible, the most exposed and blatantly obvious of finds, lit up and on show all the time.*
> D. E. Harding

> *Seeing is not seeing others but oneself.*
> Chauang-Tzu

> *There is not reality except the one contained within us. ... [Most] take the images outside them for reality ...*
> H. Hesse

> *Everyone thinks of changing the world, but no one thinks of changing himself.*
> L. Tolstoy

He begins to realize that the world was never outside of himself, that it was his own dualistic attitude, the separating of 'I' and 'others,' that created the problem ...
                                C. Trungpa

We can see through others only when we see through ourselves. ... Our preoccupation with other people ... is at bottom a means of getting away from ourselves ...
                                E. Hoffer

Our worst fault is our preoccupation with the faults of others.
                                K. Gibran

The trouble with happiness is that it is often linked to the behavior of others.
                                Anonymous

IN/DEPENDENCE, SELF-RELIANCE

Dependency on the outside is, after all, only one extreme of the full range of possibilities. It's a merely one-sided and all-or-nothing duality. In truth, we can't avoid, put off, abdicate, or delegate our own ultimate responsibility for the unfolding of the entirety of our own lives. Even if we're a fully disabled ward of the state or another; even if we're in prison; even if we're the abused and exploited subject of a tyrannical regime; even if we're permanently brain damaged; or even if we're a quadriplegic who's totally dependent on life-support; ... we still must face life squarely, honestly, and alone, if we're to solve life's deepest riddles and unite with our paradoxically wise part-selves within. At the end of the day, this is our sacred task. No one else and no outer circumstance can relieve us of this responsibility.

You can never have a greater or a lesser dominion than that over yourself.
         Leonardo da Vinci

[Neurosis is] the tendency to refuse responsibility for self. ... the realization that it is up to him to do something about his difficulties without insisting that others, or fate, or time will solve them for him.
         K. Horney

... ultimately, ... in the most important matters, we are unspeakably alone ...
         R. M. Rilke

We meet all life's greatest tests alone.
         Anonymous

You learn more on your own than from others.
         Anonymous

To get nowhere, follow the crowd.
         Anonymous

The real purpose of books is to trap the mind into doing its own thinking.
         Christopher Morley

... the real writer writes in order to teach ... [and] understand himself.
         Alfred Kazin

You carry the key to release yourself from your own chains.
         Anonymous

The wise traveler carries their own pack.
                                    Anonymous

Chop your own wood; it will warm you twice.
                                    Anonymous

To be balanced, however, a continuum exists between the extremes of dependence and independence. We're all vulnerable to the effects of outer circumstances. We all occasionally need a helping hand, but only to eventually take full responsibility for ourselves. Not one, not two. This is in/dependence. For instance, others can sometimes lend a more objective, educated, experienced, telling, advanced, or profound perspective. It's important to be able to ask for and accept help from others with some degree of grace, independence, and integrity. It's vital to both listen to and to disregard others, to seek advice and to rely solely on our own counsel, ... all with rapt in/attentiveness.

ENABLING/DEPENDENCE; DESTRUCTIVE/HELPFULNESS

The deepest resolutions are so very paradoxical. These illusions of taking care of others and of being taken care of are identical. They each cling to only one extreme of the same continuum. They constitute a mutually enthralled and mistaken duet of enabling/dependence. If we believe that we can save, rescue, mentor, or enlighten anyone over the age of sixteen, then we still believe in the concept of magical and omnipotent influence. Our underlying and preposterous illusion of personal grandiosity peeks out around the edges of these supposedly kindly and saviorish outer ministrations.

Dependency is a brief necessity during youth. It's a necessity, thereafter, only for those who are temporarily, gravely, or permanently afflicted, and even then only to a certain extent. *THERE ARE NO RESCUE HUMANS. ANY ATTEMPT TO TAKE TOTAL CARE OF ANOTHER IS ESSENTIALLY DESTRUCTIVE TO HIS OR HER VERY SOUL.* It's a well-meaning effort to blind him to his own strengths and responsibility. It imprisons him within the disastrous illusion of dependence. It cripples him in an invisible, but palpable and profound way.

The most effective physicians and psychotherapists lend a compassionate hand, indeed; and then they step back as much as possible and utilize the body and mind's innate self-healing capacities. The finest lessons we can teach our family, friends, students, or patients is for them to gradually grow out of their wish to rely on us for help; to face their own pain; to grapple with their own pathway's calamortunites; to catch on to the cosmic con-game for themselves; to make their own illuminating mistakes and errors along the way; and to painstakingly find their way as much as they can during their odysseys to their own two feet, ... to their vastly healing and paradoxically wise part-selves.

After all, the paradoxically wise parent purposely, gradually, and methodically makes him or herself into an ex-parent and lets the kids go. He or she allows the grown children to eventually fly with their own wings. This is the the most challenging and authentically loving part of parenting.

The most astute way to love others is to emulate the universe and our own paradoxically wise part-selves and give others hints, but we must let them discover the deepest truths for themselves the hard way, of course. We actually have no choice in this matter. It's the only way any of us stumble into a small measure of paradoxical wisdom. True to their own childish part-selves and to their paradoxically wise part-selves, our grown children don't and shouldn't listen to us, anyway.

We're all in this alone.
Jane Wagner & Lily Tomlin

Any pupil is fundamentally responsible for nurturing and developing his or her own deeper insights, decisions, pathways, and life, ... even while he's taking lessons from the most ultimate master teachers. In the ever-changing future, the pupil, alone, must become able to alter, innovate, and customize his teacher's lessons, in order to make them truly his, and in order to handle unanticipated, unpredictable, deceptive, and yet applicable circumstances and configurations to come. It's always an inside job. Teachers are destined to become erstwhile teachers. Further, the consummate former student naturally strives to surpass his teacher in matters of paradox. He becomes his own master.

A [good] mother is not a person to lean on, but a person to make leaning unnecessary.
Dorothy Canfield Fisher

... you don't do anything for anybody else, anyway.
Ram Dass

Every person must climb out of his own hole.
Anonymous

The Sphinx must solve her own riddle.
R. Emerson

'What have you come here for?' ... 'I have come seeking the Buddha's teaching.' 'What a fool you are! ... You have the greatest treasure in the world inside you, and yet you go around asking other people for help. I have nothing to give you.'
The Zen Teaching of Hui Hai

The only Zen you find on the tops of mountains is the Zen you bring up there.
                                    Robert Pirsig

A zen master would say, 'Kill the Buddha!' Kill the buddha if the Buddha exists somewhere else. Kill the Buddha, because you should resume your own Buddha nature.
                                    S. Suzuki

The individual who is ... self-reliant will not allow anyone to lean on him, as it would result in his enslavement. ... the one who leans and the one who allows himself to be leaned on are equally lacking in self-sufficiency.
                                    W. & M. Beecher

We know we have met such a teacher when we come away amazed not at what the teacher was thinking but at what we are thinking. ... A great teacher exposes the source, then steps back.
                                    J. Carse

To the extent that I swim for you, you never learn to take full responsibility for your life, in order to swim for yourself. If I enable you, I'm really damaging you by holding you back, thereby. It's all so paradoxically and intricately woven into the very fabric of the cosmic con-game. It couldn't be otherwise.

Many parents get caught up in a "helicoptering" dance with children over sixteen. They think that good parenting is measured by how devotedly attentive, hovering, instructive, coddling, and indulgent they are to their children, even to their middle-aged ones! They try to shelter their offspring from the ultimately healing and enlightening effects of taking full responsibility for themselves, which provides instructive consequences to their inherent and inevitable folly.

Grown kids must find out that they're not exceptional and special. They, too, are terribly fooled by that same cosmic con-game which so misleads their parents. There's no preemptive or educational end run around this. What self-aggrandizing enablers unintentionally teach is the illusion that life is fair; that we need not accept limits; that we need not find out what kind of fools we are; that we need not even attempt a change in our basic game; and that we can live a life without the healing and enlightening price of repetitive, painful, solitary, lonely and failure-ridden experience.

NO ONE ELSE AND NOTHING OUTSIDE TO BLAME

Some well-meaning, but misguided psychotherapists encourage both seriously ill and mildly neurotic individuals to cling to the disastrous belief that they're merely helpless and permanent victims of an inborn, untreatable, and incurable error of anatomy, physiology, or brain chemistry; or that they've been permanently and irretrievably warped by mistaken, neglectful, and/or malevolent parents. This interferes in a disastrous way with the patient's realization that he or she already possesses all he needs for his own recovery. It's all within, even for those who also happen to suffer from inborn, permanent, untreatable, and incurable errors of anatomy, physiology, or brain chemistry; or for those who were/or were not optimally parented.

> ... the sick in soul insist that it is humanity that is sick, and they are the surgeons to operate on it. ... once they get humanity strapped to the ... table, they operate on it with an ax. ... he who sets himself up as his brother's keeper will end up by being his jailkeeper.
> E. Hoffer

Sometimes counselors go so far as to blame a patient's present and real-life parent or partner-enabler for the patient's own one-sided dependency strivings. This is preposterous, since outer and enabling indulgence isn't what really imprisons them. They unconsciously and actively insist on imprisoning themselves, due to their own attachment to the illusion of womb-service. Each patient must rely on his or her own inner strengths and choose to seek an uncommon personal awakening. We must do our own self-soothing and find our own intrapsychic legs, even while in a wheelchair or while facing death. Even though we need outside compassion and assistance, we must simultaneously learn to go it alone.

If I politely decline to enter into an enabling and, therefore, disabling arrangement with another, it's not that I'll automatically and magically succeed, thereby, at teaching him or her a permanently insightful and life-changing lesson in self-reliance. Unfortunately, their powerful illusion of dependency is usually far too habitual and resilient for that. They usually and quickly replace me with yet another grandiose and saviorishly enabling type of helper.

Well-meaning, but unknowingly destructive enablers are everywhere, ready to step in at a moment's notice to "confirm" their unconscious, self-defeating, and other-defeating illusion of innate superiority by offering the very illusion of dependency that they think I'm so "unfairly" and "callously" withholding. These new saviors are really fostering their own vicarious dependency longings, out of their own self-aggrandizing sense of guilt. Ultimately, they harm themselves as much as they harm the other. It's all so backwards.

Said another way, we're not "curing" others by refusing to engage in well-meaning, but enabling dances. We're simply harmonizing with our own paradoxically wise part-self and with the cosmos. We're staying in the center, atop our balance-ball gizmos. Thus, we're maintaining a profound harmony with the innate wisdom of the universe. Maintaining our own centered wisdom and maturity atop the cosmos' balance-ball is simply the best way to help anyone else.

When we throw a drowning person a rope, we're no help to them if we fail to anchor ourselves and the line to a stable and reliable base. This is why airlines instruct us to secure our own face-masks, before we attempt to help others. After all, in these and all other dire instances, we're no help to others if we lose our own centered, anchored, cohesive, in/dependent, and paradoxically wise part-self awareness.

At the end of the day, we realize that we must leave it up to the dependency-seeking other to decide if they want to take the road less traveled; ... to see if they're willing to consent to pay the price to try to find their own paradoxically wise part-self within, by striving for their own balance, and by choosing to relinquish their own futile and childish notion of dependency. It's their choice. Sadly, they often choose dependency.

CHAPTER 7

INSIGHT

PART TWO

WE WRITE THE WHOLE PLAY

A most transformative, profound, and healing insight is the realization that we unconsciously write, produce, cast, direct, act out, watch, applaud, criticize, and promote the entirety of our life's melodrama. We choose the entire production's direction and mood. Even amidst life's requisite failures, setbacks, ailments, disabilities, tragedies, disasters, traumas, imprisonments, and wars; we, alone, create the entire production. We, alone, are responsible for the strategies we select to play these cards. This is karma. The good news, here, is that we're also the only ones who can revise our melodramas, our plays.

You are the painter, and life is your canvas.
                                        Anonymous

The curtain is lifting. We can have triumph, or tragedy, for we are the playwrights, the actors and the audience. Let us book our seats for triumph. The world is sickened of tragedy.
John Macauley

... the Hindu-Buddhist principle of karma [is] that everything which happens to you is your own action or doing.
A. Watts

Few blame themselves until they've exhausted all other possibilities.
Anonymous

We are not only the creators of our misery, but can just as well construct our happiness.
P. Watzlawick

Your mind can either free or imprison you.
Anonymous

EQUAL OPPORTUNITY HAPPINESS-ENLIGHTENMENT; WE CAN'T MISS A THING

If we truly comprehend this principle that we create the entire melodrama or karma of our lives, ... then this insight sets us free! Exterior hindrances can't really block our ultimate inner enlightenment! Paradoxical wisdom can take place amidst literally any external setting, circumstance, or time. We humans can't miss it, as long as we're receptive, humble, and inner-directed. Our inner, instructive, and paradoxically wise part-self is ready to be discovered, even to our last breath. It's a gift, and it's also earned. We can discover it, but only if we seek it.

This is truly wonderful news! It means that no one has an advantage or disadvantage when it comes to life's most sacred responsibility of finding ourselves, ... our integrated and paradoxically wise part-selves, that is. It's foolproof! Think of it! No one has a leg up! ... not the rich, the powerful, the advantaged, cared-for, cloistered, well-raised, educated, famous, beautiful, free, intact, healthy, or talented. No one. We can't miss a thing; that is, we can't miss out on the one thing that really matters; and yet, ... most people do.

The grass may be greener on the other side, but it still has to be mowed.
Anonymous

Riches and poverty are a thick or thin costume; ... our life [is] ... identical
R. Emerson

The real measure of our wealth is how much we'd be worth if we lost all our money.
John Hewett Jowett

Within this setting of universal inner equality, envy becomes obsolete. Think of the seemingly preposterous possibility of a life without envy! There's actually no one out there to admire, idolize, or worship. We can serve as our own role models. What would *our* paradoxically wise part-selves do? We each have the same teeming and enriching supplies of ultimate and world-class paradoxical wisdom within, just waiting to be tapped. We each possess this same, equal, and profoundly integrated self. No one is deprived or inferior. It's standard issue.

PSYCHOLOGICAL AFFLICTION AS A CHOICE: NO EXCUSES

This also means, however, that there are NO MORE EXCUSES. Our entire state of mind and self-esteem are totally in our own hands. It's our choice. We can no longer blame afflictions, others, accidents, traumas, losses, tragedies, abuses, or the outside, dang it. We thought that was what parents, home towns, partners, friends, governments, tragedies, and past histories were there for. Where's the ogre to blame? Where's our entitled, demanding, and dependent victim role? Our very psychological afflictions, other than extreme biological and/or post-traumatic ones, are of our own creation. We unconsciously and meticulously concoct them all. This is good news. It means we can choose to climb out of them, as well.

This is a huge windfall/and a terrible loss. It's revolutionary/and catastrophic. What will we do without our cherished and dualistic excuses, PROJECTIONS, illusions, ideals, PROJECTIONS, victim roles, PROJECTIONS, and envy? Did I mention projections?

B.E. K.I.N.D. TIME

Let's consider an example of how to put our **B.E. K.I.N.D.** mantra-mnemonic to work in regards to **INSIGHT**. We could use many examples of conflicts with others. These hurt our feelings. Let's look at a common instance of such conflict. Imagine that I'm in a very upsetting and urgent argument with my lover. I've been misunderstood, mistreated, betrayed, insulted, and such, ... at least in my own mind. I feel deeply wronged, and I resent this. It's time to apply the "**I.**" portion of **B.E. K.I.N.D.: INSIGHT**.

As always, the first step in the drill is to pause and give the inner five-year-old an all-**EMBRACING, ACCEPTING**, and healing **S.P.A.C.E.: Silence, Pause, Acceptance, Compassion,** and **Empathy**.

Compassion is probably the only antitoxin of the soul. Where there is compassion even the most poisonous impulses are relatively harmless.

E. Hoffer

It's time to keep our mouths shut, turn off our projectoscope, metaphorically grab our child part-self by the shoulders, push him or her away from the "poised-to-eject-him-from-the-game" umpire, and let the child rant and rave in the safety of our mind:

> I can't believe you did that or think that about me. What injustice! How can I ever be happy with you while you treat me like that? How can you do this to me? I've told you a thousand times not to do that. This makes me crazy. I'll shake you by the shoulders and teach you a lesson. You can't do this to me any more! I'll never be happy, until you stop it!
>
> I'll just withdraw my love and sulk and fume, in order to demonstrate how badly you've mistreated me. I'll do this until you realize what you've done, and until you apologize and promise not to do it, again. If you don't come around to my way of seeing things, I'll just have to leave you, forever. Then, I'll have my revenge on you! You'll be sorry!

Now it's **B.E. K.I.N.D.** time in regards to **INSIGHT**. It's time to pause and have an enlightening sit-down consultation with our paradoxically wise part-self. It's time to soothe, comfort, confront, and guide our inner child with the healing perspective of our experienced, mature, profound, and paradoxical wisdom. It's time to gently remind the child that our paradoxically wise self is best equipped to drive the bus.

We can remind the child that when he or she is angry, afraid, and projective, he's using childlike and dualistic thinking. He's seeing reality in polarized, either-or ways, rather than in centered and realistic ways. He sees the vexation as arising outside himself, and thus he chases his tail with outer, not inner, solutions. More often than not, this is a total waste of time.

We can remind the child that apart from basic food, water, oxygen, shelter, and such, we have all we need within. Let's roll up our sleeves and see what we can accomplish ourselves, rather than relying on our partner or the outside to change. What can we change about ourselves?

In other words, how can we get over our own illusion of dependency? We control how we feel. It's not another's job. We can learn to adjust to and maneuver with our partner in internal ways. All relationships require compromises. We can see how we stir his or her upsets in this circumstance, for example. We can use our skills of observation to anticipate his hot buttons, so that we can learn to adeptly maneuver around and accommodate to them. We can thus take the reins ourselves and use preventative diplomacy to avert a fight before it develops, as much as possible.

For instance, it's best to just listen to our partner when he or she complains about a conflict they had today with a friend, co-worker, or boss. Instead of offering him a solution, we can keep our mouths shut, give him S.P. A.C.E., and say to ourselves:

> Just listen. Just let him or her vent and complain. This is what I do for my own five-year-old part-self, so I'll do this with him, too. Besides, I know from painful experience that if I run in with a solution or suggestion, he resents that every time, and then I've succeeded in turning his ire away from the upsetting external situation and onto me. Then, if I defend myself by saying my usual, 'I was just trying to help,' I succeed in stirring his anger all the more.

He or she just wants to be heard and comforted. I need to trust that he'll eventually come to his own more wise judgement and solutions, himself. My job is to soothe and comfort him. He's told me time and again not to solve things for him. It makes him feel like he's being parented. It's time to just keep quiet, soothe, and love him. It's so counter-productive to be competitive and to parade my supposedly superior and "told-you-so" problem-solving abilities. Sympathetic, loving, and empathic silence is nearly always a good start.

In this way, we've unilaterally solved the relationship problem, without relying on another to change or to solve it for us. We've paused and used **INSIGHT** to avert stirring up the entire conflict, ourselves. This prevention strategy works so much better than our old, externalizing, impulsive, dependent, well-meaning, and yet conflict-provoking ways.

Although our own five-year-old could easily provoke our partner, again, and set up the same old endless arguments with him or her, wherein the other represents a past parent or sibling, and wherein our inner child thinks he can win, this time; … it's useless and foolish to repeat and perpetuate this ancient, unresolvable, and interminable argument. We can stay in the present moment, put away our fancy projectoscope, look within, overcome our repetition compulsion, seek inner resources, and perform more astute and profound maneuvers, ourselves. This is the result of profound **INSIGHT**, of self-reliance.

This reliance on inner solutions reinforces the rest of the six **B.E. K.I.N.D.** measures. It keeps us centered and **BALANCED**, instead of imbalanced and extreme. It assists our **EMBRACING ACCEPTANCE** of what is, rather than insisting on our tidy and dualistic illusions. It reinforces that the illusion of revenge is truly counterproductive, provocative, and useless. This is **D**ISILLUSIONMENT. **I**NNER solutions help us to be humble, to **D**EFLATE our big-shot selves, and to concentrate on changing the only person we can change, ... ourselves. It enables us to be **K**IND, rather than resentful and vengeful. Finally, it enables us to seek here-and-**NOW** solutions, instead of relying on the past, or on theoretical future developments.

CHAPTER 8

B & E: BALANCE AND EMBRACING

PART ONE

Let's consider the first two letters of the **B.E. K.I.N.D.** mnemonic, the "**B**." and "**E**.", the **B**ALANCE and **E**MBRACING. These initial letters could be called the "**B**reaking and **E**ntering" letters. In essence, the universe must force us to break and enter into the universe's paradoxical wisdom, as a result of the healing and transformative fierce-teacher-rug-pulling calamortunities of life. Without these healing and painful provocations and rug-pullings, it just wouldn't occur to us to inquire further than our shallow, dualistic, misleading, and unfulfillable illusions. We would settle for the frantic, meager, and sadomasochistic joys within our self-created and immense misery. We must break down already unlocked and open doors to get into unreasonably happy paradoxical rooms.

We must be broken into life.
                                                    Charles Raven

The essence of being human is ... that one is prepared in the end to be defeated and broken by life.
George Orwell

EMBRACING ACCEPTANCE AS THE FIRST STEP TOWARDS CHANGE

Let's take up the "**E**" letter, first. Paradoxical wisdom enables us to accept and **EMBRACE** reality's paired identical twin/opposites, ... the good-bad, divine-horrid, inspired-depraved, beautiful-terrible. It's an equal acceptance of all the positive and negative paired elements of the full catastrophe of painfully/ecstatic reality. In fact, the three most important factors in awakening are: ACCEPTANCE, ACCEPTANCE, and ACCEPTANCE. It's really a totally accepting/effort to transform, ... an acceptance of what is, while also trying to bring about imperfect increments of change.

Acceptance means that we cease the futile project of giving reality, ourselves, and others a drastic, extremist, utopian, and curative make-over. It means that we accept the fullness and messiness of reality as it is. Paradoxical acceptance is philosophical and emotional jujitsu. It's a totally accepting/need for change, a surrendering/resistance.

Life is a roller-coaster. ... Either you get dragged along behind the car ... Or you ... climb into the car and choose to have things be exactly as they are ...
G. Claxton

... literally absorbing pain and insecurity ... like judo, the gentle ... way ... of mastering an opposing force by giving in to it.
Alan Watts

> *If a doctor wishes to help a human being he must be able to accept him ... and ... himself as he is.*
> C. Jung

WE LOSE IT ALL, ANYWAY

We're destined to lose everything in the end. In fact, a season during which we lose everything we think we have; ... this is one of the universe's finest and harshest teaching and healing calamortunities. Like children, we want what we want. We want what we artificially separate out as the good part: life's abundant pleasures, gains, trinkets, loves, successes, youth, health, justice, and victories. When it comes to the so-called bad stuff: the pains, losses, deformities, illnesses, defeats, decay, and inequities; ... all that should happen to the other guy, but not to us.

> *There is praise and blame, gain and loss, pleasure and pain, fame and disrepute. Did you think this would not happen to you?*
> The Buddha

> *I'd like to live like a poor man - only with lots of money.*
> Pablo Picasso

What are we to do when we're stripped clean, hurt, ill, defeated, betrayed, lost, abandoned, rejected, and desperate? What happens after life takes away our "happily ever after" fantasy? Stiff upper lip? Do we fight back? Do we kvetch, wring our hands, and complain about the existential unfairness of it all? Do we just give up, take it, and lose hope? Do we struggle to get back to the "good?" Do we strive for a fresh new life, career, location, or partner, and start all over? Do we try to use setbacks to improve ourselves, others, laws, and politics? Do we lead a deadly rebellion, or do we just live within the system, let the tyrants and bullies have their self-corrupting bounty, and make the best of it? Do we run for our lives, leave our belongings behind, keep our families as safe as possible, and dare to hope for more equitable new circumstances, elsewhere?

How can we remain unreasonably happy and hopeful amidst life's inescapable elements of agony? How can we reconcile, persevere, and maintain a mature, realistic, compromised, and ironic sense of gratitude, hope, and resilience? How can we teach this to the children?

BALANCE: TRANSCENDING DUALITY: WELCOMING GOOD AND EVIL EQUALLY

Now we come to the "**B**" letter of the mnemonic: **BALANCE-PARADOX**. We've already spent three chapters exploring PARADOX. The equidistant **BALANCE** at the stable and paradoxical center of the spinning cosmic wheel amidst apparent extremes; ... this is our most profound existential and enigmatic position. Initially, we cling to an overly-simplified, dualistic, split-up, either-or, good-or-evil, and "one-eye-blind" world of illusion. In so doing, we stunt our own growth or awakening. We remain fixated, thereby, as flat-earth, two-dimensional "children grown tall," as Milton Erickson said.

The very distinctions between good and evil, and pleasure and pain are the culprits. It's this unintentionally destructive dungeon of either-or, right-wrong, win-lose, happy-sad perception which keeps us so very half-blinded and imprisoned. "It's all good."

Every angel is terrible.
                                        R. Rilke

Centered and paradoxical awakening is all about accepting life's negatives and positives equally. How can we accept all this pain, loss, decline, disability, and even death without becoming irretrievably resentful, bitter, broken, and hopeless? Perhaps this is the central dilemma for all of humanity and its philosophers, clergy, writers, gurus, and psychologists.

> *If a lonely man's final scream*
> *Before he hangs himself*
> *And the Nightingale's perfect lyric*
> *Of happiness*
> *All become an equal cause to dance,*
>
> *Then the Sun has at last parted*
> *Its curtain before you —*
>
> *God has stopped playing child's games*
> *With your mind*
> *And dragged you backstage by*
> *The hair,*
>
> *Shown to you the only possible*
> *Reason*
> *For this bizarre and spectacular*
> *Existence.*
>
> Hafez

Some existentialists are rather eloquent about balanced and paradoxical acceptance. Although most existentialists seem at first glance as rather one-sided, negative, pessimistic, bitter, and resigned, some of them can actually go beyond the acceptance-rejection realm and into an additional dimension of active, enthusiastic, and paradoxical acceptance of life's full beauty and horror. They even manage to respect, welcome, and celebrate the negatives equally with the positives. In this way, they transcend merely linear logic.

This centered and balanced embracing of the wholeness of reality frees us from our self-imposed, win-lose, and dualistically distorted lenses. Paradoxical acceptance enables us to become quietly, unreasonably, and unconditionally happy. We can accept and enjoy what we have, and get over our grief about what we've lost. We can then celebrate the miraculous gift of life, itself, in all its terrible/beauty. We come to enjoy the pathway. Isn't this resilient and unreasonably happy sense of gratitude the point of an awakening?

"CALAMORTUNITY"

Acceptance is where paradox really shines. Consider this. Some have over-simplified the translation of the Chinese word for "crisis" as a combination of two characters, one for "danger," and one for "opportunity." Hence, the derivation of my made-up term for the opportunity within every crisis, "calamortunity," which we've discussed.

When the cosmos provocatively pulls the rug out, it's giving us a benevolently/painful "whack on the side of the head." It gets our attention and invites us to wake up and think outside of our dualistic box. This awakening or insight makes it possible for us to choose to detach from our self-defeating illusions or misassumptions. We can replace or expand them, in order to include those opposite aspects of life that we had denied, repressed, and projected. We can thus stop playing in a half-blinded manner. The tinny and hollow solos of mere illusion transform into the multidimensional, integrated, enriched, and harmonic symphony that we call enlightenment.

Seen in this way, each adversity or setback can be considered as both a curse and a blessing. Each calamortunity is a white-hot crucible, which can destroy our old view and create the new, enriched, resilient, integrated, and unreasonably happy alloy of paradoxical wisdom. We can achieve an epiphany, thereby, and forge maladies into melodies. There's an old saying among meditators that affliction is the finest pathway to enlightenment. I would add that it's also the finest pathway to unreasonable happiness. Again, it's all in appreciating the pathway, not the destination.

> *Your pain is the breaking of the shell that encloses your understanding.*
> K. Gibran

> *We want to run away from the pain rather than regard it as a source of inspiration.*
> C. Trungpa

> *In the middle of difficulty lies opportunity.*
> A. Einstein

> *The difficulty we meet with in reaching our goal is the shortest path to it.*
> K. Gibran

> *All misfortune is but a stepping stone to fortune.*
> Anonymous

> *I do not believe that true optimism can come about except through tragedy.*
> Madeleine L'Engle

> *Our hearts can grow strong at the broken places.*
> Buddhist saying

> *In life it is more necessary to lose than to gain.*
> Boris Pasternak

When you understand what you see, you will no longer be children. You will know that life is pain, that each of us hangs always upon the Cross of himself. And when you know that this is true of every[one] ..., you will be wise.
Whittaker Chambers

The true way goes over a rope which is not stretched at any great height but just above the ground. It seems more designed to make men stumble than to be walked upon.
F. Kafka

Be grateful for the darkness ... that's when you can see the stars.
Anonymous

All my major works have been written in prison. ... I would recommend prison not only to aspiring writers but to aspiring politicians, too.
Nehru

GOING INTO THE PAIN, INTO THE FIRE

Life separates out the strong from the weak primarily through adversity and pain. These are the rug-pullings. This is when ultimate secrets can be revealed to us. We must train ourselves, therefore, to go into the healing and fiery crucible, into the pain, rather than being scared away.

> *[A] Chinese sage ... was asked, 'How shall we escape the heat?' ... He answered, 'Go right into the middle of the fire.' ... in* **The Divine Comedy**, *Dante and Virgil find that the way out of Hell lies a its very center.*
> A. Watts

Only great pain, the long, slow pain that takes its time ... compels us to descend to our ultimate depths. ... I doubt that such pain makes us 'better,' but I know it makes us more profound.
F. Nietzsche

... the only thing that's taught one anything is suffering. Not success, not happiness, not anything like that.
Malcolm Muggeridge

God whispers to us in our pleasures, speaks in our conscience, but shouts in our pain: it is His megaphone to rouse a deaf world.
C. S. Lewis

Without suffering there is no salvation.
C. Jung

He has seen but half the universe who never has been shown the house of Pain.
R. Emerson

The model which you are stuck in ... is shaken by pain and suffering. ... At that point you recognize the bizarre phenomenon that suffering is grace.
Ram Dass

No artist or scientist reaches the peak of his accomplishments as long as he has been spared great suffering.
Theodor Reik

Suffering only hurts because you fear it. ... It pursues you only because you flee from it. You must not flee, ... you must not fear ... love your suffering. ... Listen to me, and remember: suffering is nothing, suffering is illusion. Only you yourself create it, only you cause yourself pain.

Herman Hesse

The wisdom of others remains dull till it is writ over with our own blood. ... it bursts into our consciousness only when it sinks its teeth and nails into us.

E. Hoffer

Why do you want to shut out of your life any uneasiness, any misery, any depression? ... sickness is the means by which an organism frees itself from what is alien; ... that is the way it gets better."

R. Rilke

All psychological disorders are caused not by the painfulness of living but by the misguided and unfounded belief that pain is always avoidable.

G. Claxton

Think of your problems as a challenge in a game you enjoy playing.

Anonymous

Pain makes man think. Thought makes man wise. Wisdom makes life endurable.

John Patrick

There's no need, by the way, to become breast-beating and card-carrying masochists and, thereby, to actively and heroically seek out, create, or make a permanent home within such unavoidable and illuminating pain and suffering. Adolescents and young adults often make this tactical, dualistic, and tragic error. Like us and our ancestors, they run off to pursue their brave and masochistic foreign crusades. Life supplies abundant painful opportunities right where we are, without our assistance. Pain is a required lesson along the way. It's not the destination.

FIERCE TEACHERS; NOTHING TO LOSE

What about that special category of extreme, excruciating, unendurable, and unbearable pain? This pain goes far beyond life's normal measure of pain and suffering. It's the kind of pain that moves us to scream to whatever gods may be, "Enough! I can't take it any more! Haven't you made me suffer enough? You surely can't expect me to go on!" How can such unbearable pain possibly be construed as an opportunity for growth? To the severely afflicted, the mere suggestion of such a "look-at-the-bright-side" attitude seems to be downright calloused and cruel.

Surely, the only reasonable response during such extreme pain is to throw ourselves on the ground or bed, and beg for relief at any cost. Nevertheless, the greater the pain, the greater the potential for learning. As we've discussed, this is nature's most ultimate crucible, its most destructive/creativity.

In fact, reality does us a great service if it visits us with extreme and unavoidable pain, suffering, discouragement, betrayal, injustice, abandonment, illness, and loss when we're young enough to learn, poor enough to have little to lose, and resilient enough to recover and/or adjust. We need these fiercest of teachers, these crucibles, in order to get our attention and knock some sense into us. The universe holds our hands to the fire so that we can awaken and wise up to the cosmic con-game. "IT'S ONLY UNBEARABLE

PAIN." We must trust it and go with it. This extreme, sadistic, and fierce teacher is a healing gift from the universe.

We may as well not whine, complain, and "catastrophize." Just as there's no crying in baseball, there's no whining in enlightenment. Pain doesn't confer special privileges or exceptions. Our inevitable measure of almost unbearable suffering gives us no excuse to become childishly, passively, and melodramatically breast-beating and demanding about life. Besides, losing everything is absolutely guaranteed.

The down side of any fate we can imagine doesn't compare with our death. This calamortunity reveals to us that WE ACTUALLY HAVE NOTHING TO LOSE. We don't get to keep these bodies, minds, families, friends, enjoyments, skills, wisdoms, positions, or halcyon times. We have to move on. All things come and go, ebb and flow.

Until we lose ourselves there is no hope of finding ourselves.
Henry Miller

Nature's first green is gold, *Then leaf subsides to leaf.*
Her hardest hue to hold. *So eden sank to grief,*
Her early leaf's a flower; *So dawn goes down to day.*
But only so an hour. *Nothing gold can stay.*
R. Frost

There's another staggering paradox, here. It turns out that losing everything is actually and routinely *required*. We must hit bottom. We must lose all our illusions if we're to attempt this huge and CON/FUSING project called paradoxical wisdom. All of them. Any nearly unbearable fierce teacher is simply presenting us with this standard bill for the seemingly impossible and exorbitant price of admission to our unreasonable happiness.

The expanded fullness and richness of life that loosing everything introduces us to; ... these are well worth it. I've had the privilege to assist several individuals' attempts to consciously embrace their own approaching deaths within this degree of profound, courageous, and paradoxical acceptance. They invariably say that they wish they'd done this during the years before. They enter, thereby, into the present moment/eternal realm of quiet, modest, unreasonable, and unconditional happiness.

WE'RE NOT ALONE; WE'RE ALL FOOLED

It's somewhat consoling that everyone is equally and completely fooled by life's cosmic con-game. No one escapes. We all must learn that we're so terribly, chronically, and repeatedly fooled about almost everything that really matters in life. No one gets to do an end run around this terribly/beautiful and mortifyingly/exhilarating realization. No one is just handed great wisdom without this fall, and without realizing what lifelong fools we are. We find out what we're really worth after we've lost everything, ... at least everything we think we have.

Therefore, if we choose to embrace this painfully/enjoyable brand of paradoxical wisdom, we're not taking a harder, worthier, more noble, more deprived, or more humiliating pathway than anyone else. We're not being superior. Paradox is the path that we all must choose to embrace, sooner or later, but one which very few have the courage to even contemplate, let alone attempt. We're all on a paradoxically level playing field, here. We're identical twin brothers and sisters.

If we meet a fellow awakening pilgrim, we know that he or she is amidst the lifelong process of emerging from the same disappointing, humiliating, defeating, confusing, painful, and illuminating rug-pullings. They, too, hit bottom at times, so that they can find out what kind of fools they and we are. They, too, are foolishly and paradoxically wise.

IT'S ALREADY GONE

Life demands that if we aspire to any degree of profound and paradoxical wisdom, we must willingly relinquish all that really matters to us; that is, all that we mistakenly think gives our life its very meaning, relief, and hope. As some Buddhists say, "They're already gone." This is transformative and curative disillusionment. "This is unbearable!" we say. "I can't do without my precious and idealistic philosophy, religion, ease, comfort, child, spouse, parent, friend, love, money, house, security, safety, possession, luxury, power, occupation, respect, dignity, reputation, youth, beauty, health, status, freedom," and so on. "That's too much to ask of me," we cry.

It turns out that losing everything is one of life's finest learning opportunities. It's the ultimate shakedown fierce teacher. These are the times when life strips us down to bare essentials. These times help us, thereby, to discover just what we're really made of. It's not a fate reserved only for those other unfortunates out there. It's reserved for us all.

The cosmos takes everything away; that is, all our most cherished illusions and ideals. Then it steps back and watches to see if we can not only take it, but even utilize it to become reborn into a larger, more ultimately fulfilling, more unreasonably happy, and more paradoxical reality. Can we emerge, like the Phoenix, with even more strength, wisdom, gratitude, depth, and happiness?

> ... *those who have been ... [afflicted] beyond belief ... achieve a real reunion, a reconciliation of the deepest ... kind.*
>
> Oliver Sacks

> *Everything we lose is Buddhist truth. ...We can mourn it, but we don't have to get down in the grave with it.*
>
> Anne Lamott

A "WILLING-HAND-ON-THE-TRIGGER" TYPE OF AWAKENING

At times of terrible loss, we suffer such agony that we sometimes consider the relief of taking our own lives, of course. We research and devise specific and efficient suicidal plans. We tell ourselves that suicide is really the best thing for ourselves and others. We just can't stand it a moment longer. In fact, now that we've decided to end it all, and, therefore, to let go of everything in life, ... this decision, itself, gives us the very peace of mind that we so desperately crave. This seems to confirm our plan, ... or so we think. We should have realized this sooner. "Ah, the relief to come," we think, as we grow impatient with any delays or impediments to our plan for permanent entrance into the sweet relief of this-or-that and losing-it-all oblivion.

At these times, when we're willingly and enthusiastically pointing the loaded gun at ourselves; when we're staring down the gun barrel; when we're even eager to pull the trigger; when we're at the moment of certain death; and when we're at that pause between the in-breath and the out-breath, ... that's when we've actually given ourselves the answer! It's that simple. All-too-often, people don't stop and listen to this ultimate, present-moment, and inner awakening or satori. Instead, they rush ahead and pull the trigger. It's too bad, because they actually give themselves the ultimate answer at this "willing-hand-on-the-trigger" moment of awakening. All they need to do is to let go, pause, and have a conference with their paradoxically wise part-selves.

THAT'S THE ANSWER! If we're willing to literally die, then in essence we're willing to let go of everything, everyone, and all our convictions! We've given ourselves the ultimate zen moment of detachment! We've essentially solved life's central mystery. The truth at that very moment is that we don't need to actually pull the trigger and rush into the relief of oblivion, or into an imaginary, halcyon, and eternal afterlife future. We don't need to literally die. We'll do that soon enough, anyhow. All we need to do is to stay in the present and newly awakened moment and listen to our own desperate, accidental, unanticipated, backwards, and ultimate "giving-up-everything" wisdom! Suicide is actually an instance of over-kill. Such a near-death experience is very illuminating.

All we need to do is to let go of all the illusions that we hold so dear. All of them! It's not things, people, positions, or our very lives that we need to relinquish. Rather, it's all our precious and terribly mistaken mirages or illusions. Just let them all go and live a truly and authentically new, stripped down, humble, and modest life, one based on the abundant/deprivations of the sacred and paradoxical center of the cosmic wheel. We must relinquish the merely linear, pleasurable, and ever-receding mirages of the wheel's spinning outer edges. We truly do need to die to our old dualistic selves, so to speak, thoroughly and completely, so that we can be "reborn" into the expanded and enriched center of paradox. Let it all go.

... when we no longer know what to do ... or which way to go, ... we have [begun] our real work and ... journey. The mind that is not baffled is not [profound].
                                    Wendell Berry

In truth, however, and paradoxically, when we do this, we don't actually let go of anything. After all, illusions have no real substance. "They're already gone." There's nothing to lose, because illusions are merely ever-receding mirages. They're figments of our imagination. Thus, we're really only required to relinquish that which we could never have obtained in the first place! We just need to add acceptance of the other harsher half of life. Less is more. It's time to discard our blindfolds. I'll cover this later under "**DISILLUSIONMENT**," as I have in the previous book.

CHAPTER 8

B & E: BALANCE AND EMBRACING

PART TWO

WE ESCAPE TO UTOPIAN PRISONS

We humans tend to live such catastrophically self-imprisoned/and escapist lives. We think we can escape from life's abundantly abhorrent aspects. Rather than facing and accepting the disillusioning, messy, illuminating, and curative fullness of reality, we construct protective, compensatory, and idealistic utopias in our minds. These merely imprison us all the more within our self-imposed and dualistic blindness. Ironically, thereby, we inadvertently jump from the frying pan into the fire.

Each sneaky and unconscious defensive maneuver merely solidifies our attachment to the corruptive siren songs of our fondest and most impossible illusions. These prevent our awakening into the expanded vision and unreasonable happiness of centered and reconciling paradox. Thus, each attempt to escape merely seals us all the more within the catastrophically wrong game; renders us increasingly lost and irredeemable; and intensifies our desperation and devastation. We end up running away from precisely those things which can ultimately free and heal us.

In fact, the initially dreaded process of disillusionment turns out to be our finest and most curative resolution. We must, therefore, relinquish the imprisoning illusion of escape, altogether. Indeed, the only way out of the fire is directly into it. It's all so amazingly and beautifully backwards!

> *We feel free when we escape - even if it be but from the frying pan into the fire.*
> E. Hoffer

We construct these utopian prisons all our lives within our so-called "normal" split-up model of thinking. There's no "head-in-the-sand" escape from life's fully integrated reality of terrible/beauty. Each escape attempt earns us even longer prison sentences within the ever deepening dungeons of our self-created and linear hell. It turns out that we are the most heinous wardens of our meticulously self-created prisons.

"COULDA-WOULDA-SHOULDA"

One of our favorite escape attempts is to obsess about those ever-popular "coulda-woulda-shoulda's," as we review past mistakes, defeats, failures, losses, injuries, humiliations, and so on. In effect, we chide ourselves, thereby, about how we could or should have seen things coming and handled them differently.

This "told-you-so" hindsight is so much clearer than boots-on-the-ground, real-time, and here-and-now vision. Hindsight allows us to review our all-too-human errors repeatedly and in slow motion on the post-game films. This gives us much more data than we could have known at the time. In this way, hindsight is a preposterously grandiose, unfair, cowardly, and fraudulent way to judge past actions.

"Told-you-so's" are the unconscious five year old's way of magically expecting too much, too soon. He or she can't accept and forgive the reality that we're merely human, and that even the wisest among us do the best we can within the inevitably limited knowledge, information, and skill that we have on hand in real time. Of course we'll later know the outcome and see the answer in the back of the book, but we can't know it ahead of time. The five-year-old part-self can't accept that most actions are well-intended, that all accidents are "stupid," and that we all must have the courage to forgive ourselves and discover just what kind of fools we are.

Such "coulda-woulda" ruminations amount to our unconscious five-year-old's way of reviewing the films and reliving the past; but this time, he or she magically and unconsciously "undoes" past limitations, immaturity, naivete, ignorance, damages, and injuries by second-guessing the ego, and by endowing himself, thereby, with magical, all-knowing, and perfect foresight, ... foresight, that is, via the artificial advantage of a non-existent rear-view mirror. It's all a narcissistic, larger-than-life, and super-heroic-do-over parade to "an audience of one." It's the way the inner five year-old part-self thinks it can magically create a better past.

This unconscious five-year-old part-self is a self-aggrandizing, cheating, and strutting coward. He or she can't accept the concept of gradual and hard earned growth and knowledge through those inevitable and painful lessons of defeats and failures. That's why he says, "I told you so," when things go south. He thus imagines that he's never wrong and that he saw it coming.

This self-inflation is a huge unconscious and illusory payoff. To the child part-self, this self-aggrandizing fantasy is well worth the painful regret that it inevitably induces in the ego. As the manipulated ego rants on and on about what could have been, his invisible and instigating five year old part self secretly *enjoys* this illusion of his own superior and magical ability to foresee the future. It's a perfect "do-nothing-himself" and endlessly "re-do-the-past" type of illusion. This is part of his underlying "secret victory of self-defeat."

In contrast, it's better to face the past squarely, as it really was. We must relinquish this notion of grandiose prescience, of never having to stumble and learn from mistakes. We're only human. Stumbling is how we learn.

Learn to wish that everything should come to pass exactly as it does.
                                Epictetus

FORGIVENESS:
IT COULDN'T HAVE BEEN OTHERWISE

The antidote to such endless, pointless, and self-deceiving obsessing, which is unconsciously so grandiose, larcenous, and pleasurable, ... is to realize that "it couldn't have been otherwise." Let it be. The "bad" or unfortunate thing happened. There's no escaping that reality. We fell short, period.

We must forgive ourselves. We were not God. We were ignorant or fooled, indeed. That's how we learn. Let it go. Time has moved on; it happened; and no amount of imagining it otherwise will magically change it. It's now etched in stone. The "coulda-woulda-shoulda" really "couldn't-a, wouldn't-a, and shouldn't-a," because it didn't. It was what it was. We were what we are, ... merely, irretrievably, and fallibly human.

REPLAYS IN THE SERVICE OF
HUMBLE NEW LEARNING

Although we can't change and undo the past, we can use

memory as a way of learning and growing from past experience. We can now recognize similar such situations and enjoy the wisdom of knowing how to better anticipate and resolve them in real and present time. We can practice better things to say and not say, do and not do, in such instances. That's the closest we mere and limited humans get to prescience.

Experience is often bad experience, isn't it? Spontaneous and clever come-back lines are usually well-rehearsed and perfected lines in the endlessly re-written scripts of life's plays. We've learned these lines the hard way, through past failures and defeats. We learned them when we didn't say them at the time. We may as well make, forgive, and learn from our rookie and veteran mistakes, like everyone else, instead of ruminating endlessly about some utopian, perfectionistic, and always successful fantasy of "what could have been." It's much more realistic and courageous to take our lumps and be humble enough to learn from bad experience, like anyone else.

This "it couldn't have been otherwise" mantra is a handy tool to use, in order to manage setbacks with some degree of acceptance, grace, and utility. It's useless to complain that we and life are not perfect and fair. This mantra helps us to accept a merely realistic and human win-loss record. We can stay in the present moment and let the past go. More about that, later.

Adversity introduces a man to himself.
Horace

Experience is a hard teacher. She gives the test first, the lesson afterwards.
Anonymous

Things falling apart is a kind of testing and also a kind of healing.
P. Chodron

Success is the ability to go from one failure to another with no loss of enthusiasm.
W. Churchill

At the cost of one failure, the wise can learn a lesson for a whole lifetime.
Sufi Inayat Khan

LEARNING TO ACCEPT AND EVEN ENJOY DILEMMA, ITSELF

Life is served up only in packages of dilemma, yet most never accept this. At first, this truth is quite obnoxious to us. We build our lives on dualistic and black-and-white notions, all of which we've made up. It's only when we train ourselves to adopt a modest and paradoxical acceptance of the true and integrated fullness of life and of ourselves that we can "break through" into a much deeper comprehension of and harmony with the expanded and messy fullness of reality.

Dilemma or paradox is the only reality there is. It's all we get. We can never emerge from this confusing, ironic, painful, and even absurd reality of paradox, so we may as well learn to accept it. Further, we're required to gradually acquire a taste for unending dilemma. We can even learn to prefer it, to prefer what is.

There is no cure for birth or death except to enjoy the interval.
George Santayana

We are all here for a spell, get all the good laughs you can.
W. Rogers

The ultimate sense of humor is a free way of relating with life situations in their full absurdity. It is seeing things clearly, including self-deception, without blinders, without barriers, without excuses ... Joy ... is an ultimate and fundamental sense of freedom, a sense of humor, the ability to see the ironical aspect of the game of ego, the playing of polarities.

C. Trungpa

Man is ill prepared to put up with sheer bliss.
P. Watzlawick

B.E. K.I.N.D. TIME

It's now **B.E. K.I.N.D.** time in regards to the **B.** and **E.** letters: **BALANCE** and **EMBRACING**. We often have to accept the harsh, abhorrent, and nearly unacceptable elements of life. This runs counter to our dualistic illusion of smooth-sailing, or cost-free living. Many such obnoxious predicaments involve illness, aging, death, loss, tragedy, betrayal, injustice, limits, defeat, compromise, and so on. For example, I could find myself in a wheel chair after a permanent spinal injury. Worse, it could be the result of another's malevolence or neglect. This is an extreme test of my ability to embrace uncommon acceptance and adaptation in the face of a grievous and mortifying reality.

GIVE THE FIVE-YEAR-OLD
A TOTALLY LOVING AND CARESSING "S.P. A.C.E."

Our best initial strategy after such an unfortunate injury is to give our inner five-year-old some "**S.P. A.C.E.**" It's time to be **S**ilent, to **P**ause, and to **A**ccept the child's complaining, ranting, and raving with **C**ompassion and **E**mpathy. After all, it's understandable that our inner child is grief-stricken, mortified, frightened, and outraged. He or she full of self-pity, fury, and vengefulness. It's best to sit him on our lap and let him cry, complain, and threaten without criticism. It's time to give him a good listening to. Just hold, soothe, caress, and contain his seemingly endless, inconsolable, and unbearable pain. This loving and containing **EMBRACE** is how healing begins.

Consider the beautiful image of a parent who gently, quietly, casually, and lovingly carries their exhausted and fast-asleep two year old child in their arms in public. The small child is so completely trusting that his little arms and legs hang limp, and his mouth may even be lax and open. What wondrous trust! It touches that part of us which remembers how this felt for us when we, too, relaxed into this all-trusting and vulnerable slumber.

This is how we should treat ourselves, with totally ACCEPTING and kindly love. We should strive to be so kind as to be able to trust ourselves completely, like a small child trusts his or her parents. This totally accepting and kindly listening is how we begin to soothe, comfort, and heal our upset and ranting little five year-old, as he complains:

> This is so unfair! I was following the rules, and now look at me! I'm injured and crippled for life. I'll never walk or dance or play sports again. I'm just a freak. No one will ever want to be with me. The very sight of me will gross them out! Worse, I'll be a burden on everyone.
>
> I hate being like this. I hate my life, now. I'm filled with envy and hatred every time I see intact people. They're everywhere! They can afford to take their bodies for granted. They have no idea what it's really like to be suddenly cut down like this. They better not say "make the the best of it." That makes

me so furious! It's so easy for them to say that. I just hate them! I even hate God!

Most of all, I hate me. There's no place in my world for a cripple. My pain is unbearable. Why didn't I just die in the accident? I just want to die, now. That'll end my misery. I'll just lay low and plan it all out, so that I can leave this hell-hole of a life. No one can stop me.

Such a childish, furious, hateful, spiteful, revengeful, tragic, pitiful, and hopeless rant is understandable. It's perfectly safe. The first step in helping anyone who's so hopelessly bereft is to listen without judgment and with endless compassion and love. Let him or her get it all out. It's a healing catharsis.

Let the passionate inner child rant on and on, within the privacy, capacity, safety, tolerance, acceptance, love, forgiveness, resilience, and silence of our own mind. Let the inaudible child shout the most vile, ghoulish, extremist, impulsive, aggressive, inciting, frightening, and foolish concepts possible. Remember, all thoughts are acceptable, as long as they're later seen in a larger context. They're harmless enough. There's no need to criticize them, but there is a requirement to use judgment and strategy about when and if to believe them, say them out loud, or act on them. Once again, we are not merely our thoughts and feelings.

> *Feelings are like children. You can't let them drive the car, but you can't just stuff them in the trunk.*
>
> Alcoholics Anonymous

THE B.E. K.I.N.D. DRILL

After pausing and listening, it's now paradoxical wisdom or **B.E. K.I.N.D.** time. It's time to have a consultation with our more profound and paradoxically wise part-self, who can offer the soothing and comfort the child needs. We've let the child have his or her say, but now it's time for our profound and integrated self to drive the car.

We can remind ourselves that we're not merely our inner child's thoughts and feelings. Our most profound part-self is our ultimately paradoxical self. It has far broader and deeper perspective, wisdom, hope, experience, resilience, and perseverance. It's large enough to be patient with and abide the child's rants. Our integrated self has the capacity to astutely choose just which of our thoughts to believe and which actions or inactions to take.

This is **B.E. K.I.N.D.** time. How would our integrated self respond to these thoughts? Specifically, it's time to practice the "**B**," or BALANCING-PARADOXICAL principle, as well as the "**E**", or EMBRACING-ACCEPTANCE part of **B.E. K.I.N.D.** Acceptance, acceptance, acceptance. IT'S ONLY UNBEARABLE PAIN. It's time to come into our center, to be our own finer and soothing self. Anyone can be immature and give up. Negativity only leads to more pain and suffering. There's no profound enjoyment or fulfillment in that. It's time to define ourselves by what we have now, not by what we've lost. It's time to persevere and be intrepid.

After all, the most profound task in life is to find our way back to our integrated and paradoxically wise part-self, as much as we can. Nothing outside can block this task. Moreover, losses and tragedies even enhance this sacred quest, all the more. Even without the use of half of our body, we can still accomplish this. We can still find a deeper meaning for life. There's no need to envy others, because we still can come into a vast, soothing, and healing inner harmony with the same disembodied and integrated self that resides in others. No one has an advantage about this. In fact, these times of loss, discouragement, and pain are opportunities to enhance the coming into our finest and most paradoxical self.

Our integrated self can sit our five-year-old down on his or her lap and talk soothingly to him. It can remind him that it's now time to grow up, go on with life, and make the best of it. We've cried and complained, but now it's time to settle for living in the limited present, not in the mere illusion of an endlessly revisable and intact past and future. It's time to convert hopelessness into mature and realistic hope. Anyone can give up. It takes real courage to accept what happened and just go on with energy, hope, curiosity, and enthusiasm.

After all it's merely an illusion that we can have a life without loss and pain. There's no guarantee that any of us will make it to the end of our lives with these bodies and minds intact. The dances, parties, and ball games are fun, but the real joy and fulfillment are within. It's time to accept loss as merely part of life. There's no such thing as an endlessly cost-free life. Sooner or later, we all lose everything and everyone, anyhow. "They're already gone."

> *There is praise and blame, gain and loss, pleasure and pain, fame and disrepute. Did you think this would not happen to you?*
>
> The Buddha

Further, the most profound paradoxical wisdom is measured more by what we relinquish than by what we gain or keep. We must lose all our illusions, anyhow. All things come with a cost. It's time to get away from an illusory, purely dualistic, win-lose, smooth-sailing, and utopian mentality. It's time to come into the paradoxical wisdom of the center, beyond such false and dualistic distinctions. As Nietzsche said, "It's all good."

After this self-soothing and self-coaching pause, we're ready to speak, remain silent, act, or remain still, ... all in harmony with the wisdom of our centered and paradoxical self. This is the compromised result of a cooperative, collaborative, and wise inner congress, which synchronizes with the perfectly balanced and paradoxical universe. We can harmonize with our paradoxically wise part-self. We can learn to live and love, in spite of losses, humiliations, and failures.

Anyone can be miserable. That takes no courage or talent. Despite our disability, there are many fulfilling things we can learn to do. There's nothing to do, so let's get started. Loss and gain fuse in the center, the unreasonably or unconditionally happy center and **BALANCE** of paradox. That's where we can learn to surrender unconditionally to life as it really exists. This is a "take-no-prisoners" and "enter-into-the-fire" type of EMBRACING ACCEPTANCE. In the years to come, and if we live long enough, we'll have many more such seemingly insurmountable and grievous realities and losses to accept.

Now that we've gone through the breaking and entering, **B** and **E** parts of the **B.E. K.I.N.D.** mantra-mnemonic, we can proceed to apply the rest of its principles, as well, ... some of which I've already mentioned. Although it's awkward and clumsy at first, we'll get the hang of it. Starting with the already-mentioned **KINDNESS** element, we can be loving and kind to ourselves, rather than being self-hating and blaming. We can forgive and embrace being merely limited and human.

Moving on to other **B.E. K.I.N.D.** elements, we can seek **INNER** solutions, not external ones. If we're paraplegics who can no longer walk, dance, or play conventional sports, we can, nevertheless, seek out enriching, enjoyable, and fulfilling wheelchair types of exercises, sports, loves, and readings. After all, the most profound solutions in life are inner ones. We can let ourselves be dependent on the help of others to a reasonable extent, since we're disabled, but we can also cultivate an inner strength of self-reliance.

We can seek here-and-**NOW**, present moment solutions. Rather than forever mourning what we've lost, and instead of idealizing and mourning what we were, then, ... we can move on to embrace and celebrate the teeming abundance of what we are and what we have, right here and right now. Life, itself, is such a gift!

As I mentioned, we can embrace **DISILLUSIONMENT**. We can let go of illusions, such as perfection, cost-free living, and so on. We can **DEFLATE** this larger-than-life sense of entitlement and embrace a more humble, realistic, and limited view of ourselves. Injured and handicapped individuals can be worthy, vigorous, enriched, fulfilled, loving, inspired, and inspiring.

By applying all seven elements of **B.E. K.I.N.D.**, we can, thereby, come into a larger and more spacious synchrony with our paradoxically wise part-self, and we can enjoy the depths of a mature inner peace which far eclipses the frantic, frustrating, superficial, and misery-inducing strivings of merely dualistic consciousness. It's all good.

CHAPTER 9

DISILLUSIONMENT

PART ONE

Let's consider the first "**D.**" of **B.E. K.I.N.D.**: **D**ISILLUSIONMENT. My first book explored the numerous wired-in illusions we all seem to have about life. These include perfection, purity, justice, unconditional love, dependency, security, certainty, permanence, smooth-sailing, superiority, and center-of-the-universe specialness. All these illusions thrive during youth and thereafter when we remain imprisoned within our normal, extremist, split-up, and dualistic model of thinking. We insist on trying to live in some sort of self-concocted and perfectible version of heaven or utopia on earth.

While we chase mere illusion, we think we're getting the good stuff. In so doing, we actually miss out on all that's more profoundly rewarding in life. Practically the only thing that's "perfect" on this tiny and messy planet is the perfect misery we induce when we try to give reality such an ambitious and idealistic make-over. These visions of pretend and counterfeit pay-offs are simply not worth it. They decoy us into mere fool's errands. They shallow us out.

The sooner we embrace a curative **DISILLUSIONMENT** and **DETACH** from these impossible pipe dreams, the better.

Lower your expectations of earth. This isn't heaven.
Max Lucado

When one sees that everything exists in illusion, one can live in a higher sphere.
The Buddha

Everywhere you turn ... you see people who are ... caught in the closets of their own perceptions.
Alexander Eliot

The basic psychological problem is trying to be what we are not.
Schaeffer

People will cease to commit atrocities only when they cease to believe absurdities.
Voltaire

Beware lest you lose the substance by grasping at the shadow.
Aesop

"SIN" ORIGINALLY MEANT "MISTAKENNESS"

This folly reflects what the ancients really meant by the term "sin." Scholars tell us that "sin" didn't originally mean "bad deeds" or "transgressions." Rather, it meant "mistakenness." It meant that we missed the mark, were on the wrong track, were unrealistic, and were going against the possible. If we chase after unrealistic illusions, swim against the current, and try to improve on reality by attempting to re-engineer life and humans according to our own mistaken, foolish, split-apart, and perfectionistic specifications; then objective reality, itself, automatically "punishes" us, every time. "Sin carries its own retribution." We thus create our own bad "karma."

DISILLUSIONMENT AS A THERAPEUTIC TRIUMPH

Seen in this way, disillusionment is not so disappointing, depressing, and insufferable, after all. It's actually essential to our very awakening. Indeed, it enables a therapeutic breakthrough. This is truly great news! We need to be stripped clean of such misleading illusions about life, as soon, abruptly, harshly, and humanely as possible. Disillusionment is a necessary step in our awakening. We can learn to embrace and even celebrate it.

Discontent is the first step in the progress of a man ...
O. Wilde

The opposite of reality ... is the world of illusion, which is also that of our ordinary state of consciousness. ... Enlightenment is a ... dissipation of illusion ...
Claudio Naranjo

We must surrender our hopes and expectations ... and march directly into disappointment ... we ... begin to see that our expectations are irrelevant compared with the reality ... Disappointment is the best chariot to use on the path of [enlightenment].
C. Trungpa

You must be ready to postulate that all your beliefs may be wrong, ...
Ali

Our life is an apprenticeship to the truth.
                                    R. Emerson

The mystic's view ... : he regards the many earthly desires of common man as substitutes for what he really wants, a groping in all directions for waters that do not quench his thirst.
                                    C. Naranjo

Lost Illusion is the undisclosed title of every novel.
                                    Andre Maurois

If we decipher the cosmic con-game, and if we allow ourselves to be therapeutically disillusioned and illuminated as a result of reality's rug-pulling calamortunities, we can then move on to the unreasonable happiness of more accurate, useful, astute, centered, and paradoxical wisdom. If not, we endlessly chase after seductive siren songs and steer our lives onto the destructive shoreline rocks. Amidst the wreckage of our boats, cargo, and bodies, we then do what humans usually do. We refuse to admit to our original error in strategy. Instead, we crow in defiance all the more about the pseudo-veracity our precious illusions. "I did it *my* way!"

This self-justifying and childish nonsense is the larger-than-life pay-off to the massive folly of chasing illusions. We convince ourselves, thereby, that we're right, regardless of all objective evidence to the contrary. This makes us feel immune to the shackles of reality. This is a sad, pitiful, and illusory payoff to our half-blinded failure to stop and question our basic and self-defeating misassumptions.

Man is like a swimmer who is fully dressed and hampered by his clinging clothes. ... To have the impression that he is swimming properly; ... may make him feel better, and [yet it drowns] him ...
                                                            Latif Ahmad

Amidst the ruins of our lives, we even make the preposterous boast that we're really happy. We'd rather convince ourselves that we're right than strive to embrace the pain of disillusionment, which can lead to authentic happiness. We often fool ourselves for a lifetime. It's all in the service of our own foolish and self-aggrandizing auto-hoodwinking.

THE DISILLUSIONMENT ZONE

If we commit to the healing process of letting go of illusions, these new steps seem so awkward and backwards, at first. Our performance gets worse, for a while. It seems we'll never get the hang of this awkward new way. This is no fun. It seems like a bad idea from the start.

In contrast, the old and comfortable way feels so natural and intuitive, and it works well enough, we say. It calls to us. It's our comfort zone or default mode. Maybe we should just skitter back to it and make do. We tell ourselves it's too late to retool and learn a whole new way. Maybe we can just put our blinders back on and believe those illusions, again. Maybe that's the best we can do. Most others agree. They say we've "recovered."

In fact, if we gain too much uncommon and enlightening insight at this point, we come to feel hopelessly trapped in what I call the "disillusionment zone." This is Kafka's point of no return. At this point, the inaccuracy our previous vision of reality is now so exposed that we can no longer revive our belief in it. In addition, we can't reprise the abilities, agilities, and counterfeit happiness that it inspired. We want our magic back. Even worse, we can't yet trust the new paradoxically wise vision, either. Now we can't seem to get comfortable either way, neither forwards nor backwards. It seems we've entered into an endless, inescapable, and miserable morass.

Amidst this disillusionment zone, enlightenment seems even more elusive than ever. We come to hate that we ever got talked into such a damnable and impossible pursuit. What were we thinking? Reality's seemingly perverse, painful, and involuntary head-banging lessons thus drag us all kicking, screaming, and damning whatever gods may be, as we approach what eventually turns out to be the far more fulfilling realm of paradoxical wisdom on the other side.

Unfortunately, this entrapped and seemingly hopeless predicament is a necessary step towards enlightenment. Twelve step programs call it a "dry drunk." There's no short-cut to bypass this. The regrettably prolonged disillusionment zone must be engaged, endured, trusted, and then even cherished. In this zone, we're up against the centrifugal, regressive pull of our illusory habits. We must resist that pull and reassure ourselves, somehow and against our intuition otherwise, that we're on the right track.

Ideals are dangerous things. Realities wound, but they are better.
O. Wilde

I find that the fewer illusions I have about myself or the world around me, the better company I am for myself.
Noel Coward

We should stop kidding ourselves. We should let go of things that aren't true. It's always better with the truth.
R. Buckminster Fuller

Better to be wounded than to always walk in armor.
Margaret Fuller

As any recovering addict can testify, it turns out that it's not the avoidance of pain or negative consequences that drives us to change. You can't be scared out of an addiction. In enlightenment, as well as in self-defeat, it's the lure of enhanced pleasure that really fuels a change. When we're enmeshed in the doldrums of this disillusionment zone, we must trust that initial, fleeting, and pleasant taste we had of the heightened and expanded pleasure of awakening. That will be the carrot. Despite the seemingly interminable and miserable angst that follows, we must trust that this tiny initial kernel of joy will eventually grow and prevail. This is what really drives us to persevere, to have faith, to achieve an uncommon awakening, and to refuse to settle for less.

WE MUST "SPOIL" OUR ILLUSORY FUN; IT'S GOOD FOR US

Fixated chess players fear that such a radical and seemingly backwards change of strategy will burst their bubble; spoil their counterfeit, make-believe, feverish, childish, fragile, and fleeting fun; and destroy their so-called true, natural, spontaneous, and free selves, forever. They have a point, ... a single, dualistic, and incomplete point, that is.

Therapeutic disillusionment is how the fortunate one out of ten among us begin to awaken and learn practically all that really matters in life. This is an uncommon secret. Disillusionment is, indeed, very painful, insufferable, frightening, and even terrifying. It always hurts our feelings. It takes courage to even consider changing our basic game. Worse, it's not for everyone. Most are not willing or able to persevere through this seemingly-interminable disillusionment zone to get to the elusive and paradoxical "good stuff" on the other side.

You cannot discover new oceans unless you have the courage to lose sight of the shore.
                              Anonymous

Taking a risk is central to everything worthwhile in life.
                              David Viscott

No decision of any consequence can be made in our lives without some form of surrender.
                              Theodore Rubin

Many teens and young adults make another fundamental and terribly self-defeating error when faced with this disillusionment zone. They take the easy way and simply "go over to the dark side." If all positive pursuits are so hard and failure-ridden, these types simply choose the inflated and nihilistic stance of declaring that nothing really matters. They choose to embody and parade all that's negative, profane, and abhorrent about human nature. They've thus attained a counterfeit, cost-free, and negative sense of mastery, pleasure, superiority, and grandiosity. I'll get to this, soon.

Enlightenment is free, but it costs us everything, that is, all our comfortable habits and illusions, which, by the way, are far too emotionally futile and expensive to sustain. In order to make real progress, we have to let go of all that we think we know. All of it! The journey towards paradoxical wisdom is the best journey we'll ever hate. It has nearly nothing to do with outer adventures or challenges. It's an inside job.

The at once intoxicating and agonizing knowledge, that life involves process, that process entails change and suffering, and that there can be no creative progress except by defeat of the preceding stage.
                              Anonymous

Learning to live is learning to let go.
                               Sogyal Rinpoche

Most of our assumptions have outlived their usefulness.
                               Marshall McLuhan

For the garden is the only place there is, but you will
   not find it
Until you have looked for it everywhere and found
   nowhere that is not a desert.
And life is the destiny you are bound to refuse until you
   have consented to die.
                               W. H. Auden

THE DEPRIVATION/OF SELF-INDULGENCE

Profound and ultimate wisdom is such a backwards thing. It's defined more by what we give up than by what we acquire. In fact, accepting limits greatly enhances our boundless, unreasonable, and unconditional happiness. Self-deprivation and renunciation are necessary disciplines along that very long way, until we discover that self-deprivation is really the most ultimate and extravagant self-indulgence.

This "jumping-into-the-fire" disillusionment leads to an expanded realm of wholly unanticipated joy. This is really good news! Our busy, desperate, and miserable two-dimensional world expands into an exponentially enlarged, enriched, pleasurable, and multi-dimensional hologram. Our acceptance of limits sets us free, while illusions of unlimited freedom keep us imprisoned.

Losing an illusion makes you wiser than finding a truth.
                               Ludwig Borne

To be without some of the things you want is an indispensable part of happiness.
                                B. Russell

It is impossible to arrive anywhere but at renunciation ...
                                T. Reik

If you are irritated at every rub, how will you be polished?
                                Rumi

Renunciation is not giving up the things of this world, it is accepting that they go away ... In the Buddhist texts, ... renunciation is prescribed as a cure for all human suffering.
                                A. Deikman

The adventure the hero is ready for is the one he gets. ... the adventure evokes a quality of his character that he hadn't known he possessed. ... there's no reward without renunciation, without paying the price.
                                J. Campbell

Perfection is finally attained, not when there is no longer anything to add, but when there is no longer anything to take away.
                                A. de Saint-Exupery

*For every soul the final victory
in the battle of life comes
when he has risen above the things
which he once most valued.*
                                Sufi Inayat Khan

Children, old people, vagabonds laugh easily and heartily: they have nothing to lose. ... In renunciation lies a delicious taste of simplicity and deep peace.
Matthieu Ricard

GOING AGAINST LAZY HUMAN NATURE

The more one analyses people, ... one comes to that dreadful ... thing called human nature.
O. Wilde

Fixated chess players understandably lack faith in the curative nature of this persevering and jumping-into-the-fire type of training. It takes such long and strenuous practice to learn worthy and counter-intuitive disciplines during our youth, such as writing, spelling, grammar, music, dance, mathematics, languages, or athletics. We must endure endless lessons and rote exercises, until we so thoroughly master these awkward and unnatural skills that they become automatic habits, preferences, and muscle memory movements, themselves. They become our new "wisdom muscle memory."

God makes nothing easy on purpose - we must suffer to be beautiful.
Allen Wier

He who would learn to fly one day must learn to stand and walk and run and climb and dance; one cannot fly into flying.
F. Nietzshe

> *If an experiment fails ninety-nine times, then I now know ninety-nine things that don't work.*
> T. A. Edison

> *An expert is a man who has made all the mistakes which can be made, in a very narrow field.*
> N. Bohr

> *Nothing fails like success.*
> Gerald Nachman

There comes a point amidst this prolonged practicing and learning process that we transition into a new and intuitive level. We emerge from the devotee-follower who doggedly trains and practices, into the astute master, who *is* the practice, who is paradoxical wisdom. A human doing has transformed into a human **B.E.**ing. Arduous discipline has transformed into artful and effortless joy. This is the expanded exuberance we've been after.

> *Fall seven times, stand up eight.*
> Japanese proverb

> *Great people fail as often as ordinary people.*
> Anonymous

> *Even the best writer has to erase.*
> Anonymous

> *Falling is part of learning.*
> Anonymous

> *All misfortune is but a stepping stone to fortune.*
> Anonymous

The brook would lose its song if you removed the rocks.
　　　　　　　　　Anonymous

Adversity introduces a man to himself.
　　　　　　　　　Horace

Experience is a hard teacher. She gives the test first, the lesson afterwards.
　　　　　　　　　Anonymous

Perseverance, patience, and the courage to endure endless mistakes allow us to develop a taste for challenging, worthy, and hard-won pursuits. These just happen to be the most worthwhile, advanced, and fulfilling of endeavors. After all, air guitar is not really very impressive.

Think of your problems as a challenge in a game you enjoy playing.
　　　　　　　　　Anonymous

Difficulties exist to be surmounted. ... A strenuous soul hates cheap successes. ... The great are not tender at being obscure, despised, insulted. Such only feel themselves in adverse fortune. Strong men greet war, tempests, hard times ...
　　　　　　　　　R. Emerson

WORTHY PURSUITS AND DISCIPLINES AS NECESSARY

It truly doesn't matter what our primary pursuits in life may be. We all arrive at the same generic and centered paradoxical wisdom, no matter what specific paths we take. One mountain... many pathways. What matters is that we leave our comfort zone and challenge ourselves with any available, difficult, worthy, virtuous, and non-harmful devotion or practice of our own choice and taste.

This is why some Zen masters teach ultimate truths and wisdoms only if students agree to commit to such a practice. The master doesn't care which we choose. Choosing a discipline, any discipline, is imperative.

> *It's not the pursuit of happiness ...; it's the happiness of pursuit.*
>
> Denis Waitley

THE PUER AETERNUS - "KING" OR "QUEEN BABY"

Let's reconsider those who give up on positive, strenuous, and constructive pursuits. These are the masses of humanity who take the easy, lazy, and negative pathway. It turns out that we can't awaken in this passive and effortless way, without lifting a finger on our own behalf, and hoping for enlightenment to just land or dawn on us, while we remain on a shelf, and while we contemplate our navel, out of the fray. Jungians call this fixation the puer or puella aeternus, or "eternal child." Twelve step programs call it the "king or queen baby." Entitled passivity leads to a life-long, complaining, whining, resentful, and miserable childhood.

There's no such thing as a free ride, or womb-service. Everything comes with a price, even enlightenment. The king or queen baby is the strategy of:

> waiting for enlightenment to come to me automatically; so I'll not settle or make any compromised choices; I'll not lift a finger to train myself and learn more challenging skills; I'll concentrate on criticizing those others who have the strength, endurance, and courage to strive for excellence; I'll keep practicing my

counterfeit air guitar skills; I'll keep all options open forever; I'll convince myself that I *can* have and become everything and God when I grow up; I'll try to live forever without any cost, anxiety, or risk; and, when deprived, I'll take on such depressed moods and throw such grand hissy fits that others will eventually give in and do anything to keep the baby quiet.

I am entitled to have things done for me. ... to have happiness fall into my lap. ... life should be easy, painless, and effortless. ... **[I] should not be bothered.**
K. Horney

The problem is that we tend to seek an easy and painless answer. ... the spiritual path ... is very painful and we are in for it. ... It will be terrible, excruciating, but that is the way it is.
C. Trungpa

They always look on the dark side of things. Or they dismiss the whole matter by calling themselves 'pessimistic.' This ... puts ... a pseudophilosophical basis [on] an entirely personal incapacity to [engage,] tolerate, [and rise above] adversities.
K. Horney

Life's a pretty precious and wonderful thing. You can't sit down and let it lap around you. ... you have to plunge into it; you have to dive through it! And you can't save it, you can't store it up; you can't horde it in a vault. You've got to taste it; you've got to use it. The more you use, the more you have. ... that's the miracle of it!
Kyle Crichton

NO DELUSION, NO AWAKENING; WE MUST CONSENT TO BEING FOOLED

On the contrary, we must push the envelope and wholeheartedly attempt a strenuous, flawed, and messy external pursuit or "occupational therapy," in order to discover that the answers are within. We must actually consent to being fooled by the cosmic con-game. "No delusion, no awakening." Psychotherapists say that we must build up an ego in order to deflate and transcend it.

There's nothing to do, so do it.
                                        R. Dass

PUER AETERNUS NIHILISM: THE "SOUR GRAPES" SHORT-CUT

King and queen babies resort to nihilism, as they say:

> I don't really want that finer discipline or paradoxical wisdom thing, anyhow. Nothing really matters. Why waste all those years studying and training? That's for suckers. I'm already an instant, self-proclaimed, and entitled world-class genius, without even having to lift a finger.

This "sour grapes" maneuver is their lazy and cowardly attempt to do an arrogant and frightened end run around the humble, strenuous, and prolonged effort that it takes to attain mastery or enlightenment. There are no short-cuts.

Good people are good because they've come to wisdom through failure. We get very little wisdom from success, you know. Success makes a fool of you, but failure can come only from great effort. **One who doesn't try cannot fail and become wise.**

William Saroyan

He is like a person who believes he has a warranted claim to an inheritance; instead of making constructive efforts in living, he puts all his energies into a more effective assertion of his claims. In the meantime his actual life loses interest for him; he becomes impoverished; he neglects all that could make life worth living. ... he has the underlying feeling that he would lose his title [entitlement] for future fulfillment if he became interested in himself and his growth. ... It would mean seeing himself as a mortal like everybody else, harassed by difficulties; it would mean assuming responsibility for himself and recognizing that it is up to him to outgrow his difficulties and to develop whatever potentialities he has. It is deterring because it would make him feel as though he were losing everything. ... [Unreasonable] claims seem to solve many problems for him. [They] ... perpetuate his illusions about himself, and ... shift responsibility to factors outside himself.

K. Horney

CHAPTER 9

DISILLUSIONMENT

PART TWO

LESS/IS MORE

It's not that psychotherapists want patients to become permanently fixated in the discouraged, confused, hopeless, and miserable disillusionment zone. Rather, the objective is to relinquish illusions on the way to graduating, as much as we can, into paradoxical realms. Thereby, we can embrace the wholeness and enjoyment of a much larger and inclusive reality, rather than limiting ourselves to one tiny and restricted extreme or the other. That's the point of paradoxical integration and growth, isn't it?

ILLUSION, DISILLUSIONMENT, AND INTEGRATION: "THESIS, ANTITHESIS, AND SYNTHESIS"

Maybe some examples of the therapeutic and transformative process made possible by disillusionment will help. In all such instances, the healing process can be summed up as: "illusion, disillusionment, integration." These steps are comparable to philosophy's classical triad: "thesis, antithesis, synthesis." Neither extreme is the resolution. The answer lies in the paradoxical center.

Whenever we find ourselves in a painful and frustrating dilemma or quandary, the first step is to decipher just which unconscious and impossible illusion, or "thesis," we're trying to fulfill that drives us to bang our head against the immovable brick walls of reality. This useless quest for that which is essentially unfulfillable is how we create and fuel our misery. The "antithesis" in this instance is the resulting and disappointing disillusionment we experience when we realize the futility of such efforts. The final step is to confer with our paradoxically wise part-self, which can offer an all-embracing, integrating, centered, and healing "synthesis" of paradox. This resolves the pain of disillusionment by guiding us towards the multidimensional region of centered and paradoxical wisdom.

PERFECTION, FALLIBILITY, IM/PERFECTION

Consider the illusion or "thesis" of perfection. We often fantasize about performing extraordinary feats flawlessly, effortlessly, and without prior training. We long to be pure and effortless naturals. Whenever we engage in any challenging or worthy endeavor, however, we're confronted with our fallibility. Everything we do and know is limited, flawed, and, ... well, ... human. Indeed, we always have a lot to learn. This arena of limits is our "antithesis," our disillusionment.

We often compensate by turning our perfectionistic imagination towards the outside, instead. We idealize some fetching and pure quest, model, devotion, creed, principle, icon, hero, prophet, or god. Unfortunately, this strategy is merely an externalized version of the same self-defeating illusions of perfection and purity.

The real awakening is to give up on such impossible illusions, altogether. Instead, we can settle for merely human im/purity and im/perfection, ... for the attainable standard of "not bad for a human." Our realistic, messy, and compromised performances can then fall within acceptable limits and tolerances. At such a point, we've reached the healing "synthesis" of paradox. Amidst this compromising and settling, we arrive at a far more authentic and satisfying sense of accomplishment, mature hopefulness, and even unreasonable happiness. Less is more.

JUSTICE, INJUSTICE, IN/JUSTICE

The same three principles apply when we give up on our naive insistence on the illusion or "thesis" of pure justice. The universe doesn't promise or manifest anything even approaching such a one-sided notion. After all, this whole "I'm-right-and-you're-wrong" game is just another linear version of either-or dualism. The strongest, smartest, most skilled, and most virtuous among us suffer deserved and undeserved defeats, setbacks, obstacles, insults, slights, criticisms, rejections, deprivations, betrayals, injuries, tragedies, and such. These comprise the disappointing and disillusioning "antithesis," the embracing of life's inequity.

The universe is what it is: random, harsh, impartial, impersonal, and exquisite. It does not take sides. It just lets the whole range of events and possibilities play out. It straddles and embraces the sacred, unmoved, and impersonal "synthesis" of the paradoxical center. Nature doesn't care that some are blessed and others are deprived; that some are predators and exploiters, and others prey and victims; that some groups, species, civilizations, planets, and galaxies survive, while others vanish; and so on. Nature isn't concerned with our artificially one-sided and pristine notions of justice or fairness. It doesn't give victims any special passes, compensation, or restitution. It's not interested in our utopian notion of meritocracy.

The immature and linear response to such disillusioning cosmic injustice and indifference is to refuse to play the game, if it's going to be so impure, and if it's going to have no regard for our personal notions of fairness. We often complain that it's rigged against us from the start, so we quit, often in a vengeful or nihilistic snit.

In contrast, the healing and illuminating "synthesis" is the embracing of in/justice. Paradoxical wisdom allows us to participate in realistic and compromised endeavors as earnestly, enthusiastically, and deeply as possible, while accepting our share of defeats and setbacks along the way, whether they're merited or not. Real champions are those who can take losses, even unfair ones, and just get on with it. There's no whining in enlightenment. Let's just pick ourselves up and try again. Let's embody perseverance and resilience. Let's be intrepid.

> *Success is the ability to go from one failure to another with no loss of enthusiasm.*
> W. Churchill

JUSTICE, REVENGE, RECONCILIATION

Another of our favorite unawakened responses when our perfectionistic "thesis" of justice is thwarted, is to demand the "antithesis" of retaliation, revenge, compensation, and reparation. We insist that the perpetrator must be punished, and that we must be made whole. "You owe me!" These are among our favorite illusions. We often nurse such self-confirming "I'm-right-and-you're-wrong" grudges for a lifetime.

Such one-sided duality gives us a falsely clarified and projective sense of identity. We really know who we are when we know what and whom to fight against. It becomes our "raison d'etre." We fail to grasp, however, that the designated enemy or perpetrator is often a mere projection of our own dark side.

There are many who find a good alibi far more attractive than an achievement. ... when we have a valid alibi for not achieving anything we are fixed, so to speak, for life.

E. Hoffer

Melville wrote that revenge, itself, is foolish. It's just another self-defeating illusion. There's no need to pay back or reform the designated bad guys. Life does that for us, although it may annoy us by taking its time. Life often lets meanies bully their way to seemingly endless, undeserved, and unearned treasure, position, fame, and glory. Much to our chagrin, life lets them have their empty and external prizes, riches, power, and applause in prolonged abundance, sometimes without requiring them to face eventual adverse consequences.

Life then lets them choke on these victories and spoils. They cement their dualistic consciousness upon outer, extremist, and illusory pursuits, until they're so corrupted and fixated that it's usually too late for them to turn back and find the authentic abundance within. What they "win" is the right to live irredeemable and horrid lives of half-blinded, self-created, and ever-escalating inner misery. As a result, they often expel themselves permanently from the sacred and redeeming inner garden, from the expanded center of paradox.

This condemns them to a lifelong pursuit of that which doesn't really matter or satisfy. It'll never be enough. This wisdom is revealed within the old turned-on-its-head adage: "Time wounds all heels."

You can never have enough of that which you really do not want.

E. Hoffer

There is only one thing worse than not giving a man what he wants. It's giving him what he wants.
G. B. Shaw

Sooner or later, we all sit down at the banquet of consequences.
Robert Louis Stevenson

There are those who make the pursuit of revenge a life-long occupation. They walk around with projective chips on their shoulders, searching the horizon for someone to avenge for the slightest and imaginary hint of an insult or mistreatment. They love nothing better than a self-justified and outraged rant or fight.

They conclude that if life is inherently unfair and unrewarding, then they'll henceforth embody all that's purely negative and horrid about us humans. They'll parade it around and rub our noses in it. In fact, they rationalize this by explaining that the very essence of human nature is the child's unbridled dark side of raw, self-serving, and self-absorbed impulses and drives. They thus elevate their self-justified and self-indulgent pursuit of evil and selfishness to a negative religion or nihilism. They worship raw destruction, greed, impulsiveness, cruelty, and anarchy; and then they recruit others to join the ranks of this infantile and sadistic cause.

This amounts to a short-cut, lazy, and negative parody of wisdom. It allows such deluded individuals to play the easiest, most god-like, and externalizing role of all; that is, the self-appointed, cynical, and horrid devil's advocate. They go around bursting others' idealistic bubbles. Thereby, they become self-righteous disillusionment machines.

This is an all-too-easy and sinister endeavor. Our dark side is already on display everywhere and in plain view. Exposing and indulging humanity's admittedly prodigious and collective dark side is far too easy. It's child's play. It distracts these individuals from any worthy quest to attain inner wisdom. It's more challenging and rewarding to try to integrate the two sides of human nature into that glorious amalgamation, integration, and "synthesis" which attempts to approach paradoxical wisdom. That's where the real and centered fun resides.

SELF-AGGRANDIZED, HUMILIATED, PROUDLY/HUMBLE

Then there's the naive quest to be larger than life, to be grand and awesome. This is such an enormous and prevalent "thesis," or illusion, that I devote the next two chapters and the second "**D.**," (**DEFLATION**), to it. Suffice it to say at this point that when we're faced with our realistically tiny and insignificant status in this enormous and powerful universe, we experience a painful sense of humiliation. As a result, we often install and justify the life-long "antithesis" of an inferiority complex. We feel that we're nothing, despicable, unworthy, awful, and so on. We jump, thereby, from one illusory extreme to the paradoxically identical other, from "thesis" to "antithesis." As Kohut explored, inferiority is merely a disguised form of superiority.

He who despises himself, nevertheless esteems himself, thereby, as a despiser.
Nietzsche

The compromised, integrative, and healing paradoxical alternative, or "synthesis," is that we can be realistically mindful and humble about our rather insignificant status in the cosmos, and yet we can also strive, nevertheless, to be all that mere mortals can be. We become proudly/humble. We're not the big shot centers of the universe that we thought we were, but we're still quite unique and important in our humble, modest, equal, mortal, and merely human realms. We can accept being much less, so that we can be so much more.

HOPE, DESPAIR, HOPE/LESS

Let's consider the illusion of boundless hopefulness. We humans need to preserve an enduring sense of hope, in order to go on with life in a positive way. This is our "thesis." Nevertheless, we notice that all beings experience setbacks, defeats, losses, obsolescence, deterioration, and death. This negative side of life, or "antithesis," can seem overwhelming and mortifying. We can attempt to deny and soothe the daunting reality of this inevitably hopeless destiny by installing compensatory illusions of nirvana or heaven. This is our imaginary and eternal pension program. It's a most powerful salve and antidote, indeed. It's a major motivation for religion. It's an illusion which all governments attempt to exploit.

The more maturely and modestly hopeful resolution to this dilemma is to accept and even embrace the middle ground of our inevitable limits and mortality. In so doing, we discover that the present moment is the closest thing we humans can taste of eternity. The present moment is timeless. Perhaps we could even argue that the present moment *is* eternity. Again, less is more. This is the hidden and paradoxical "synthesis" of a hope/less attitude. Instead of losing all hope, we gain a more realistic, limited, temporarily/eternal, resilient, and paradoxical sense of hopefulness. There's that still space between breaths, that sacred center of paradox, again.

You cease to be afraid when you cease to hope; ... hope is accompanied by fear.
                                            Seneca

... he who holds hope ... for the human condition is a fool.
                    Camus

It is only by knowing how little life has in store for us that we are able to look on the bright side and avoid disappointment.
                    Ellen Glasgow

I feel so much better now that I've given up hope.
                    Ashley Brilliant

MEANING, NIHILISM, MEANING/LESS

Our "thesis" is that we can't live a life without meaning or purpose. We occupying ourselves with a series of external quests, duties, devotions, and obsessions. These give us a feeling of purpose, meaning, fulfillment, identity, progress, and success. We say we must acquire that degree, that career, that spouse, children, home, car, religion, recognition, fame, power, accomplishment, and so on. We say we must live long enough to see that child or grandchild born, grow, graduate, marry, procreate, or even grow old. This self-concocted bucket list can be endless. It's never enough. This is the ever-receding carrot of our lifelong "occupational therapy."

When this frantic sense of purpose is dashed, we're disillusioned. We're thrown towards the painful "antithesis" of meaninglessness, or nihilism, and we give up on all positive pursuits and ambitions, altogether. On the other hand, perhaps the most profoundly meaningful pursuit in life is to retrieve and find ourselves; that is, our integrated selves, right here and right now. Maybe it's a subtle mix of both. After all, the real meaning to life is that which we give it. Your choice is as valid as anyone else's. Life is both meaningful and meaningless. This is the healing "synthesis" of the meaning/less paradox. Along any of life's pathways, we can synchronize in this way with the paradoxical wisdom of the universe. Isn't that our highest ambition?

I like what is in work - the chance to find yourself.
Joseph Conrad

Disillusionment starts the process that sets us free. It's agonizing and discouraging at first, as we let go, but it leads to exponentially enhanced enjoyment, fulfillment, and authenticity.

CHAPTER 9

DISILLUSIONMENT

PART THREE

PLEASURE/PAIN; HARD-WORKING/PLAY

While we remain unawakened, we desperately chase our tails and pursue the unattainable and dualistic illusion of pure and cost-free pleasure. On the other hand, if we work hard to achieve a measure of the paradoxical wisdom which we already possess, we can enter into the healing process of disillusionment to transcend such a merely either-or illusion. Thereby, we can embrace the paradox of un/reasonable, ir/rational, and un/conditional happiness; that is, happiness within and beyond normal and dualistic reason, logic, and conditions.

As a result, we can enter into the paradoxical center of the maelstrom, where we can embrace pleasure and pain equally. Equally! Can you imagine? It's like being quietly, playfully, kindly, and non-judgmentally "blissed-out" all the time. In this enhanced and relaxed state of mind, the distinction between work and play disappears. They become integrated and fused. I have to work with some patients for years to overcome their prodigious resistances and persuade them to discard their illusion-based misery, so that they can enter into such enhanced bliss.

Man is ill-prepared to put up with sheer bliss.
P. Watzlawick

For the growingly wise individual, this quiet and disillusioned bliss has a war-torn, poignant, pained, sad, and experienced expression on its face. After all, losses and defeats still hurt. Un/reasonable happiness is cynically/optimistic, tempered by the acceptance of life's defeats, fallibility, compromises, tragedies, and mortality. This quiet and adept jujitsu of un/reasonable or boundless happiness amidst negatives is by no means easy to attain, maintain, or teach.

The greatest happiness is to know the source of unhappiness.
F. Dostoevsky

The universe has to trick and drag us towards such paradoxical joy and peace. At first, we settle for what we mistakenly perceive to be merely second best. This compromise is a grave and profound disappointment to us. Only much later do we appreciate compromise as the truly unlimited bounty, ... as the sacred center of paradox. Un/reasonable happiness is thus a counter-intuitive and hard-won taste.

We find that such cynical/optimism embraces the full beauty and horror of reality, the "full catastrophe." The universe waits to see if we can get out of our own way long enough to learn to actually prefer and enjoy the disillusioned, compromised, and magnificent paradise that we've been in all along. We must acquire a taste for being so much less, so that we can be so much more. There's that hoodwinking of the cosmic con-game, again. It couldn't have been otherwise.

PRESENT MOMENT/ETERNITY

When we drop into this healing **DISILLUSIONMENT** of holographic and unreasonable happiness, we seem to have dropped into that realm of present moment/eternity which gurus the world over describe in various ways. As the edited Beatles' lyric goes, "This must be the moment ... [we've] been waiting to arise." This is the closest we humans get to an expansive nirvana feeling, to a sense of oneness with the universe. Best of all, it doesn't require drugs, possessions, money, advantage, trances, trips, or costumes. It can endure. It's always in the present moment center of paradox.

This is only our truly uncanny, god-like, and paradoxically wise part-self emerging. It's only our piece of cosmic consciousness. That's all. It seems magical, but it's just ordinary enlightenment, ... and it's also remarkable. I'll expand on the concept of this here-and-**NOW**/eternity in Chapter 11.

IN "THE ZONE," THE HOLOGRAM APPEARS

Let's get back to the metaphor of the hologram. We can point a laser at any random point of a holographic image, and it evokes the entire three-dimensional image. Alternatively, we can gaze at a two-dimensional holographic surface pattern and change our focus to just the right point ahead or behind it, so that a whole new and expanded three-dimensional image emerges.

> *The real voyage of discovery consists not in seeing new landscapes, but in having new eyes.*
> M. Proust

This is analogous, again, to the fact that we can have an awakening disillusionment at any time or place. All humans are redeemable, even to the last breath. In fact, when we change our focus and decipher the cosmic con-game, a whole new, enjoyable, multidimensional, and expanded vision and wisdom appear. Suddenly, we're stripped of our illusions. A previously invisible, unanticipated, pleasurable, intricate, vast, and expansive vista of new insight appears from behind the veil of our previously dualistic vision. We were blind, and now we see!

This may reflect the possibility that the entire holographic universe is, itself, composed solely of pure consciousness. Further, such pure and intrinsic cosmic awareness may emerge, die, and re-emerge within each present moment breath or heartbeat, as a result of the endlessly repetitive, cyclical, in-and-out, systolic-and-diastolic rhythm of opposites merging and splitting apart, merging and splitting apart.

This happens, for example, at a biochemical level, when pairs of DNA strands come together, copy themselves, and then split apart during the processes of cell-division and reproduction. The very phenomena which we call life and death may have to do with this endlessly fusing and splitting apart cosmic breathing and pulsating rhythm, or reverberation. Life and death may be rhythmic, reverberating, and spiraling portions of a larger and paradoxical unity. Transcendentalism comes to mind. Prose is inadequate, here; … at least my prose is.

This is the hidden ecstasy of a disillusioning epiphany or awakening. It has nearly nothing to do with superficial or surface appearances. We can start where we are now, along any path, and amidst any company. We don't have to find a special place and special people. In fact, harsh circumstances and bad company are provocatively illuminating, as well. This harmonizes with the harsh and abrasive rug-pullings of the cosmos. It's right here and now. We just need to drop in.

The healing "synthesis" and integration of paradoxical vision that results from this disillusionment process turns out to be way too much fun. When we break into this expanded arena of awareness, it's uncanny, even eerie. We feel like we're cheating and looking at the answers in the back of the book. We look around to see if anyone sees us peeking.

Unreasonable, unconditional, present moment, and disillusioned happiness feels like we're in the presence of God; like we can see and experience eternity; and like we can see and know the ultimate secrets that God sees and knows. In fact, it feels like we are God. In a way, we are, but let's not get carried away with ourselves. It's only our ordinarily/and amazingly paradoxically wise part-self emerging. Anyone can do this.

When we **B.E.**come **D**ISILLUSIONMENT and break into this present moment/eternity or ecstasy, we arrive into a realm that athletes, meditators, and thinkers call "the zone," or "the flow." Our sense of time slows down in these states; and previously difficult moves, feats, and insights seem to take place easily, without great effort or hurry. At these times, we can just "let it happen." It's like being a child who's in an endless "play" mode.

Man is most nearly himself when he achieves the seriousness of a child at play.
                                            Heraclitus

JUST B.E. K.I.N.D.

Let's do the **B.E. K.I.N.D.** drill about the first "**D**.:" **D**ISILLUSIONMENT. We're so automatically committed to so many illusions that we'll likely have the opportunity to perform this exercise several times each hour. When faced with life's eye-opening rug-pullings, we need to stop and ask ourselves, "Where's my mistaken, dualistic, and naive illusion. How can I let it go, so that I can change?"

For example, let's consider times when we must embrace the paradox of in/security. This arises when we're about to make one of life's crucial choices. This paralyzes us with the anxiety, indecision, and fear of "what if's." Let's say, for example, we're about to decide on a somewhat permanent home. After looking through dozens of choices, we're now at the point of submitting a formal written offer and putting down a deposit. We're about to make a commitment. This is frightening.

EMBRACE THE FIVE-YEAR-OLD WITH HEALING S.P.A.C.E.

As usual, it's best to pause and allow the inner child to fully express his or her fear. Give him or her **S.P.A.C.E.**. **S**ilence, **P**ause, **A**cceptance, **C**ompassion, and **E**mpathy. This is a portion of the **E.**, EMBRACING part of **B.E. K.I.N.D.** This is when we grant our inner child that marvelous, healing, and loving EMBRACE of total ACCEPTANCE. We can grant him this healing S.P.A.C.E. and let him rant and catastrophize to his heart's content.

> I'm scared! I've never risked so much money, before. What if this is a disaster? What if there's a hidden awful neighbor, a flood, a roof leak, an earthquake? What if I lose my job or get a divorce? Then, I'll have to support two homes! I'm committing myself to a huge mortgage. What if I find a better place, and then I'm stuck? I'll look like such a fool.
>
> What if I find out that I've been conned? What if I paid too much? What if I bought a lemon? What if its value declines and I can't get my money back, later? What if I can't afford repairs? What if the schools are not as good as advertised? What if this whole move thing turns out to be a first-rate disaster? What if I find out, later, that I really want to live elsewhere?

I'd rather keep my freedom intact; thank you very much. I'll just rent. That way, I can play it safe, keep my options forever open, stay fast on my feet, escape from any negative consequences, and let someone else take the risks. This commitment thing feels like I'm putting my head in a noose.

In the face of this or any commitment, these dualistic, terrifying, and inhibiting "what-if's" can go on and on. The inner child is confronting his or her illusions of security, guarantees, smooth-sailing, cost-free living, endless options, and womb-service. Of course he or she's scared. Anyone would be. This type of commitment and decision is best left for adults to consider, not for kids.

B.E. K.I.N.D. TIME

It's time for our paradoxically wise part-self to step in and consult with the inner congress of the self, by using the **B.E. K.I.N.D.** method. It's time for this part to reason with the inner child and practice the first "**D**:" **D**isillusionment. Our paradoxically wise part-self can soothe the child and let him or her know that it's not their job to drive the bus. This is the adult's job to accept and resolve life's dilemmas. We can only do the best we can. Leave this job to us.

This wise part can counsel that in adult reality, there's no guarantee that our decisions will always be totally and endlessly correct, successful, or profitable. We need to relinquish illusions of certainty and security. Indeed, we do the best we can to make correctly calculated decisions, and then we have to stand up and face the full mix of positive and negative consequences. We must grow up and accept the healing paradox of in/security. Any mere child can simply run away from challenging adult dilemmas. This is a job for our adult side.

When we take this elusive and unattainable illusion of security off the child's mind, his anxiety naturally calms down, and he trusts the paradoxically wise part-self a bit more to guide things in a workable, astute, and compromised way. Life's risks can't be avoided. It's permissible to try and fail, at times. These things help us to keep on learning. Failures are part of the gig. In fact, losing everything we think we have is a useful calamortunity. It clears the air. It helps us to discover the abundance within that we already possess.

After this healing and Zen moment of **DISILLUSIONMENT**, we can proceed through the rest of the elements of the **B.E. K.I.N.D.** drill. We can practice predominant and forgiving **K**INDNESS to ourselves about having to make merely limited, faulty, risky, and 52-48 decisions. We can **DEFLATE** our larger-than-life ambitions and play the mere and realistic odds. After all, we can't guarantee universally successful outcomes in advance of unforeseeable circumstances. We also promise to not sit back on our self-imagined and all-seeing after-the-game perch, where we can assume the unfair, larger-than-life, and condescending role of the "told-you-so" critic of ourselves about the unavoidable negative consequences of any predominantly good decision.

We can stay in paradoxical **BALANCE** amidst such decisions, knowing that we can cultivate an **EMBRACING ACCEPTANCE** of the outcomes of all our choices, whether they work out or not. We can ACCEPT that we're only human. We can embrace **INNER** solutions, rather than relying on external reality and others to supply us with endless smooth-sailing. We can do the best we can to accept the results of here-and-**NOW** decisions, instead of putting off all decisions until that theoretical and ever-receding time in the illusory eternity of the future when we will supposedly (that is, never) capture the rainbow and achieve perfect clarity and foresight.

By embracing all seven elements of the **B.E. K.I.N.D.** mantra-mnemonic, we can thus relax, go with the flow, and **B.E.** our finer self.

CHAPTER 10

DEFLATION

PART ONE

SELF-AGGRANDIZING INFLATION

Now we come to **B.E. K.I.N.D.**'s second "**D.**": **D**EFLATION. The most foolish of all our seven categories of illusions, and the worst of the proverbial seven deadly sins, is the sin of pride. In essence, this is our innate and thinly-disguised quest to be an all-powerful and larger-than-life god when we grow up. In the final analysis, we all want this, regardless of our status in life. It could be said that this is the unconscious aim of all neuroses. We touched on this in Chapter 9.

This illusion of grandeur seems to be an intrinsic part of our DNA. Newborns and young infants are not yet developed enough to perceive that another person, such as mother, even exists. They operate on the misperception that they're literally the center of the universe. Psychologists call this "primary narcissism." Later, the young child continues to see him or herself as outstanding, awesome, and so on, as they act out the roles within their make-believe games of kings and queens, heroes and heroines.

Unfortunately and at deeply unconscious levels, most adults don't entirely outgrow this childish center-of-the-universe misassumption. This wish remains a lens through which we unknowingly distort all perceptions. In fact, all other illusions could be considered as mere sub-illusions.

> *[The neurotic's] entire self-esteem rests on being admired. ... inflating his ego ... for the sake of protecting himself against a feeling of insignificance and humiliation. ...*
> K. Horney

> *All neurosis is vanity.*
> Alfred Adler

> *Man needs self-esteem more than anything; he wants to be a cosmic hero.*
> Ernest Becker

> *It is an evil thing to expect too much either from ourselves or from others.*
> E. Hoffer

> *Power will become ultimately demonic ...*
> Joseph Chilton Pearce

> *Half the harm that is done in the world*
> *Is due to people who want to feel important.*
> T. S. Eliot

> *The graveyards are full of indispensable men.*
> Charles de Gaulle

INFLATED AND LARCENOUS ILLUSIONS SPELLED OUT

In essence, we chase after various illusions of grandeur, in order to steal more from life than it has to offer. Just what are these inflated illusions? A short list of them exposes them as silly and child-like, ... because they are. Nevertheless, most humans choose to live endlessly miserable lives; fight needless and devastating battles; and die dramatic and terrible deaths, all in pursuit of such ever receding mirages. In the end, we enthusiastically defeat ourselves in exchange for these inflated, unattainable, unsustainable, empty, and childish illusions and pleasures!

> *All men seek happiness. This is without exception. ... this is the motive of every action of every man, even of those who hang themselves.*
> B. Pascal

So here's a short list of our inflated and illusory quests: We feel entitled to our every whim and demand. We want unlimited and magical power. We want to be instantly and endlessly celebrated, admired, adored, loved, respected, confirmed, and protected, without preparation, merit, or effort. We want to be ever dominant, in control, correct, and authoritative. We want to determine what's right and wrong for everyone else. We want to be above blame at all times. We want endless revenge, compensation, reparation, and apology whenever we've been "wronged," ignored, betrayed, insulted, deprived, or disrespected.

If we're not supplied with these "center-of-the-universe" demands, we throw giant hissy-fits, until others will gladly "do anything to keep the baby quiet."

> *[Neurotics] want to be right all the time, and are irritated at being proved wrong, even if only in an insignificant detail. They have to know everything better than anyone else. ...*
>
> K. Horney

Any immature, narcissistic, and pretentious adult can prance around, toot his own horn, and pretend to be larger-than-life, especially if he comes from out of town. An all-too-large proportion of adults naturally fall for such a ruse. They long to adore their or another's illusory and magical omnipotence. It effect, both the narcissist and his or her fawning admirers pursue reciprocally/identical illusions of grandeur. They form a mutually enthralled consortium. They need each other. In tandem, they conspire to remain unawakened, misled, and self-aggrandized.

THE KING OR QUEEN BABY: SELLING OUR SOUL TO THE DEVIL

In fact, we sometimes take our unconscious illusions of grandeur to such an extreme that we meticulously avoid engaging in any objective task which could burst our bubble and expose us as merely limited humans who have a lot to learn from failure, just like anyone else. We become perfectly and defensively passive. We become a lifetime king or queen baby, who sits on his or her self-proclaimed throne and does nothing, and yet who's a superior, know-it-all, "told-you-so," demanding, entitled, and ever critical monarch over those others who have the courage to actually attempt something. This is a full-time, do-nothing-yourself job.

King and queen babies make a pact with the Faustian devil. They sell their soul for mere fool's gold. They sucker for the lure of life's illusory forbidden fruit. Of course, this is a staggeringly bad deal. No one can steal more from life than it has to offer. Forbidden fruit is forbidden, because it's impossible to acquire. Nevertheless, self-defeaters ignore that annoying and inconvenient piece of reality. In truth, they've settled for mere smoke and mirrors. Such a choice "shallows them out," often for life.

This is a huge folly. After all, we can't actually re-design the universe according to our own self-aggrandizing and self-serving specifications. At the end of the day, we get away with nothing on this planet. We can't steal more from life than it has to offer. We may as well face reality squarely. By pursuing the mere illusion of personal grandness, we ignore the neon sign on this rotten tree limb which says, "YOU CAN'T GET THERE FROM HERE." The further we go, the more we make matters worse, and the more desperately we must try to convince ourselves of that which can never be true for anyone.

> *The most pertinent symbol ... for the neurotic process is ... the devil's pact. ... The devil ... tempts a person with the offer of unlimited powers ... on the condition of selling his soul. ...the easy way to infinite glory is ... also the way to an inner hell of self-contempt and self-torment. By taking this road, the individual is in fact losing his soul - his real self.*
> K. Horney

> *The mystic ... regards the many earthly desires of common man as substitutes for what he really wants, a groping ... for waters that do not quench his thirst ...*
> C. Naranjo

> *You can never get enough of that which you really do not want.*
> E. Hoffer

Once you base your whole life-striving on a desperate lie, and try to implement that lie, ... then you instrument your own undoing.
E. Becker

Human nature ... can endure no restraint; if it binds itself it soon begins to tear madly at its bonds, until it rends everything asunder, the wall, the bonds, and its very self.
F. Kafka

The fool's paradise is the wise man's hell.
Anonymous

THE INFLATED COST

Sadly, such imaginary and wildly exaggerated grandiosity turns out to be a mere consolation or booby-prize. It takes too much energy to drag around, feed, maintain, polish, defend, and promote these over-sized little self-esteems. We waste such grievous and ever escalating time and energy trying to fool ourselves by denying and filtering out any real or imaginary perception, manifestation, or accusation to the contrary. Worse, the very endeavor to obtain such "forbidden-fruit" fool's gold entraps us, all the more, within the endless misery and shallowness of this dualistic, and half-blinded mentality.

While we think we're getting the good stuff by maintaining this preposterous illusion of grandeur, we're really distracting and blocking ourselves from the authentic pleasure and fulfillment of quiet, humble, and yet expanded paradoxical wisdom. We attain such wisdom only by proceeding along modest, gentle, hard-working, one-step-at-a-time, and non-showy pathways.

In this realistic, healing, and deflated realm, we can relax and take a load off our minds. We no longer feel the need to lug around an over-sized self-esteem. We no longer need to swim against the current. Indeed, we actually have no larger-than-life attributes to prove or defend. We can relax and be the merely flawed, foolish, curious, learning, compromised, and non-magical humans that we are. This is the real freedom, relief, and cure of an inner awakening. Less is more.

The great ... introduce us to facts; small men introduce us ... to themselves.
S. Hendricks

A bore is a fellow who opens his mouth and puts his feats in it.
Henry Ford

The mark of the immature man is that he wants to die nobly for a cause, while the mark of the mature man is that he wants to live humbly for one.
Wilhelm Stekel

FAILURE AS A HEALING DEFLATION

Failure is an opportunity.
If you blame someone else,
There is no end to the blame
Lao Tzu

During the process of striving for the realistically compromised and limited success of any endeavor, king and queen babies are automatically forced to settle for what is, for being merely small, limited, flawed, and human amidst similarly imperfect others and societies. They have to learn to take the daily and hourly failures and defeats, large and small, that the rest of us have to endure during the process of any worthy positive endeavor. They're thus forced, within any active striving, to confront their illusion of self-grandeur. This throws them into that long, dreaded, and resentful disillusionment zone, when such merely positive efforts seem so pale, puny, plain, boring, and unexciting in comparison to their previous and imaginary heroic passivity. They miss their illusion of grandeur. Twelve step programs call this a "dry drunk." It's no fun. This irritability can last for years, or even a lifetime.

This courage to take real and positive risks amidst inevitable and acknowledged failures is a hard-earned and acquired taste. It takes a very long time before king and queen baby self-defeaters can learn that merely limited, modest, and positive efforts turn out to be exponentially more fun, possible, and fulfilling. They lose their chronic air of resentment, in exchange for the realistic humility of gratitude.

Talking highly committed self-aggrandizers into trying to make such a transition is no small feat. It usually requires the services of a seasoned, wily and talented professional and/or twelve step group, who can skillfully counter their every clever resistance. Most drop out and return to their more comfortable and illusory rewards of passive, self-aggrandizing, entitled, resentful, and king or queen baby self-defeat. Oh well.

So, the non-personified universe enlightens us by deflating our over-sized little self-esteems. Thereby we become humble enough to realize that *WE*, not the world, must adapt, get smaller, settle, compromise, surrender, learn, and change. We can't reengineer the whole world in order to delude ourselves that we're always right, and in order to suit our idealistic, childlike, and self-serving wish list.

Paradoxical wisdom thus requires that we take a pathway that seems, at first, to go in precisely the wrong direction. The way out is to dive right in. On the surface, this seems to be another dreaded and disastrous entrapment. It can never be popular.

HUMILITY: THE ESSENCE OF THERAPEUTIC DEFLATION

Like Icarus, we're naturally driven to fly too high and too dangerously close to the sun. In so doing, we singe our wings, and we plummet back to the ground. Deflation is an essential task of profound wisdom. This is why Irving Yalom taught therapists to be subtle and unimpressive. Any self-aggrandizement on the therapist's part is unrealistic. It merely encourages the patient's own habitual self-inflation. This is drastically counter-therapeutic.

Life is ... a long lesson in humility.
    Max Shulman

The most solid stone in the structure is the lowest one in the foundation.
    K. Gibran

... the secret of my success is that at an early age I discovered I was not God. ... Humility is the first of the virtues - for other people.
    O. Holmes

There is a rule in sailing where the more maneuverable ship should give way to the less maneuverable craft. I think this is sometimes a good rule to follow in human relationships as well.
    Joyce Brothers

Actually there's no ego-trip to match the spiritual ego-trip! Satan is said to be the most enlightened of all the angels: he lacks [only] ... humility.
D. E. Harding

Neither an egg nor an ego is any good until you break it.
Anonymous

Except during the nine months before he draws his first breath, no man manages his affairs as well as a tree does.
G. B. Shaw

Knowledge is knowing as little as possible.
Charles Bukowski

Sometimes it proves the highest understanding not to understand.
B. Gracian

We don't know one millionth of one percent about anything.
T. Edison

All men are ordinary men; the extraordinary men are those who know it.
Chesterton

Submission is the ability to lay down the terrible burden of always needing to get your own way.
Richard Foster

Wear your learning like your watch, in a private pocket; and do not pull it out and strike it merely to show that you have one.
Earl of Chesterfield

WE ENDLESSLY RESIST TURNING BACK TO THE SACRED CENTER

Unfortunately, however, when faced with this dilemma or choice about deflation, we instinctively and deliberately ignore all evidence to the contrary. Moreover, we don't even notice the "YOU CAN'T GET THERE FROM HERE" sign. After all, that sign can't possibly apply to us, we say, since we're so positively or negatively special, exceptional, and entitled. We consider ourselves to be above all the rules.

If we take heed of the warning sign, then we have to stop and have the humility to admit that the cosmic con-game fooled us, too; that we've been so terribly wrong and confused; that we have to give up our superior and self-aggrandizing air of resentful superiority; or inferiority; and, worse, that we have to start at the beginning, like anyone else. We'll have none of that.

> How embarrassing! All those years of time and effort! What a waste! It can't be true! I'll just continue on and whistle in the dark, thank you very much, so that I can prove to myself that I really was right, all along. That feels better. That's the ticket!

> *Man is like a swimmer who is fully dressed and hampered ... by his clinging clothes. ... To have the impression that he is swimming properly; ... may make him feel better and [yet it drowns] him. .*
> Latif Ahmad

We hate to realize that we now have a choice, which is, indeed, our only realistic choice, no matter how distasteful it may be. Life teaches us best when we get ourselves out on a limb and into these desperate and larger-than-life predicaments. Life confronts us with the reality that we must stop at this point; turn around; double back to the metaphorical tree trunk; waste even more time climbing higher; get even further behind; choose other seemingly grandiose but rotten branches; turn around again and again; hopefully even withdraw from the illusory and larger-than-life "race," altogether; and finally choose a more substantial, sturdy, reliable, internal, humble, healthy, realistic, and lower branch. This is a huge fall in our illusory sense of status.

We must defy our natural instinct to just go ahead with our useless, competitive quest to be the larger-than-life "one-and-only." We must admit that like all humans, we so totally fell for the self-aggrandizing cosmic con-game. At this crucial juncture, do we humans usually stop, re-evaluate, and do this? NOOOOO! Instead, we'd rather save face; throw good money, time, effort, heart, and soul after bad; keep pretending; and just push on endlessly and irrationally, out onto this obviously rotten, sagging, useless, and now even hazardous branch.

Lugging around this booby-prize-sized self-esteem gets heavier and heavier. Awakened others can see right through us. We're only fooling ourselves. For most humans, however, that's enough.

CHAPTER 10

DEFLATION

PART TWO

NEGATION CONFIRMS ILLUSIONS ALL THE MORE

Most healthy individuals strive for a feeling of positive and even inflated self-esteem by participating in constructive and positive endeavors. These allow us to compare ourselves with others in a forthright manner. We can take the risk of being embarrassed, if we fall short. If we agree to play the game of life out in the open, we can learn from a normal mix of successes and failures along the way. Such healthy and normal self-aggrandizing efforts are easy to comprehend.

In contrast, it takes much more paradoxical insight to understand those strivings for superiority which are hidden within negative, ineffective, frightened, and self-defeating behaviors. These acts are backwards attempts to resolve the superiority-inferiority dilemma by one-sidedly giving up on most positive and productive pursuits, altogether. Let's explore how this self-defeating sleight-of-hand works.

A prominent aspect of the unconscious mind is that it doesn't distinguish between positive and negative, or any other opposites, for that matter. To the unconscious, less is more; inner is outer; inferior is superior; and so on. To the unconscious, each extreme of this either-or linear continuum thus confirms, supports, encourages, incites, and even inflates its opposite, all the more. As a result, while self-defeaters are consciously preoccupied all day with feeling that they're inferior and unworthy; they are, nevertheless, simultaneously, and unconsciously coveting, striving for, and even demanding to be seen as superior.

The unconscious mind can reverse any trait in this fashion hundreds of times each day. It can slip such flip-flop distortions into our more logical conscious minds within the hard drives of its sneaky and unperceived repetition-compulsions. That small and unperceived five-year-old elephant riding on the back of our neck can thereby so easily wear down, fool, and commandeer us.

> *[The neurotic's] capacity for this unconscious reversal ... is ... amazing. ... Thus inconsistency turns into unlimited freedom, blind rebellion ... into being above ... prejudice, a taboo on doing anything for oneself into saintly unselfishness, ... dependency into love, exploiting others into astuteness, ... vindictiveness as justice, ... and so on.*
> K. Horney

> *[The] ego's intelligence is tremendously talented. It can distort anything.*
> C. Trungpa

This infantile distortion and reversal is a crucial factor in cementing self-defeaters' tragic, compulsive, and often unconscious self-aggrandizement. Since he or she has no insight about his unconscious error of logic, any explanation of this backwards form of inflation makes no conscious sense to him. This makes it all the less likely that he'll choose the only reasonable and available pathway towards paradoxical wisdom: which is to stop, look at himself, admit to himself that he's essentially mistaken, turn himself around, and choose to awaken and deflate his unconsciously inflated self-esteem.

NEGATIVE INFLATION: THE LAZY AND EVEN MORE GRANDIOSE FOOL'S GOLD

My first book explores what I call "negative inflation." Any negative turns out to be far easier to "verify" than a positive. After all, everything in life is a mix of positive and negative. It's all too easy, therefore, to point out the intrinsic negative aspects of anything or anyone. They're always there! All positives can be so totally rejected and dismissed as being merely flawed and imperfect, because they always are. If we're negative and critical, we're always perfectly correct to some extent, at least in our own minds.

It's easy to live a bad life.
Anonymous

There is nothing clever about not being happy.
Arnaud Desjardins

It's easier to dump the cart than to load it.
Anonymous

Knots are easier to tie than to unravel.
Anonymous

In contrast, being positive about any realistic matter or endeavor requires strenuous compromise. It takes much more maturity to settle for "good enough" or "not-bad-for-a-human." Compromise is what allows us to live on this planet with some measure of grace, hope, and reality. On the other hand, if we're too lazy to develop a healthy capacity for compromise, we must convince ourselves, against all objective evidence to the contrary, that our impossible illusions of "Planet Utopia" and self-aggrandizement are accurate and eventually feasible. We must become dedicated, desperate, and half-blinded idealists.

The negative individual makes himself perfectly miserable, while he thinks he's making himself happy with the lazy and artificially amped up pleasure of the mere forbidden fruit of passive, negative, and entitled certainty and largeness. Since such illusory grandiosity can't be attained in the real world, he or she dares not even venture forth and lift a constructive finger on his own behalf. That would risk having to take the trouble to develop a capacity to settle. It's easy to hold himself out as having such negative, demanding, remarkable, superior, and sophisticated standards and tastes that no one else can live up to, either. He's the perfect "do-nothing-himself-connoisseur-impresario-critic" of all others. That's quite a lofty perch. It's the ultimate king or queen baby stance.

Rather than risking looking at himself critically, he busies himself with mowing everyone else down who tries to actually accomplish something worthwhile. This can be quite intimidating, but only to those friends or partners who have the reciprocal, hand-in-glove, unconscious, and masochistic need to be mowed down. In contrast, awakened, self-reliant, and authentic others have no interest in such "super-critic" and king or queen baby partnering. They aren't impressed.

Never satisfiable and negative inflation is thus exposed as a secret route to an imaginary level of unassailable self-aggrandizement. Its imaginary dimensions dwarf the compromised and realistic measures of self-esteem which are actually available via positive, modest, and practical effort. This is not a mere academic or semantic splitting of hairs. It's actually nearly the whole ball game about self-defeat. It explains why mental illnesses of all kinds are so paradoxically gratifying and resistant to change. To king and queen babies, mental health seems like an enormous and irreversible setback. If we try to do anything positive, we achieve a mere win-lose batting average, not a perfect record. We're only human.

On the other hand, nothing can block negatively inflated individuals' efforts to defeat, harm, or even destroy themselves. They're so much larger than life if they simply pursue the negative. If humans don't try for any positive goal; if we do nothing and just sit on the shelf as a king or queen baby and criticize others who have the courage to risk merely human endeavors; and if we even actively pursue self-defeat and hatred; ... then we succeed a hundred percent of the time. We bat a thousand. Thereby, we're undeniable heros in our own mind, at least in a backwards sort of way.

> *A writer may produce little more than half-finished manuscripts ..., or an ... artist may dawdle for years, and never quite get together a portfolio or exhibit. ... The net result is the maintenance of a grandiose conception of one's ability: For if nothing is completed, then one's ability cannot be tested, judged, or found wanting. ...*
> **To be free to succeed, one must be free to fail**, *for creative effort always occurs within the context of possible failure.*
> Samuel Warner

This baffling concept of negative inflation is at the heart of many mental illnesses. It took me years of listening and puzzling to decipher it. It turns out that this seemingly small piece of the puzzle may be my only entirely original contribution to the field. I'll likely be disabused of this conceit, too, when better informed readers cite the several ancients who said this in other, better, shorter, and simpler ways centuries ago.

Negative inflation explains why self-defeaters of all kinds are so very resistant to the humbling and deflating effects of treatment. At deeply unconscious levels, they sense that they have such huge cascades of illusory, "larger-than-life," and negative payoffs to lose, if they improve. Converting them to merely positive, and, therefore, compromised, modest, humble, and productive efforts feels to them like a tremendous come-down or deprivation. In reality, they're the ones who miss out, usually for life.

> *That popular notion that 'of course, a person who suffers wants to be helped if only someone is able to help him' is not really so. ... there is the humiliation of simply having to yield to another person, of giving up being himself as long as he is seeking help. ... the self nonetheless ... fundamentally prefers the suffering along with the retention of being itself.*
>
> *... Once he would gladly have given everything to be rid of this agony, but he was kept waiting; now it is too late, now he would rather rage against everything and be the wronged victim of the whole world and of all life, [he] has his torment on hand ... no one takes it away from him for then he would not be able to demonstrate and prove to himself that he is right ... The person in despair believes that he himself is the evidence ... and therefore he wants to be himself, himself in his torment, in order to protest against all existence with this torment.*
>   Soren Kierkegaard

FALSE HUMILITY

Self-aggrandizement comes in many convincing disguises. Just when we think we've deflated the grandiose and entitled five year-old king baby, he or she flares up in new, hidden, disguised, and baffling ways. A prominent example is false humility. We tell ourselves,

> Look at how outstandingly and admirably pious, humble, and meek I am! I'm so superior in my world-record-setting renunciation. In fact, I can "do without" longer and better than you can. I can bow lower; sit in the lotus position longer; and endure more pain, poverty, humiliation, and self-deprivation.

Chogyam Trungpa called this "spiritual materialism." This is just ego inflation turned on its head and packaged as its opposite. Like the Hunchback of Notre Dame, self-defeaters cry out, "I am unworthy! I am unworthy!" Paradoxically, this is the disguised cry of a deeply hidden and backwards sense of intense pride and self-aggrandizement.

> *He who despises himself, nevertheless esteems himself, thereby, as a despiser.*
> Nietzsche

> *We must be willing to be completely ordinary people, which means accepting ourselves as we are without trying to become greater, purer, more spiritual, more insightful.*
> C. Trungpa

> *... on seeing through the illusion of the ego, it is impossible to think of oneself as better than, or superior to, others for having done so.*
> A. Watts

Again, the paradox is that superiority and inferiority are identical. The comparison mind of extremist and either-or dualism, itself, is the trap. While in this trap, we're living, thereby, in the artificially split-up and exclusive land of "better-or-less-than," instead of graduating to the paradoxical equality of "contrastingly/identical." In the land of paradoxically wise humility, there are no winners or losers. We are, indeed, equals, ... equal fools, that is.

> *Humility is just as much the opposite of self-abasement as it is of self-exaltation.*
> Dag Hammarskjold

> *Humility does not mean believing oneself to be inferior, but to be freed from [the illusion of] self-importance.*
> Matthieu Ricard

> *... we do not hate ourselves because we are worthless, but because we are driven to reach beyond ourselves.*
> K. Horney

> *My idea of the experience of God ... led to religious elitism. ... a special revelation of my own, ... a direct route to spiritual arrogance.*
> J. Carse

> *... many people who tried to overcome pride were doing so because in this way they would be able to inflate themselves with such a victory.*
> Hakim Jami

> *Insisting that I am someone special only leads to needless suffering.*
> S. Kopp

UNIQUELY/NOTHING SPECIAL; EXTRA/ORDINARY

As we've seen, the resolution or "synthesis" of this illusion of grandiosity is a paradox. The healing, integrating, and paradoxical jujitsu trick is to recognize that we're all unique and amazing individuals, but we're *also* nothing special. We're extra/ordinary. Not one, not two. We each possess all that's divine and sublime within, to be sure, but we also come equipped with the seeds of all that's horrid and depraved about our unimportant and temporary little species.

> *All we know is nothing, ... unless we are in touch with that which laughs at all our knowing.*
> D. H. Lawrence

> *The game is not about becoming somebody, it's about becoming nobody.*
> Ram Dass

> *When you soar like an eagle, you attract the hunters.*
> Milton Gould

> *The higher a monkey climbs, the more you see of its behind.*
> Joseph Stillwell

> *The nail that sticks up gets hammered down.*
> Japanese proverb

> *We feel that we are ... very extraordinary, that we are different from everyone else. This ... attempt to prove our own uniqueness is just an attempt to validate ... self-deception.*
> C. Trungpa

... he must lose himself (his neurotic glorified self) in order to find himself.
K. Horney

This fall from special status doesn't detract from our individual and unique place in the universe. There will never be another identical human being, and yet we are each also the basically the same. In fact, beneath all the apparent, unimportant, and superficial differences, which, unfortunately, we tend to harm and kill each other over; ... beneath all that, we're really identical twin brothers and sisters.

Angels can fly because they take themselves lightly.
G. K. Chesterton

It is in the knowledge of his follies that man shows his superior wisdom.
French proverb

GENTLENESS: DON'T PUSH THE RIVER

Do you remember that old-fashioned term, "gentleman?" During my youth, this quiet and modest manner of being strong but gentle, considerate, modest, and humble was highly prized. It was the ideal of the "strong and silent type," perhaps best portrayed by those winsome and understated Gary Cooper, Gregory Peck, or Donna Reed types of movie characters. During the "look-at-me!" decades since, this humble ideal has lost favor. Too bad. We could use a few more gentlemen and gentlewomen, these days. Only the strong can afford to be gentle.

> *Nothing in the world,*
> *Is as yielding and receptive as water;*
> *Yet in attacking the firm and inflexible.*
> *Nothing triumphs so well ...*
>
> Lao Tzu

> *Gentleness is a divine trait: nothing is so strong as gentleness, and nothing is so gentle as real strength.*
>
> Ralph W. Sockman

> *Study hard, think quietly, talk gently.*
>
> Anonymous

When we begin to awaken, we can just let it happen naturally and without effort. There's no need to fight the seemingly heroic, egotistical, and showy battle against reality by being such big shots and swimming against the current. The gigantic universe remains unimpressed. Seen in this way, real strength is displayed by gentleness, not by impressive shows of power.

> *If you use one iota of strength to make the slightest effort to obtain Enlightenment, you will never get it.*
>
> Tsung Kao

> *... the greatest power is available to those who do not seek power and who do not use force.*
>
> A. Watts

B.E. K.I.N.D. TIME

Let's apply the profoundly healing quality of **B.E. K.I.N.D.** to this process of **DEFLATION**. Imagine that we're on the verge of over-reacting, as usual, to a negative situation. For example, our lover has just criticized us in a way which we feel is unfair. Our inflated inner five-year-old part-self feels insulted and outraged. He or she's on the verge of escalating a minor criticism into a major confrontation and even conflagration.

Here's when we can take the pregnant pause and let the inner child rant and rage in the inaudible and invisible privacy and safety of our mind, while we remain silent and still. We can give him a healthy, EMBRACING, and healing S.P.A.C.E.: **S**ilence, **P**ause, **A**cceptance, **C**ompassion, **E**mpathy. In so doing, we're providing him with the "E." part of **B.E. K.I.N.D.**

> How dare he or she? Can't he see I've been working hard all day? Can't he see that I've got our best interests in mind, ... that I've done all these other things so well, today? He doesn't appreciate or love me! We've gone through this a thousand times! He'll never learn. I can't take it any more. Our relationship is OVER! I'm out'a here. He'll be sorry!

This childish hissy-fit is perfectly harmless and safe, as long as it's contained within the spacious, silent, and private congress of the mind. A kindly and therapeutic pause enables us to stop and consult with our paradoxically wise part-self. He or she can apply the healing and larger logic of paradox, in order to soothe the insulted child's hurt feelings.

We can be compassionate to this injured child part-self. We're not merely our five year-old's thoughts. We can pause to reconsider and reframe the situation in silence, without causing a needless outer conflict by saying these childish and impulsive things out loud. What would our paradoxically wise self say or do, in order to **B.E. K.I.N.D.**? He or she can calm the child down by saying something like:

Of course our lover feels the need to criticize us. He or she's just trying to help. Often his criticisms actually offer better ideas or alternatives, and often we're even grateful for them.

Perhaps his or her day's been rougher than ours. Maybe we can come from our finer part-self to soothe and calm him. Since all partners become peevish at times, it's nothing personal. This isn't an outrageous insult to our grandness, lovingness, or helpfulness. It doesn't mean that he no longer loves us, that he even hates us, that he doesn't know the real us, that he's an impossible mate, or that he's about to leave us. He just didn't hold his tongue. We all do that from time to time.

We're just being overly-sensitive. That's all. Our partner's a merely fallible human. He or she can be moody. We don't have to exaggerate the importance of this truly petty argument. We don't have to escalate it. Ten years from now, will we even remember what this little snit was all about?

During this all-embracing, accepting, and healing pause, we can talk our impulsive and aggressive five year-old part-self off the inflated, self-important, and center-of-the-universe ledge. We can block his attempt to drive the bus and soothe his or her hurt feelings. We can come from our paradoxically wise part-selves and employ centered and kindly concepts and maneuvers, in order to escort this calamortunity into more calm, positive, productive, non-provocative, and compassionate waters. We can convert this contentious and useless fight into a mutually enjoyable dance. We can salvage the rest of this day, instead of ruining it, so that we can spend a more loving time with our partner.

We can stop being so needlessly and overly outraged, and start to **B.E. K.I.N.D.** We can overcome our larger-than-life illusions about ourselves and just be humble. We can pause and deflate our own huge and insulted self, before we respond in some impulsive, unfortunate, destructive, snippy, alienating, and ill-advised way. This is the **DEFLATION** part of the **B.E. K.I.N.D.** method. The paradoxically wise part-self's intervention is at a level of equality, not in the service of condescending/or yielding to a lover we've assumed to be so very inferior/or superior to us.

We can now apply the rest of the **B.E. K.I.N.D.** elements. Some of this is implicit in what we've already mentioned. First, and above all else, we can be **KIND** to our lover and, therefore. to ourselves. It was an unkindness to ourselves to expect that all our behaviors must be so ultimately perfect as to be above any reproach.

For example, we can just be kind and keep smiling. We've done this to preserve our love, before, when we've been childish and impatient. We can kindly remind our lover that we already thought of that, or that his or her idea is a good one, or that he has a point, or that we always appreciate his insights and inputs, or that he always has such good ideas, or that we love him, or that we're lucky to have his opinion, and so on.

We can add a little humor by saying that we so need this sixth reminder about this same issue; or we appreciate his criticisms for things we've already finished or have on the schedule. We can use gentle irony and ask if this is one of those times we've previously agreed should be handled without criticism or harshness? We can ask him or her to take a pause and pretend that they still like us. We can just be silent, or we can say, "Yes, dear." We can gently and lovingly caress him.

All this is a **DISILLUSIONMENT** and **EMBRACING ACCEPTANCE**, as well. We can use the **BALANCE of PARADOX** to embrace praise and criticism as equivalents. We can seek **INNER** solutions and self-soothing, rather than relying on external approval and support. Finally, we can seek present moment, here-and-**NOW** solutions, rather than externalizing and trying to train our lover to be uniformly and permanently non-critical. We don't need to seek eternal and perfect future solutions in order to be happy.

CHAPTER 11

THE PRESENT MOMENT/ ETERNITY OF NOW

PART ONE

Sages across many cultures and centuries agree that the most profoundly awakened consciousness exists in this present moment. In fact, some consider the present moment to be the only moment in all of eternity. Worries about the past or future are misleading and distracting. All we have is this present breath, and, even more ultimately, this still and sacred point between breaths. It lies precariously suspended and balanced between the realms of life and death.

Inhale and exhale, inhale and exhale, … life and death, life and death. Isn't it synchronous that such a profound, paradoxical, and balanced secret to the enigma of life is so well hidden between the millions of unnoticed inhales and exhales that take place automatically each year, while we tend to what we think are more important matters? This suspended pause between breaths is the ultimate and centered paradoxical point of Buddhist detachment. It's the sacred, central, glorious, and present moment experience. *Be Here Now.*

Tomorrow's life is too late. Live today.
                                    Martial

Sign outside a casino in Las Vegas: 'You must be present to win.' ... Living fully means jumping into the unknown, dying to all our past and future ideals, and being present with things just as they are.
                         Joseph Goldstein & Jack Kornfield

Nothing is worth more than this day.
                                    Goethe

Treat all things as if they were loaned to you; ... everything.
                                 M. Eckhart

We cannot put off living until we are ready. ... life is always urgent, 'here and now' without any possible postponement. Life is fired at us point-blank.
                              Jose Ortega Gasset

Time is the most valuable thing one can spend.
                                 Theophrastus

PRESENT AND TIMELESS/ETERNITY

This is more than just a mildly interesting academic point. Some sages, such as Thich Nhat Hahn or Ram Dass, say that this present moment is the whole ball game. One might say that it's all too convenient for an old man like me to have such a view. After all, my back's against the existential wall. Nevertheless, the present moment essence between breaths was just as crucial when I was five. Our puny lifespan is only an instant of time within this fourteen and a half billion year-old universe. Sooner or later, we must come to the realization that all we have is right here and right now.

This secret is hidden in the most obscurely/obvious place. There's no need to strive for future inner peace, wisdom, and happiness. We already have them. We're already in paradise, or paradox. It's so deceptively simple. We can take our time, literally. There's no need to rush. We have an eternity, this present moment/eternity.

> *'Today' means boundless and inexhaustible eternity. Periods ... are ideas of men, who calculate by number; but the true name of eternity is Today.*
> Philo

> *The present is the only reality. There is no other.*
> K. Wilber

> *Eternal life belongs to those who live in the present moment.*
> L. Wittgenstein

> *There can be no hurry to be in the moment. There is no rush to reassume our true nature.*
> J. Goldstein & J. Kornfield

> *A day is a miniature eternity.*
> R. Emerson

> *For the Present is the point at which time touches eternity ...*
> C. S. Lewis

> *To come into the present is to stop the war.*
> J. Kornfield

SAVORING THE PATHWAY, ITSELF

We're so programmed to strive towards "that" goal, "then," "someday." That's when we'll be happy. This keeps us in the repetition-compulsion "war," in the dualistic and misery-inducing realm of this-or-that, now-and-then, hope-and-fear, win-or-lose, right-and-wrong. When we drop into the expanded, non-dualistic, and here-and-now center of paradox; that is, when we straddle the abyss; ... we find ourselves savoring the pathway, itself, rather than the goal. This is when apparent opposites come together. This is the realm of un/reasonable happiness.

The journey is home.
                                    Basho

Consider the tale of a man alone in the jungle. Suddenly, he's attacked by a ferocious man-eating tiger. While desperately trying to escape, he slips and falls over a cliff, barely saving himself by clutching the very last bush. He hangs just out of reach from the murderous tiger above. Boulders loom far below. Such a fall would certainly be fatal. The shrub begins to pull out by its roots. With nothing else to hold, and amidst his terrible desperation, the man notices a strawberry growing on the plant, so he plucks and savors it.

Can we be similarly content to just enjoy the trip, in the midst of its various, daily, and distracting pendulum swings? All things come to pass. Can we train ourselves to stay in, and even savor, this present moment?

This centered stillness isn't really a "settling," or compromising, at all. It turns out that this "mere" present moment pathway is a limitless bounty! This is the secret to paradoxical and unreasonable happiness. It takes place when we become like children, again, who simply look around and find a way to enjoy each precious moment. It's adults who remain so dutifully and seriously attached to getting themselves and the kids dressed, equipped, and transported on time.

Buddhists speak about detaching. They're not merely advocating a detachment from things, others, or pleasures. That would amount to yet another attachment to an opposing and extremist illusion. They mean a detachment from our blinding, limiting, dualistic, and self-imposed prison of either-or misassumptions. Fully embracing the present is the real and centered Buddhist moment of detachment.

> *... yet the cure is simply to die to the world.*
> S. Kierkegaard

OBSTACLES BECOME THE MEDITATION AND THE PATH

What a backwards thing! Along our daily pathway, obstacles become our best teachers. Adversities are teaching koans, which can dislodge us from our dualistic comparison mind. They present us with illuminating opportunities to awaken, to experience an epiphany, a therapeutic disillusionment. Preposterous as it sounds, obstacles are treasures. Thus, instead of dreading and avoiding hindrances, we can embrace, revere, and learn from them. They illuminate the paradoxical pathway. This is what's meant by going into the pain and fire.

> *There is no way to happiness: happiness is the way.*
> Anonymous

> *Think of your problems as a challenge in a game you enjoy playing.*
> Anonymous

> *Stop acting so small. You are the universe in ecstatic motion.*
> R.M. Rilke

THE PAST: "IT COULDN'T HAVE BEEN OTHERWISE"

In addition to our preoccupation with the future, we have an obsession with the past. This preoccupation is the basis of our repetition-compulsion. Our attachment to the past is a most distracting and disabling excuse. We hide behind it. We mistakenly blame it for what we are and do now. We tell ourselves we aren't able to attempt innovative and illuminating new adjustments, because we're so irretrievably trapped within the habitual ones. We inherited this or that trait, or we were trained to do so in our youths. We claim that all people in our religious, ethnic, or national group are just that way. After all, we say, we can't change our specific identity, essence, and destiny.

We tell ourselves that we've been this way so long that it's too late to change. We demand to be accepted just as we are. Such seemingly reasonable, justifiable, and even idealized distortions are ingeniously self-imprisoning and self-manipulating excuses. They allow us to justify not lifting a finger on our own behalves to illuminate the ways we think and maneuver. They mire us in our customary, self-justified, and self-aggrandized misery. They keep us fixated in what we were, then, instead of graduating into being fully and gloriously what we already are, now. We don't have to let go of illusions; "they're already gone."

We also revisit the past in order to magically rewrite, relive, manipulate, or spin it in a positive way, this time. This is an essential ingredient of the repetition compulsion. Psychologists call it "undoing." We want to somehow magically undo what went wrong then, at least in our own minds, so that we can sooth, rehabilitate, re-inflate, and, unfortunately, re-inflame our injured and inflated little self-esteems. This can also occur in a backwards sort of way during negative inflation, when we devise and justify our self-created victim role.

To make matters even more confusing, neuroscientists tell us that there's no such thing as completely accurate and objective memory. We inevitably distort and spin the facts of past events ever so slightly, and, thereby, we depict ourselves as having been less thoroughly defeated, conned, humiliated, or mistaken. We depict ourselves as having been much more victorious, admirable, heroic, heroically-victimized, and correct, then. We tell ourselves that we saw it coming all along. That's the ticket! We weren't really fooled at all. We were just being cagey. We feel so much better when we tell ourselves such self-congratulating and self-aggrandizing lies.

As with all illusions, this preposterous effort to rewrite and re-invent past events has no actual substance or reality. Like rainbows, its positively or negatively inflated mirages remain ever-unattainable. They recede just out of reach. It's never enough. As with all addictions, each retelling can never end the matter. The stark and deflating reality of what actually happened keeps intruding, and the self-inflating mirage keeps fading away in the distance. Thus, self-deceptions must be repeated and embellished compulsively and endlessly, as we obsess on the past. Paradoxically, such repetitive and escapist efforts to re-write the past keep us all the more imprisoned within it. They block us from living actively, fully, and authentically in the present.

It would be healthier and more honest to choose to face the past squarely. Let it be as it actually was. Let it end there. Let it go. **B.E.** here now. "It couldn't have been otherwise." It was what it was, and we were what we were: human, flawed, naive, foolish, mistaken, learning, and not yet awakened, ... pure and simple. Indeed, we were terribly, thoroughly, and mortifyingly fooled about almost everything that really matters; and no amount of revision and wishful thinking will change that. In fact, the full acceptance of our inevitable failure to grasp the trickery of the cosmic con-game during our youth; ... this is key to our most profound and enlivening awakening. A central task of enlightenment is to let the past be, without regret, blame, excuses, replays, spins, or victimization. Acceptance, acceptance, acceptance.

> *Only by acceptance of the past will you alter its meaning.*
> T. S. Eliot

There's another essential element about this constant, self-deceptive, and self-aggrandizing obsessing about the past. As I've explained, each time we create these fictitious do-overs, the inner five year-old part-self is able to utilize them to slip in his or her childish "I-was-never-really-fooled" illusion. He's thereby able to further cement this self-aggrandizing and "told-you-so" distortion into our consciousness in a sneaky and unnoticed way, hundreds of times each day.

This amounts to an enormous, constant, and ever-renewing process of self-brainwashing, of self-inflation. As a result, while the conscious mind is being decoyed into ruminating and complaining about a past and troubling event, it's automatically and unconsciously being conned by our five-year-old's fondest, most self-aggrandizing, and most childish illusions. What an ingenious and efficient hoodwinking. It occurs all day, every day.

RESILIENCE AND LEARNING FROM THE PAST

If something or someone in the past got the best of us, it's useless to punish ourselves or others. It's useless to beat ourselves up with imaginary "coulda-woulda-shouldas." It's unrealistic to re-invent the past scene in our minds as per the distortion of our repetition compulsion, so that we can picture ourselves as having been much stronger, cagey, larger-than-life, alert, aware, prescient, and astute than we could possibly have been. That just keeps us in endless self-defeating re-runs, wherein we unconsciously and repetitively set up the old situation, with the same illusions, and in the futile hope of winning, this time.

Regrets cement our sneaky and impossible misassumptions all the more by indulging in endless, painful, humiliating, guilt-ridden, self-aggrandizing, "coulda-woulda-shoulda," self-victimizing, "I-am-unworthy," and self-imprisoning self-flagellation.

This stunts our inner growth and keeps us fixated. It leaves the car in neutral, while we loudly and impressively rev the engines, all the more. It's like cruising through the quiet village with our motorcycle engines blaring. It's an all-too-cheap, adolescent, and empty way to beat our self-aggrandizing and hyper-inflated breasts, for all to see. It's time to get over ourselves, our grandiose selves, that is.

Instead, it's more healthy and resilient to become humble enough to actually put the car into gear. It's best to use that painful memory as a learning opportunity to let go of obsolete illusions, to change ourselves, to get on with life, to forgive our ever-foolish selves, and to learn to accept a messy and compromised reality as it is, right here, and right now. It's best to review past set-backs in order to replace these illusions with practical, centered, deflated, humble, and paradoxical principles. This makes it possible for us to take control back from the unrealistic inner five year-old part-self and accept ourselves as the inevitably and acceptably flawed, limited, multifaceted, and foolish humans that we are. We can learn to simply accept what is.

Accepting the past enables us to proceed as more tested, experienced, adept, disillusioned, deflated, modest, humble, and, therefore, savvy travelers. Now we know the ropes. We're veterans. We can avoid the same mistakes in the future, because we've already made and learned from them. This is how we recover.

The past does not determine the future.
         Anonymous

Be willing to shed parts of your previous life.
         Anonymous

Whenever we act as the genius of ourselves, it will be in the spirit of allowing the past to be the past. …
         J. Carse

It is perfectly possible to make the past into a reliable source of unhappiness.
         P. Watzlawick

LIVE NOW; GET OVER IT

If we remain negatively obsessed with the past, we idealize, thereby, the "good old days" and demand that nothing should change. All things change, however, and we, too, must keep growing, no matter what our age or level of expertise.

We can choose to stay in the self-created hell of wishing we still had those lost times, youth, loved-ones, friends, health, body parts, opportunities, careers, jobs, status, homes, and so on. We can make ourselves perfectly miserable by wishing that things hadn't changed. In contrast, we can let the past go and choose to make this supremely precious life worthwhile and enjoyable as it exists today, in an ever changing, growing, compromised, limited, and sometimes even deteriorating present state.

As they say in golf, "play 'em where they lie." While we're standing over the next shot, if we're still upset about that last mistake, we're too distracted to deal effectively with this present moment swing. We've let the past "get into our heads," so to speak. Rather than dwelling on what we've lost, we can focus on and make the best of the opportunity we have right here and right now.

We lose everything and everyone in the end, anyway. Life's job is to knock us off balance, poke us in the eye, break our hearts, and take everything away. That's a given. In reality, we literally have nothing to lose. It's already gone. Without knowing it, we've actually been free to play the game of life with total and earnestly/indifferent abandon, all along.

As with all things, it's a matter of choice. We can be bitter and complaining; or we can get over it, walk it off, suck it up, and make the best of it. Just as "there's no crying in baseball," there's no whining or kvetching in enlightenment. There are, indeed, abundant pains, losses, illnesses, defeats, tears, and grief, ... but no whining. Enlightenment is quiet, non-ceremonious, and non-melodramatic. It simply and casually picks itself up, dusts itself off, and moves on from here. Surprisingly, it moves on to something far better, ... within.

THE PARADOXICAL VOICE OF EXPERIENCE

As we age, we're not what we were then, to be sure. That's the good and bad news. Along the way, we lose so many people, possessions, and abilities. Nevertheless, we gain experience, centeredness, balance, wisdom, insight, skills, come-back lines, and perspectives. We become so much more, ... and less.

As a forty-four year veteran psychotherapist, I can see for miles, and yet I'm also still curious and learning. I've seen it all with present moment new eyes. I'm an old pro/beginner. The longer and experienced view from here is both beautiful and terrible. I can utilize my elderly skills and perspectives to see through my and others' illusions and self-deceptions so much faster. I've been there. I know every move from the inside. I can dis/regard my and others' useless and self-defeating musings. I focus, instead, on essential awakening and self-forgiving opportunities during each present moment of each session.

I gain rapport more easily and quickly, as I use gentle and

self-effacing humor to harmonize with a patient's hidden and paradoxically wise part-self. I take into account an individual's multiple and conflicting levels and centers of motivation, consciousness, and needs. Sometimes, I manage to outwit patients' unconscious resistances with an effortless and seemingly casual or offhand phrase or gesture, while I'm making another seemingly more important point.

I know when to be frank or vague, blunt or soothing, revealing or concealing, open or conniving, delving or letting go, persistent or relenting. I know when enough is enough. I know what and whom to take on or let pass by. When I inevitably err or mis-speak, as humans do, I know the fixes. That's the best we flawed humans can manage.

I'm predominantly gentle, non-threatening, and kind, even when I'm abrupt and confrontative. I call this collaborative, kindly, and stealthy confrontation. I'm supportively/indifferent, soothingly/harsh, and sympathetically/disinterested, all in harmony with the patient's paradoxically wise part-self, which happens to be an all-inclusive and holographic chard of the immense, im/personal, and paradoxical consciousness of the universe.

I let go from the very start of any case, since I have a merely limited number of sessions left. I assume that after therapy is over, each patient will have years to utilize these insights and embrace life in innovative and creative ways of their own. I proceed to the crucial, essential, internal, paradoxical, and impermanent fixes, right here and right now. In addition, I leave some things unsaid, so that the patient him- or herself can come up with his or her own paradoxically wise conclusions.

THE PHOENIX:
NEW EACH SECOND; DIE TO THE PAST

Enlightenment is free, but it costs us everything. Like the Phoenix, we die to our past. We're reborn each moment.

Every moment is the last moment ... a rebirth.
                                        Ippen

Throughout the whole of life one must continue to learn to live, and what will amaze you even more, throughout life one must learn to die.
                                        Seneca

To live is to be slowly born.
                                        A. de Saint-Exupery

Work and interest in worthwhile things are the best remedy for age. Each day I am reborn. Each day I must begin again.
                                        Pablo Casals

*As long as you do not know
how to die and come to life again,
you are but a sorry traveler on this dark earth.*
                                        Goethe

You only grow by coming to the end of something and by beginning something else.
                                        John Irwin

Be ready at any moment to sacrifice what you are for what you could become.
                                        Charles Dubois

... to exist is to change, to change is to mature, to mature is to go on creating oneself endlessly.
Bergson

When does God create heaven and earth? In the beginning. And when is the beginning? At every moment. Dying to past and future, we are born into the creative Now. Beginner's mind is the mind of God.
S. Suzuki

The only person who behaves sensibly is my tailor. He takes my measure anew every time he sees me. All the rest go on with their old measurements.
G. B. Shaw

CHAPTER 11

THE PRESENT MOMENT/ ETERNITY OF NOW

PART TWO

LET'S START NOW

This "all-are-fooled" vision of reality actually sets us free. We needn't be tied in any way to specific past melodramas, tragedies, "poor me's," and losses. What matters is how we grapple with the essential enigmas of reality in this present moment, right here, and right now. One of my patients put it well. He said that when he was abandoned and mistreated from earliest childhood, it was good for him. He felt that he'd been endowed, thereby, with a head start; ... that he'd been "predisastered." He knew that it's an eventual advantage for all of us to be defeated, abused, abandoned, and disillusioned early in life, so that we can expose our illusions to the light of day, wise up to the cosmic con-game, look within, and start to resume the form of our integrated and paradoxically wise part-selves.

When I evaluate new patients, especially those over forty, I can easily discern the tracks of their past and present losses, tragedies, wounds, family histories, and adversities. I need no specifics. I can see the cumulative results of their self-defeat within their present moment and dualistic misassumptions, stories, projections, and complaints. Their illusions parade repeatedly, proudly, and loudly, right in front of me. It really doesn't matter how they started. I'm not an historian.

In fact, I try to seem somewhat dis/interested in exploring patients' specific past slings and arrows. Although I listen with patience and compassion, there's little time for such wasteful reminiscences and grandiose "could-have-beens." Indeed, we must pay attention to the past to some extent, to be sure, but only so far as it empowers us to detach from misassumptions and to proceed to the inner and wholesale positive change and transformation the patient needs, one step at a time, and right now. Let's just roll up our sleeves and get to work. We have so much to learn. There's no time for excuses.

The real job is to help patients to learn to stop getting in their own way, right here and right now. Imagine! I actually have to persuade patients, against their will, to learn to have more fun, fulfillment, and love. They'd rather wallow in the past and enjoy their endless, self-aggrandizing, and do-over misery. Let's just get to the fix of inner change.

NO FUTURE AND SMOOTH-SAILING UTOPIA

In review, we can't suspend our lives, enjoyment, and fulfillment indefinitely, until the illusion of some future perfect Camelot or Utopia arrives on the scene. This life on earth and in the midst of our more or less deluded fellow humans has and always will exist as it is. It's always going to be imperfect, messy, unfinished, unclear, controversial, competitive, enigmatic, frustrating, frightening, uncooperative, insulting, deceptive, painful, and confusing. It's not going to change in any ideal, substantial, or transforming way.

Individuals, groups, organizations, and governments are not going to progress into those unerringly loving, caring, concerned, compassionate, cooperative, honest, efficient, intelligent, mature, thoughtful, equitable, just, and enlightened models we so fervently imagine. Those are just our utopian, perfectionistic, and, therefore, self-destructive illusions. It's our very attachment to such dualistic illusions that produces endless self-inflicted misery.

Lower your expectations of earth. This isn't heaven.
Max Lucado

If you are not happy here and now, you never will be.
Taisen Deshimaru

[We] have all been waiting for this moment to arise.
Paul McCartney

Madness and sanity, folly and wisdom, vice and virtue, injustice and justice, cruelty and kindness, horror and glory, and war and peace have always taken their turns in the cyclical affairs of humanity. In fact, madness, folly, ignorance, vice, injustice, cruelty, horror, and war prevail much of the time. They're louder and more persuasive. It's virtuous to try to effect positive change, indeed, but it's also wise to be modest about what we really can accomplish, often one person at a time, and amidst such merely cyclical, flawed, and collective consciousness and industry.

A patient was complaining about his workplace. He went on and on about the misbehavior, distrust, dishonesty, larceny, prejudice, incompetence, irresponsibility, disregard, laziness, mismanagement, betrayal, and such. I answered that when he finds a place where people behave in a predominantly ethical, ideal, and enlightened way, please let me know. I've never been to such a place.

This man hadn't yet fully accepted the messy and unalterable reality of basic, universal, collective, and unfortunate human nature. He thought humanity should be tidied up, updated, and populated by enlightened selves, only. He was thus hoping to recreate humanity and reality according to his own idealistic and utopian specifications, so that he could then be happy. He wanted to give humanity a purifying make-over. In effect, he was making himself perfectly and endlessly miserable, since such wholesale perfectionistic changes never have and never will take place. This man was also promoting, thereby, and not incidentally, the implied illusion of his contrasting, all-knowing, and all-powerful superiority. His smug and holier-than-thou inner five-year-old part-self was peeking out, behind the distraction of his painful complaints about the negative aspects of inevitable human nature.

As per the cosmic con-game, we're already in paradise, or paradox, right here and right now, as we have been, all along. We just don't know it. There never has been anything even remotely resembling our illusions of "smooth-sailing," utopia, perfection, or womb-service. Adversity, pain, conflict, war, injustice, and fallibility are woven into the very fabric of our lives. They never go away. In fact, they're even necessary and indispensable ingredients of the process of our awakening. We must learn to embrace them.

Adversities can be our most profound, illuminating, and demanding instructors. We must relinquish the flat-earth illusion of peaceful, halcyon, and perpetual smooth-sailing. Such a mirage of eternal womb-service only holds us back. Instead, we can challenge reality to "hit me with your best shot." That's when the rubber really meets the road. That's when we really grow.

What is crucial to Nietzschean thought is what Rosset calls beatitude. ... refusing to speak about another "truer" world beyond what exists here and now.

commentary on C. Rosset

The more certain the end, the more tempting the minute.
                                    Theodro Fontane

DISTANT/PRESENT MOMENT ENLIGHTENMENT

William James wrote that we can have an ultimate and life-changing awakening in a variety of ways. It can be a sudden, melodramatic, showy, and "burning bush" type of epiphany. It can take place in gradations of more gradual and quiet ways, too. It can even arrive with no dramatic, pivotal, or even discernible awakening moment at all, amidst a lifetime of the diligent, routine, rote, ordinary, and mundane study and practice of any worthy or unworthy discipline. All routes and roles are valid. They can all get us to the same mountain top.

There's no need to indulge our comparison mind and feel "better-than" or "worse-than" others about our specific path. There's no need to fret about just which route is best. It's time to just get on with it, on whatever path we choose. We can't miss out on anything that really matters. Enlightenment is enlightenment, regardless of the specific pathway, costume, belongings, abodes, curriculum, setting, era, group, or time span. It's the same now as it was in the beginning. Through the ages, we're all identical twins, grappling with the same essential enigmas of life, and arriving at the same all-too-limited portions of paradoxical wisdom.

Because we humans are such consummately self-confirming, self-aggrandizing, and projecting machines, we usually languish for a lifetime within our highly prized, seemingly special, seemingly unique, and yet ultimately ordinary, identical, and self-defeating soup of extremist illusions. Those who repeatedly, gradually, partially, and finally awaken and re-awaken from this folly usually do so in the fourth or fifth decade, or later. That's when enough of life's rug-pullings have finally occurred in a painful and confrontative enough way to give us a confluence of compelling evidence to redirect our focus to inner, present moment, centered, and paradoxical realms. That's when we learn that the most profound objective in life is to contradict our own favorite misassumptions. It's nothing personal.

> *Life is a journey up a spiral staircase; ... we cover the ground we have covered before, only higher up; as we look down ... we measure our progress by the number of places where we were but no longer are. The journey is both repetitious and progressive; we go both round and upward.*
> John Butler Yeats

> *... people ... are always making new beginnings. Yet it is not a matter of tedious repetition, because each new beginning is an invitation to enter a genuinely new situation. The making of souls is neither linear nor circular; rather it is spiral. We seem to repeat our lives, but at different levels and in different ways.*
> Alan Jones

This spiral, tedious, spacious, and repetitive awakening can and does take place for anyone along any pathway. It can happen in a hospice, prison, asylum, or war. Once again, "How many psychiatrists does it take to change a lightbulb? ... One, but it has to want to be changed."

B.E. K.I.N.D. TIME

Let's consider an example situation which forces us to ponder the here-and-**NOW**, "**N**." portion of **B.E. K.I.N.D.** Consider the normal and daily circumstance in adult life when we face a difficult, vexing, annoying, scary, and challenging test or adversity. How can I employ my paradoxically wise part-self so that I can embody a "present moment" attitude, as much as possible, without worrying so much about the past and future.

As usual, the first step is to take a time out, in order to caress and ACCEPT the inner five-year-old part-self. It's time to give the child S.P.A.C.E.. **S**ilence, **P**ause, **A**cceptance, **C**ompassion, and **E**mpathy. Let him or her complain, whine, and resist. He wants an easy "womb-service." He hasn't yet redefined reality as a simultaneously hard-working and playful state. We can learn to EMBRACE the fullness of life itself as a here-and-now process, rather than as a series of win-lose and work-play goals.

I am not merely my child's thoughts and feelings. I can just listen and give him S.P.A.C.E., as he complains and justifies:

> How can anyone expect me to do this? It's too hard, and it takes so long. It interrupts my play time. This adult "adversity" thing feels like hard work, and I just want to play and be natural all the time. This particularly difficult task requires effort, study, practice, delay, risk, and so on. I'm too lazy and impatient for that. I want what I want now, without delay, without effort, and without risk. I'll just sit, whine, and pretend to be so very tired and pained, until I wear them down and they let me off the hook.
>
> Besides, I've always chosen the quick and easy fix. I'm free and spontaneous, a free spirit. I shoot from the hip. That's the way my family or clan does things. It's how we roll. We're free. We just do things naturally, without planning or preparation. We've never gone in for fancy education, preparation, or training. Those nerds stay home, study, and miss the party and life, ... but not us, and not me.

Let others take the hard way and try for those lofty and difficult goals. I'll just stick to what I already know. That way, I won't be frustrated. I hate to be frustrated. When it's too hard, I just choose the easy way. I quit.

Once again, such a childish rant is perfectly safe and harmless. It's the sound of an eternal child, a king or queen baby. In the midst of this larger, adult, and paradoxical world, I'm not merely my childish fears and thoughts. My paradoxically wise part-self can respect and even empathize with the child in an all-EMBRACING and ACCEPTING silence, until the five-year-old has had his say. The child feels heard and consoled by this. After listening, my paradoxically wise self can then quietly, compassionately, and systematically redefine adult adversity as an interesting challenge, especially in reference to this chapter's "**N**." principle: the present moment. My higher self can begin to **B.E. K.I.N.D.** and reason with my child self like this:

It's true that all deeply rewarding and worthwhile adult endeavors are difficult and frustrating. New challenges force us to try innovative, uncomfortable, and scary things. In this way, they bring out the best in us. We're all learning new skills and concepts each day. That's adult life. If I do only those things that are easy and familiar, I'll have to settle for a life of simple, basic, low-risk, and, therefore, low-reward challenges. I'll thus limit myself to a less deeply fulfilling and enriching type of enjoyment, achievement, meaning, and love.

It's true that I and my family or clan have tended to shy away from tackling truly difficult challenges. Most humans do that. We've always thrown in the towel when the going got tough. Anyone can shallow out.

Besides, my life is defined in the present moment, not by my past. I may have chosen immature, impulsive, and short-sighted solutions in the past, but I can change that **NOW**. I can learn to persevere with deeply challenging and confusing adult tasks, wherein I have to study, practice, prepare, delay, work, take risks, and fail repeatedly along the way. It's never too late to start from the beginning, enter into the "**NOW**," and learn to face things the hard way, which happens to be the only way to truly master and transcend them.

Above all, my life is here and **NOW**. I'm not defined by the self-defeating and self-limiting ways I previously mismanaged the most profound challenges of life. "When I was a child I thought like a child..." I can move on. I can learn to persevere and be intrepid.

In the same way, my paradoxically wise part-self can give the inner child **S.P.A.C.E.** about his or her "coulda-woulda-shoulda" regrets about the *past*:

I should have faced and persevered through those piano or athletic lessons and practices, those calculus or philosophy or language books, and so on. By now, I'd have been an accomplished musician, athlete, scholar, leader, or professional. I'd have become someone special.

It's too late for me, now, to start from the ground floor and develop those skills that I missed. I'll just have to keep on with this shallowed out type of work or such. I can't possibly learn to read, write, calculate, dance, and so on. It's too late. I could have really been something. "I coulda been a contenda."

Again, it's **B.E. K.I.N.D.** time. My integrated self can listen and soothe, and then take the more mature and satisfying pathway. The "coulda's" are just an excuse to remain lazy and fixated within childish, safe, and self-limiting endeavors. They merely keep us afraid and unable to face life's most difficult, important, and, therefore, most satisfying burdens and endeavors. Though it doesn't matter what route we choose in life, and though enlightenment can take place along any pathway, it's simply much more interesting to push ourselves to master one or several difficult and challenging endeavors of our own preference.

Likewise, the higher self must patiently abide the child's endless "what if" fears about the *future*:

> What if I fail? What if I embarrass myself and demonstrate just how dumb and inept I am? That would be so embarrassing and mortifying to fail right in front of everyone! I can't take that chance. I'll just stick to these simple and easy tasks and ambitions. That's much less risky and frightening.

After listening, the paradoxically wise part-self can then reframe adult reality, so as to live in the present moment and quell fears about the future. All we can do is take the small and awkward steps today which will eventually lead to greater skill, wisdom, mastery, and performance. If we keep learning and growing, we will, indeed, fall short and fail many times each day. That's just part of life. The smartest and most skillful athletes, scholars, and professionals make public mistakes and errors each day. It's just part of their growth. In fact, errors and failures are the first steps towards any challenging accomplishment. It's not so mortifying to have to admit to being merely human, foolish, and error-prone.

As usual, I can go on and on about such an example. I trust the reader can discern within this discussion the other six **B.E. K.I.N.D.** elements of the mnemonic. These combine and get so ingrained through years of practice that all seven blend and become automatic. This is what's meant by the term "integration."

CHAPTER 12

THE SECRET VICTORY OF SELF-DEFEAT, REVISITED

PART ONE

These two chapters summarize my first book, which revealed the vast unconscious origins and payoffs of self-created victimhood, or masochism. This book concentrates more on the integrative and paradoxical solutions.

Most self-defeaters' misery isn't consciously intended at all. It's the consequence of being unawakened and, therefore, of being tied to the pursuit of mere and unsatisfying illusion. Masochists unknowingly create their emotional pain in countless ways. They may be late, forgetful, offensive, provocative, obsequious, dominant, hesitant, or submissive. They may monopolize or drop the ball; have endless excuses; be pessimistic, nihilistic, and negative; be so afraid and perfectionistic as to be paralyzed at the moment of opportunity; arrange to provoke rejection or dismissal; take on needless and impossible tasks; and so on. When confronted with their own unconscious hand in meticulously setting up such disasters, they say, "What! What did I do? It wasn't *my* fault."

Openly driven masochists, on the other hand, are quite aware of their extensive, systematic, requisite, talented, and versatile self-defeat and self-destruction. They may indulge in drugs, alcohol, tobacco, binging, starvation, medical neglect, excessive cosmetic surgeries, and such. These result in accidents, failures, deterioration, degradation, infection, organ failure, dementia, illnesses, obesity, thinness, deformity, premature aging, death, and such.

They may carve up, burn, tattoo, and/or 'decorate' their skin. They may damage other body parts. Sometimes they're able to achieve and/or enhance sexual orgasms only if they go through preliminary and painful rituals. They may pursue and/or be impressed by various dare-devil, reckless, and ill-advised stunts, sports, wagers, relationships, sacrifices, or investments. They may compulsively lie and manipulate to such an extent that they lose everything, alienate everyone, serve time, and even lose track of reality, altogether. The list goes on and on.

These more conspicuous, obsessed, calculated, and systematic types of self-defeaters claim that they can't help it, or that they're just trying to enhance and amplify their pleasure. In fact, their short term enjoyment is intensified by the very pain that they seek. It's the best they can do, they say. They think that they're getting the real goods. They go out of their way to create and revel in pain. Often, they even display and sheepishly joke about it.

Such masochists are aware that their weird and extravagant behaviors are apt to cause long-term pain, illness, suffering, and death. They nurse the delusion that this will not happen to them, of course. They claim that the amped-up, frenetic, melodramatic, exhibitionistic, adolescent, and world record-setting type of pleasures they attain, thereby, are well worth it, however. They feel that such frenzied and obsessed behaviors confer a self-concocted and disdainful form of superiority over their more tame, conventional, mature, compromising, timid, sane, and "regular" brothers and sisters, whom they think have no taste or courage for these heightened, daring, brave, and supposedly sophisticated endeavors.

Their disastrous self-justifications are merely self-defeating dualisms, transparent rationalizations, false insights, and chest-beating braggadocio. Because they're chasing unattainable and ever-receding illusions, their frenzied and compulsively painful/pleasures are insatiable. That's the point. These futile and addictive preoccupations provide them with endless masochistic job security. They serve as lifelong scams or decoys. Their aim is to delude themselves. Although self-defeaters may incessantly criticize, control, vex, and victimize others, their real aim is to justify themselves to themselves. Thereby, they frantically indulge in endless and desperate auto-brainwashing.

HIDDEN PLEASURE

Centuries ago, Blaise Pascal and others broke the code and deciphered the underlying paradox of self-defeat. They discovered the sneaky, larcenous, and intensified pleasure which lies so skillfully and systematically hidden within their elaborately and melodramatically displayed and experienced suffering and complaining. Of course! It had to be! Masochists are secretly getting off on their suffering. It's all in the service of brilliant and pleasurable auto-hoodwinking.

> *All men seek happiness. This is without exception. ...*
> *this is the motive of every action of every man, even of those who hang themselves.*
> Blaise Pascal

> *No despair is entirely free of defiance.*
> S. Kierkegaard

> *He who despises himself, nevertheless esteems himself, thereby, as a despiser.*
>
> Nietzsche

In short, the secret payoff to the masochist's self-defeat is the intensely satisfying and amped-up enjoyment that the unconscious part-selves experience when they act out and thus confirm a whole host of "forbidden fruit" and impossible aims, illusions, or fantasies, all at once. They include instinctive, built-in, and archetypal illusions of perfection, purity, dependency, irresponsibility, unaccountability, freedom, unconditional love, justice, certainty, security, safety, invulnerability, power, revenge, vindication, superiority, advantage, magic, eternity, and the like.

Masochists are very reluctant, indeed, to risk the possibility of losing these intricately and delicately tricked-out pleasures during the course of effective psychotherapeutic treatment. Improvement threatens them with terrible and devastating deprivation or loss. That's why they call us "shrinks." Masochists prefer their superficial, frenzied, and desperate addictions over those deeper, enlarged, subdued, safe, and serene satisfactions that result from balanced, nuanced, and mature mental health. They'll have none of that.

> *I feel like I'm winning when I'm losing, again.*
>
> Gordon Lightfoot

VICTIMIZED FANTASIES AS ALL-AT-ONCE AND POWERFUL MICRODOTS

The essentially holographic, one-part-evokes-the-whole, and all-at-once nature of fantasy is a crucial step in enhancing self-defeaters' secret and unapparent payoffs. The intensity of multiple unconscious pleasures can be exponentially amplified by bundling them all together within a single, power-packed, and melodramatic narrative or fantasy. If masochism is the all-engulfing and paradoxical maelstrom, inner fantasy is the sea craft that transports them there.

In addition to being powerful, fantasy is ultimately portable and private. Any brand of the standard, victimized, "poor me," and vengeful fantasy can be installed seamlessly and effortlessly amidst any life context, be it indulged or deprived, free or imprisoned, healthy or afflicted. It can be replayed over and over all day, within the privacy, safety, and pseudo-confirmation of one's mind. Thereby, it escapes the peer review of others' healing scrutiny, confrontation, criticism, debate, and guidance. The power of fantasy is even more enhanced if it remains out of conscious awareness, altogether. From such deep and unperceived depths, it can wreak its unsupervised havoc all the more.

Whenever the smallest unconscious masochistic illusion is fulfilled in the hidden and symbolic virtual reality of our imaginations, it automatically "confirms" and supports all the other unconscious and self-defeating illusions, as well. It's as if all childish and impossible illusions can be bundled together, evoked, and fulfilled, thereby, indirectly, and all at once. In this way, one illusion catalyzes, enlists, and evokes a veritable banquet of them all. It produces the illusion of having it all, at no cost, repeatedly, effortlessly, now, and forever. This is the quintessential, utopian, eternal child, and womb-service fantasy. This is really a good gig.

In order to illustrate the power of such instantaneous bundling, consider the following analogy. During World War II, spies devised an ingenious system for transporting secret messages across enemy lines. They used the "microdot." This consisted of a highly condensed and miniaturized photograph, which appeared to the enemy examiner's eyes at the checkpoint as an inconspicuous and innocent dot or period in a standard document. When later magnified under the microscope, it reproduced a detailed enemy map, list, blueprint, or plan. Nowadays, this power-packed miniaturization has been exponentially enhanced by computers, but the principle remains the same.

Similarly, our behavior is essentially the result of predominantly unconscious mental images, stories, or fantasies, which are the instantaneous and power-packed microchip melodramas that frame and narrate our lives. In a process comparable to the miniaturization that allows stupendous amounts of information to be stored, arranged, rearranged, and transmitted within so small an apparatus as a microdot or microchip, our brains use psychic and molecular mechanisms that work at high speeds to compress huge masses of data in a purposeful and organized way.

I'm told that this all takes place amidst the trillions of connections between a hundred billion neurons in the brain! This happens biochemically at a molecular level and at countless cell membrane locations. Imagine the colossal and unfathomable complexity and capacity of this network! We have as many connections in our amazing brains as the known stars in the universe! This dwarfs the capacity of any supercomputer. It results in the power-packed nature of fantasy.

> *Microdots are fantasies. ... 'Microdot,' more than 'fantasy,' implies all at the same instant: an ability to condense masses of data; inspiration to be moved around weightlessly and slipped into situations in which it brings about desired results. It is efficient. But the conscious experience of instantaneousness hides logical, motivated (even if unconscious) planning.*
> R. Stoller

> *Life is not governed by will or intention. Life is a question of the nerves and fibres and slowly built up cells in which thought hides itself and passion has its dreams.*
> O. Wilde

FANTASY AS THE BASIS OF THE REPETITION COMPULSION

Once a person installs a central, organizing, and power-packed fantasy-microdot-microchip in the hard drive of the mind, he or she automatically, unconsciously, and compulsively play-acts to this same psychodrama over and over, for the rest of his life. It's an endlessly self-renewing and replaying mobius strip tape-recording in his mind. This is the basis of the highly repetitive, unconscious, and self-defeating behavior patterns which we've called the repetition-compulsion. Thereby, the neurotic individual unknowingly, unconsciously, and unerringly acts out the same futile and complex scenario, amidst any circumstance. He manages to arrive at the very same pre-scripted, final, and painful ending, every time. This process is known in criminal arenas as the "modus operandi."

The self-defeater remains unaware of this inner compulsion. He or she continues to think that his conscious mind makes rational, astute, profitable, and situation-specific decisions. He can't connect the dots and realize that an unconscious part of his mind, his inner five-year-old part-self, is actually peeking out at him, installing its own C.D. or "app" in the ego's hard drive, and commandeering adult resources by replaying the same out-dated and hidden childhood play.

The inner five year-old thus manipulates the unaware and naive adult mind as if it were a musical instrument or puppet. The conscious self is unable to awaken from the highly gratifying/nightmare of this compulsive, self-imposed, self-aggrandizing, and self-victimizing prison. It's trapped in the endless cosmic con-game.

> *... it is useless to try to escape the pain he creates for himself by trying to solve adult problems with a child's tricks and evasions ...*
>
> W. & M. Beecher

THE LARCENY OF ENCODED AND AMPED-UP ILLUSIONS

Self-defeaters are unconsciously working in highly complex intrapsychic code. At a conscious level, they chase after mere illusions and windmills. Thereby, they attempt to fulfill the five year-old part-self's unfeasible, overly-ambitious, cost-free, risk-free, and unlimited childhood dreams.

Seen in this light, self-defeat emerges as an intricate and ingenious form of larceny. It's an attempt to steal more from life than life has to offer, ... to anyone. It's a refusal to relinquish that which the masochist could never have had, in the first place.

The many earthly desires of common man [are] ... substitutes for what he really wants, a groping in all directions for waters that do not quench his thirst.
C. Naranjo

VICTIM ROLE ENTITLEMENT

Beneath the deceptive sand in our eyes of the victim's carefully exhibited and consciously genuine pain, misery, worthlessness, guilt, fear, dread, inferiority, complaints, depression, and self-loathing; his unconscious inner five year-old part-self feels vastly and boundlessly arrogant, superior, and, most of all, entitled! Entitlement drives the entire enterprise of masochism. Entitlement makes it so ecstatically worthwhile to devise, stage, and act out inner, power-packed, and misery-producing sadomasochistic fantasies with others. At an unconscious level, masochists use their very failures and suffering to amplify and confirm their unreasonable and unfulfillable demands.

While thus stubbornly refusing to grow up and settle for healthy, available, and realistically limited fulfillments and skills, self-defeaters actually reveal their unconscious, hidden, imperious, inflated, and preposterous sense of entitlement. It's all backwards. It's all smoke and mirrors, bait and switch. In the land of self-defeat, nearly nothing is as it appears to be. All the ego's carefully crafted conscious explanations and self-justifications are mere self-deceptions. All too often, they fool others, as well.

Most importantly, this intricate self-deception fosters and justifies the compulsive victim's inflated sense of entitlement to unconditional and larger-than-life *love*. In one who portrays himself or herself as so unworthy and inferior, how can that be? How does this multitalented and ingenious sleight of hand, work? What's the mechanism of this magical intrapsychic card trick?

THE NEUROTIC CONTRACT: THE ILLUSION OF RESCUE HUMANS

The self-defeater accomplishes this amazing and backwards deception by employing what Berliner called "the neurotic contract." It goes something like this:

> Oh, poor me! I've suffered so much all my life at the hands of others, you, fate, the gods, or chance. I've been so unloved, deprived, neglected, rejected, deceived, betrayed, abused, traumatized, malformed, crippled, disfigured, ruined, and so on. As you can see, I'm in desperate need of rescue, healing, repair, and rehabilitation. You, on the other hand, are so strong, healthy, endowed, and successful. You're one of the lucky ones.
>
> You've had all the advantages of shelter, nurture, abundance, inheritance, guidance, education, health, attractiveness, and love. If you really love me, then, you need to *make it up to me* for all the damage that you, others, the gods, genetics, and life have done to

me. Share the bounty of your privilege and advantage with me. It's only fair, don't you see?

So, here's my deal. Be my hero or heroine. *Rescue me* from my misery. Shelter me from life's every demand and adversity. I deserve it. I'm entitled, you see, to endless guarantees and reparative smooth-sailing. I've paid my lifelong dues, up front. Henceforth, I'll gladly play the role of your caged rescue human.

Don't ever dare to be so cruel as to insinuate that I must eventually leave the cushioned and indulged safety of my self-imposed cage and find my way on my own two feet, just like anyone else. I'm special and permanently disabled, don't you see? You must do everything for me, forever. That's our deal, remember? You're the all-powerful savior-rescuer, and I'm the helpless victim-waif. Let's stick to our roles, here. Let's emphasize that word: "helpless." Say it with me.

This unwritten and unconscious contract or anthem is the neurotic's way of presenting his or her preposterously inflated, entitled, and victimized claim for "just" reparation and compensation. As you can see, this never-ending contract is in no way fair, just, realistic, or even remotely possible.

Under our paradoxical microscope, the victim role thus emerges as the most powerful, imperial, and manipulative role known to humanity. I'm not exaggerating this. The victim is the one who's in charge of these intricate melodramas. This victim-hero contract is the unconscious five-year-old's finest scam over the hapless conscious self and others.

To have a grievance is to have a purpose in life. ... We have a sense of power when we inflict pain - even if it be but on ourselves. ... The difference between the masochist's secret frenzy and the sage's quiet serenity boils down to one factor: humility.
E. Hoffer

... the weak not only survive but often triumph over the strong. The self-hatred inherent in the weak unlocks energies far more formidable than those mobilized by an ordinary struggle for existence.
E. Hoffer

The tyranny of the weak over the strong ... is the only tyranny that lasts.
O. Wilde

Neurosis is ... a substitute for legitimate suffering.
C. Jung

The magical belief that by suffering one can claim higher rewards is based on the infantile notion that one can arrest attention and obtain fulfillment ... only through ... misery and suffering ... that only the exceptional will arrest the attention and interest of the significant adult. If it cannot be achieved by positive ... performance, then it will be done by negative, destructive and self-thwarting activity.
Leon Salzman

... instead of tackling his illusions, he presents a claim to the outside world. He is entitled. ... Everyone ought to cater to his illusions. ... The neurotic feels entitled to

special attention, consideration, deference ... whatever he feels, thinks, or does ought not to carry any adverse consequences.
K. Horney

Any average citizen can ... create a difficult situation and yet remain totally unaware of having done so. ... he can suffer to his heart's content.
P. Watzlawick

The masochist feels and acts as if he were in a hostile country under a tyrannical dictator... who will allow him to live (to be loved) only on condition that he continually and actively dramatize his submissive defeat.
Charles Socarides

INJUSTICE-COLLECTING

As Adler correctly emphasized, we humans eagerly and routinely sell our souls for the illusion of larger-than-life power. The masochist isn't courageous enough to try for realistic measures of healthy and compromised power in an overt, honest, adult, aggressive, competitive, and forthright way. Instead, he or she takes a circuitous, clandestine, disguised, victimized, and uncompromising route. His aim is to collect injustices in order to shame others into trying to bestow unlimited and restorative power upon him. They must make it up to him for these wrongs.

He or she reinforces this ruse by appearing to be soothed, at first, as a result of the other's kindly and heroic ministrations. Nevertheless, at every turn thereafter, the other's efforts to help must never be accepted as "enough." In this way, by dangling the mirage of the carrot just out of reach, the masochist preserves forever the illusion of his endless "poor me" victimhood. He's just trying to fill a hole, he says, ... a hole which can never be filled, and a hole which he, himself, creates.

He's what we call a "help-rejecting complainer." It's never enough. The victim is now revealed as a highly efficient, shaming, vengeful, demanding, and power-hungry injustice-collector.

> *These people have lusciously martyrish gratifications, such as 'they'll-be-sorry-when-I'm-gone' ... which convert the ... victim into psychological victor over his tormentor. ... [to] a fantasied audience whose function is to recognize that the sadistic partner is the brute.*
> R. Stoller

> *Self-sabotage is the revenge of a dependent individual against social demands which he cannot meet as an emotionally mature person. He tries, in effect, to shame his parents when company is present.*
> W. & M. Beecher

> *The masochistic action has the purpose of enacting a phantasy of revenge by repeating the situation that justifies the feeling of revenge and defiance. It is hard for man to renounce revenge.*
> T. Reik

> *That is the only thing I have under my power - to fail! ... In self-engineered failure or in suicide, one is the master of one's fate ...*
> Samuel Warner

... how to fight parents? ... Do not function! ... this is a relatively 'safe' way to vent hostility, for it carries its own built-in camouflage: ... he causes his attack upon the parent to appear [to be] accidental, or beyond his control. ... All of us learn in childhood that we can 'get back' at others by defeating ourselves.
S. Warner

The basic dynamic of S & M is the power ..., not the pain. ... dominance is constructed from submission ... the ultimate unity of sadism and masochism.
Thomas Weinberg
& G. W. Levi Kamel

CHAPTER 12

THE SECRET VICTORY OF SELF-DEFEAT, REVISITED

PART TWO

SADOMASOCHISTIC SCENES: HAND-IN-GLOVE ENTHRALLMENTS

All of this self-defeating and entitled melodrama is acted out repeatedly in endless varieties of what I call "sadomasochistic scenes" or plays. These are the power-packed packages or microdots of the repetition compulsion. These reciprocal, hand-in-glove plays are conceived and enacted by processes which are out of the conscious awareness of each of the perfectly matched star performers.

Within these microdots, plays, or fantasies, the victim is the secret playwright-impresario-con-artist. He displays his specific wares of helpless victimhood as he stages the audition, and then he or she waits for just the right kind of co-star-sucker to show up and try out for the reciprocal role of "hero-heroine-savior-lover-rescuer." The hapless and naive co-star wanna-be buys into the never-ending "make-it-up-to-me" contract.

Once the amazingly suitable new rescuer-hero costar nails the tryout, the pair's mutual, reciprocal, and ever-escalating sadomasochistic fates are sealed. It seems like a match made in heaven. They've each unwittingly sold their souls, not to each other, actually, but to their own inner and dualistic demons. It's a perfect hand-in-glove, victim-hero, and sadomasochistic match or dance. Each player now gets to "act out" their reciprocal and well-delineated roles within the merged, well-written, rehearsed, and updated script, in order to obtain seemingly opposite, but identically/reciprocal illusions. It's an unconscious and mutual "win-win" collaboration and enthrallment, disguised as a theatrical "win-lose."

> *Life is full of internal dramas, instantaneous and sensational, played to an audience of one.*
> Anthony Powell

> *'Drama' is the intentional, although often involuntary, acting you do in life, which you believe is real. ... Being a [self-created] victim justifies anything the mind cares to act out, no matter how destructive ...*
> Ron Smotherman

The hero-heroine-savior-lover-rescuer's fatal character flaw is that he or she, too, unknowingly and vicariously enjoys the very same illusions of dependency and safety by playing the reciprocal role of the enabler-provider.

THE SADOMASOCHISTIC PLAY AS A MASSIVE, MUTUAL CON-GAME

The hero-heroine fails to notice the self-created victim's carefully hidden, deeply unconscious, and eminently larcenous agenda. It far predates Act I of their mutually satisfying and collaborating enthrallment or play. The victim's role is an unconsciously premeditated, exquisitely designed, endlessly rehearsed, and consummately executed con-game. Underneath his or her pity-ploys and postures, and unknown at a conscious level even to himself, he secretly attempts to coerce unending supplies of something none of us can actually have: total and magical shelter and exemption from having to deal with the normal adversities, risks, brutalities, responsibilities, limits, and costs of life.

Merely and maturely facing life's realistic adversities is unthinkable to the self-defeater. He or she wants no part of facing life bravely, squarely, and on a level playing field, where he must subject himself to the extensive scrutiny of peer review. He leaves that distasteful and frightening chore to the hero, his beast of burden.

THE ULTIMATE PAYOFF: ENTITLEMENT TO LIMITLESS RESTITUTION

So, both partners are heavily invested in an unperceived, symbiotic, and pleasurable con-game enthrallment. It's a hand-in-glove match made in heaven. In fact, it accurately reflects reality's cosmic con-game. Each player's unconscious five-year-old part-self enjoys veritable cascades of heroic or victimized illusory pleasures and rewards. Each five-year-old and each conscious partner feels that he or she's the one who gets the really good stuff. He projects that it's the other who blocks his full satisfaction. Projections keep both partners hooked, usually for life, in this endlessly spiraling free-fall duet.

These sadomasochistic contracts are well worth preserving and repeating for a lifetime, with this partner, and the next, and the next. There's always another group of perfectly matched, naive, and reciprocal character actors available in the wings. They're only too willing to audition for the hero-rescuer-shelterer role, if there's even the slightest hint that this plum role may be vacated and available. Hero-role typecasts go through life compulsively seeking out and even competing against others for rescue humans to enable.

Hidden beneath their identically/opposite roles, each partner unknowingly seeks the exact same unrealizable goal of unlimited and larcenous entitlement. Each is running an identical predatory con-game, really, only with opposite come-on external pitches:

> I'm so damaged or heroic that you must provide me, or I'll vicariously provide you, with never-ending supplies and shelter. It's only fair.

Each partner essentially wants the other to write him a blank check, after he or she presents his "just" bill for unlimited, "make-it-up-to-me," or "reward-me-for-my-pain-or-valor," entitlement:

> And just what fair compensation and reparation must you supply to pay me back for my pain and suffering, or for all my hard rescue work? Hmmm, ... let me see. I've got it! You owe me, ... EVERYTHING! That's the ticket! I'm entitled! It's in the contract, remember? It's only fair, don't you think? If you don't honor the contract, I may have to blame you.
>
> By my tally, here, because of my immense and virtuous victimhood or heroism, you now owe me ... hmmm, ... let's see, ... the tab comes to unconditional, endless, effortless, and risk-free

love, adoration, worship, respect, understanding, forbearance, leniency, indulgence, justice, protection, shelter, safety, security, certainty, advantage, power, superiority, and, oh yes, ... did I mention life everlasting? Let's not forget that one. Now, that's all.

I'm actually giving you a discount, here. You're really getting off lightly. I won't ask you again, I promise. Now remember, ... it's only fair. After all, I've been so injured or benevolent. Do you want me to go back over my long list? It's right here, in the contract. I happen to have a copy of it with me. It's no trouble to read it, really. Let's review ...

... his suffering accuses others and excuses himself! It excuses in his mind everything - his demands, his irritability, his dampening of the spirits of others. ... [It] also wards off the possible reproaches of others [and] ... **entitles** *him to 'understanding.' ... No matter what he does, it should arouse sympathy and the wish to help. [It] ... provides him with an over-all alibi ... for not actually making more of his life. ... Suffering ... appears as the proof of nobility.*

K. Horney

This triumphant presentation of his "just" bill for unlimited compensation is the victim or hero's finest moment. This is his or her ultimate pay-off. This is the moment he's been building up to, all along, amidst his years and tears of role-playing. It's the whole ball game. This is his "raison d'etre."

ACTS I AND II: THE SET-UP

Act I of the three act sadomasochistic play chronicles the elaborate history and set-up for both partners' con-games, amidst entertaining, melodramatic, distracting, and decoying adventures, subterfuges, and sub-plots. It establishes, develops, and installs these intricate victim-hero scenarios, or sadomasochistic contracts, complete with appropriate and reciprocal illusory conceits. Act II then moves the plot forward with intricate and interwoven actions, reactions, delays, victories, and setbacks. It allows both actors to compile, justify, polish, and present their mirror-image bills for the very same "just" and never-ending restitution or compensation. They both really want it all.

Other than during the heat of occasional bitter arguments, it wouldn't be seemly for either actor to openly present these exaggerated and even preposterous bills. "Give me everything my heart desires without requiring that I grow up; without requiring any effort or risk on my part; and simply because I've suffered so and thus earned it." Such blatant demands would be too obvious, unrealistic, and arrogant. They would contain none of the vital melodramatic elements of foreplay, buildup, distractions, setbacks, timing, surprise, subterfuge, promises, and triumph.

It's better to present such outrageous con-games as unspoken, implied, and camouflaged sadomasochistic contracts. The smoke and mirrors of their reciprocal cons allow both partners to freely cash the six-figure blank check installments on their never-ending tabs. They each get to demand it all, without any risk, scrutiny, blame, or limits. This is an extraordinarily good gig!

> *The masochist attempts to enforce his will. ... [He] is a revolutionist of self-surrender. The lambskin he wears hides a wolf. His yielding includes defiance, his submissiveness opposition.*
>
> T. Reik

In fact, these reciprocal hero-victim sadomasochistic partnerships are so powerfully and ultimately rewarding on so many unconscious levels that we humans are very loathe, indeed, to ever give them up, whether we're on the heroic or victimized wing of the contract. Where else can we get such an imaginary good deal?

ACT III: SWITCHING OF THE SCRIPTS, THE FINEST MOMENT OF DECEIT

Act III is when the victim-playwright-con-artist-impresario's superior manipulative skills really shine. After all, he or she is far more than just a star in the cast. He's also the play's secret playwright, scriptwriter, director, promoter, producer, audience, casting agent, and critic. Behind the scenes, he literally calls all the shots. In contrast, the hero-rescuer actor is merely a dispensable hired hand. He or she only seems to be the dominant partner. His power is limited only to that which the victim scripts for him.

Act III is when the victim playwright performs his "coup de gras." This is when he quietly, secretly, and skillfully SWITCHES THE SCRIPTS. This is his finest deceit; it sets up his or her ultimate moment of victory.

The victim has endlessly rationalized and begged for "just" reparations. The hero has been a good sport, indeed, about all this. In spite of his occasional objections and hissy-fits, especially when he's so inevitably and thoroughly frustrated and exhausted; he has, indeed, attempted to rise to the occasion and supply all these truly unfulfillable demands. His merely human efforts must inevitably fall short, however, as per the script. The hero or heroine is destined to let the victim down.

As a result, the victim-playwright becomes thoroughly, repeatedly, and inevitably disenchanted. This disappointment is a genuine/act. It's a required dramatic device of the whole con-game play. The self-scripted victim needs to appear to be "surprisingly" disappointed and disillusioned in the hero, in order to justify the next ultimate and treacherous Act III scene, the switching-of-the-scripts betrayal. If the intricate timing of this subterfuge is off in the slightest detail, all its persuasive leverage falls flat.

It's at this point that the victim-maestro conducts secret off-site auditions for a new hero. These auditions are attended by supporting cast members, understudies, and available actors in the neighborhood. It's easy to dupe them. Being merely and inflatedly human, they all think they can do a better job. They missed or failed to discern the victim-playwright's secret, premeditated, and pre-scripted "I-don't-really-lose-in-the-end" con-game.

One of these actors becomes the "lucky winner" in the competition and lands what he or she considers to be the plum role of "hero." He begins a secret affair with the playwright. He thinks it's an opportunity, a match made in heaven. It's really a disaster or calamortunity for him, as well. He's just the next duped and expendable hero. He begins his enthusiastic endeavor within extensive behind-closed-doors rehearsals for his upcoming public debut.

The intricately rewritten script is distributed to the entire supporting cast, as well as to the newly recruited hero. The soon-to-be erstwhile and thoroughly cuckolded original hero-costar is the only participant in the entire production who's not given a copy of this new script, of course. That would spoil the melodrama. He or she continues to act from this last existing copy of the now obsolete dummy script. He fails to notice that all the other characters are acting from a newly updated set of lines and directions, according to which he's been systematically written out of his original role. He's been recast, instead, into the dreaded role of "villain" or "perpetrator."

Ever in denial of this mortifying demotion, he or she's blindsided and confused, as his previously effective heroic lines fall flat. Instead, and in front of the entire retinue, he's relentlessly denigrated, humiliated, betrayed, dethroned, and replaced. Even worse, he's ignored. He thinks he must have delivered the lines ineffectively.

Maybe it was bad timing. Maybe he missed his marks. Being a consummate and accomplished character actor, and assuming that other actors just didn't hear him clearly, he conscientiously stays in character and redoubles his efforts to recite and enunciate his now obsolete lines even more loudly, melodramatically, eloquently, and precisely, … all to no avail, of course.

ENDLESS SWITCHINGS OF THE SCRIPTS

In the end, the now erstwhile hero or heroine is eventually, publicly, and painfully disgraced, dismissed, and divorced from the play, as the understudy or newly imported character actor moves in and takes over the coveted heroic lead. The ex-hero is understandably baffled, mortified, crestfallen, hurt, and bitter. Not yet catching on to the cosmic con-game or the switching of the scripts, he or she's not yet prone to use this experience as an opportunity to step back, re-evaluate, awaken, wise-up, and relinquish his futile, compulsive, self-defeating, and foolish fixation on playing the hero role, itself. Instead, he pushes on with his fixated, doomed, and dualistic chess game thinking. After his dismissal, he keeps on auditioning for the identical and self-defeating hero role in the next rescue human's or victim/sadist's play, … and so the cycle goes.

The original victim/sadist-playwright goes on with his or her newly-refurbished/same old play. The "truth and virtue" of his scam is "confirmed," "verified," celebrated, and promoted by the play's enabling and ever-approving chorus. Eventually, the predatory/victim will come to switch the scripts and dismiss this and subsequent heroes, too, as they take their desperate and futile turns at the hopeless project of attempting to supply the victim's every impossible illusion. The magic show or scam must go on and on, endlessly. Such an ever-refreshed and re-enacted play often enjoys a masochistically profitable lifetime run on this internal and interpersonal stage. That's show business.

INTERNAL SADOMASOCHISTIC SCENES

We've described the interpersonal sadomasochistic scenes which are so very common between reciprocal and nearly interchangeable victims and heros. Just how does all this ingenious and damaging trickery play out internally, within the individual victim or hero's unawakened mind? After all, the primary objective in this dualistic, win-lose chess game is to act out all the parts of the internal play, by fooling ourselves. This inevitably perpetuates our own folly. As with all things human, it's ultimately an inside job. That's where the most telling, tragic, and extreme damage occurs. External victims or heros are merely collateral damage.

Previous chapters have already described these internal sadomasochistic scenes between the unconscious five-year-old part-self and the conscious ego. The inner five-year-old victim-playwright dupes the ego-hero into dancing like a marionette to its unheard siren songs and CD's. As per their sadomasochistic contract, this inner child gets to enjoy the pleasures of his or her unreasonable demands, while the beast of burden and hero-shelterer ego takes the hit. The conscious ego can't fathom that there's a part-self within who secretly enjoys inflicting such pain. Both parts of the self suffer from illusion, while each considers him or herself to be the ultimate champion. For both, it's a lose-lose conceit, disguised as a win-lose.

THE ULTIMATE HEALING OF INNER INTEGRATION

As per previous chapters on balance and integration, we already know the paradoxical answer in the back of the book about this nearly inevitable and irresistible process, ... this endless, circular, and futile repetition compulsion. Of course, the answer in adult years is to gradually become aware of the deceptions and workings of our unconscious minds. The objective is to expose these hidden and childish agendas and phenomena to the objective light of day, so that they can be confronted, faced, re-evaluated, and recognized for who and what they really are. This is when we adults can have an epiphany and come to realize that we've been commandeered by the cosmic con-game and by our own immature and childish part-selves, all along. We can then pause and choose just which of our conflicting thoughts to believe and implement.

Only by owning and accepting our inborn element of inner, sadistic, self-indulgent, and conniving evil can we learn to work with it. It doesn't go away. It's a manifestation of the resentful and negative child. We must become an ultimate diplomat and learn to achieve internal peace with and supervision over this often unchangeable inner part-self. As a result of this expanded and enhanced consciousness, we can pause to weigh and balance our options. This is when we can listen and give the inner child the healing comfort and **EMBRACE** of **S.P.A.C.E.**

After this, it's time for the rest of the **B.E. K.I.N.D.** method. We can now consult with our paradoxically wise part-self, in order to formulate **BALANCED**, **KINDLY**, **INSIGHTFUL**, **DISILLUSIONED**, and **DEFLATED** behaviors and attitudes in the here-and-**NOW**. Only then can we "tame" our unconscious mind and commence to resume the form of our whole, integrated, authentic, expanded, enriched, and paradoxically wise self.

It would be ideal if all humans did this within the course of natural and normal maturation, but we're just not built that way. Nine out of ten of us keep on chasing our own tails. We're highly impulsive and intricately self-confirming little creatures. The more we're confronted with a paradoxical truth, the more we ignore half of reality and explain it away. That's why the universe must confront us so stringently with painful rug-pullings, so that we have the opportunity to be alerted to the folly of our compulsive, idealistic, and extremist misassumptions. These calamortunities can start to loosen our death grips on illusion. They can begin to enlighten us, but only if we strive to catch on to the cosmic con-game and look within.

UNCONSCIOUS PLEASURES AND SECRET PRODUCTION OF SYMPTOMS

The pivotal and self-defeating pay-off, here, is the secret, amped-up, and larger-than-life pleasure the unconscious part-selves are able to experience, while our beast-of-burden egos are busy taking the conscious hit. It's this unperceived, heightened, and internal pleasure which drives the whole engine of self-defeat. Part-selves need secrecy in order to pull off such colossal larceny. They do this by creating distractions or decoys, some of which we call "symptoms."

By creating physical and mental symptoms, the unconscious mind adds to the ego's pain. It distracts, fools, hoodwinks, preoccupies, and, thereby, commandeers the well-meaning, busy, and unaware conscious self, which is also distracted by the hundreds of ways each hour that it must deal with the complex external demands of a reality that comes at us at the speed of life.

According to the script, the conscious ego takes on the savior-provider role in this internal sadomasochistic play. The unconscious then quietly, gradually, and relentlessly switches the script and recasts the ego into the "villain" role. The unconscious part-self vindictively afflicts the hero-turned-villain with painful, baffling, punitive, and distracting symptoms, while it enjoys the illusion of pure, duty-free, pain-free, and risk-free joys.

These mental and physical symptoms are merely the trojan horse packages that make possible our unconscious mind's hidden, sneaky, hedonistic, and larcenous sadomasochistic scene agenda. This is truly brilliant hoodwinking strategy! This is the secret, hidden, and internal sadomasochistic scene which drives the external one.

The very secrecy inherent in our constitutionally split up mind thus enables us to unknowingly and freely indulge in our wildest and most unrealistic unconscious fantasies. We couldn't pull this off if we were fully aware of what we were doing. Self-defeat thus emerges as a hidden, intricate, vast, and Shakespearian bonanza! "All the world's a stage, and all the men and women merely players." As Stoller said, "She was a victim in search of a disaster."

GODS WHEN WE GROW UP

So there you have it. These endless internal sadomasochistic scenes enable us to pull off the most grandiose and preposterous illusion of all. In the end, we get to play the thinly disguised and coveted role of the long-suffering God-playwright. That's our central and most ultimate sadomasochistic superhero fantasy. It comes in endless masculine and feminine varieties.

SOUR GRAPES

We may consciously or unconsciously arrange for our own obvious failure, every time. Nevertheless, and being our own most avid and hoodwinked fans, we can always convince ourselves that we actually prefer, relish, and take pride in these sorry and defeated states.

> You can't fire me; I quit. I don't really want those grapes of success, anyhow. They're really too sour. I'm more unique, superior, and fascinating, you see, than all those ordinary, boring, tame, obedient, conventionally successful, and predictable do-gooders out there. I'm so much deeper.
> They have to make compromises, but I'm truly free! I'm above those petty quests for merely superficial and partial approval, success, and happiness. I even prefer my messy, unconventional, and uncompromising life. I pull brilliant and unexpected gems of success out

of the fire, every time. That's what makes me so much more dazzling, amazing, courageous, unpredictable, enticing, exciting, dangerous, and, therefore, fascinating. Come on in and join me. You'll love it, here!

Self-defeaters' imaginary, superior, and grandiose fantasies thus win/or lose the day, nearly every time. They can't help it. Masochists are the ultimate romantic-vengeful-victim-victors. "I did it my way." This is the ultimate in perverse, foolish, self-soothing, self-aggrandizing, entitled, and solipsistic pleasure. It's our most grandiose self-deceit and conceit. After all, "con" is short for "confidence," ... *over*-confidence, that is.

CHAPTER 13

ROMANTIC LOVE'S ILLUSIONS

PART ONE

Love is the answer, isn't it? Love brings out the best and worst in us all. It allows us to really show our stuff, ... the good, the bad, and the ugly. It's one of our most illuminating calamortunities. Love can expose our most lowly, selfish, and childish folly; as well as our most sublime, altruistic, and paradoxical wisdom.

Unawakened, and, therefore, dualistic lovers are fixated at extremist, split-up, and this-or-that levels of awareness. Unable to achieve the profound, enduring, safe, and balanced intimacy that comes with paradoxical wisdom; they fling themselves into wild, confusing, either-or, and brinksmanship oscillations between love and hate, acceptance and rejection, closeness and distance. Their impressive, larger-than-life, positive, and negative demonstrations and tempests are just not worth it.

The adversity one faces in trying to manage such an extremist and moody lover constitutes one of our finest crucible-pathways to enlightenment. I suppose, therefore, that nurturing and enjoying what one can in the midst of such a sadomasochistic and sub-optimal love relationship should make us feel grateful for such a potentially illuminating and transforming calamortunity.

TRANSFERENCE

Because such self-defeating lovers are unknowingly controlled by their unconscious five year-old part-selves, they dance like marionettes to unheard and repetitive melodies. They thus unwittingly sentence themselves to repeat seemingly adult versions of highly scripted, well-rehearsed, melodramatic, reciprocal, and sadomasochistic scenes, which they've written, directed, staged, and perfected since childhood.

the "trance" of everyday life reflects the channeling of attention into the unconscious fantasies of childhood.
... Much, if not most, of our activity consists of the un-knowing [re-]enactment of these dramas.
       A. Deikman

Instead of dancing personally and specifically with their enigmatic, multifaceted, and complex enough adult partner, they dance with their unconsciously projected image of the inner child's distorted and reconstructed version of their childhood parent, sibling, or other important figure. This dance with a mere phantom from the past is called "transference."

Their unsuspecting adult partner enters into the love dance with appropriate adult steps. The unawakened partner commences the dance in harmony with these adult moves, but he or she inevitably seizes the lead; commandeers the dance; and inserts his own unconscious music, rhythm, and choreography; ... all in order to synchronize with some long-forgotten, internal, and distorted childhood psychodrama.

This inappropriate dance step confuses the adult partner. In the name of love, he does the best he or she can to synchronize with and even develop a taste for these odd, awkward, childish, and dissonant steps and moves. He even defends them to complaining other adult partners. He has no inkling that despite his self-defeating partner's earnest claims otherwise, his partner isn't really dancing with him personally or specifically, at all. Rather, he's dancing with an ancient and self-created phantom from the past, ... a mere shadow on the back wall of Plato's cave.

This perverse and uncoordinated attempt at a love dance spins out of control and into a predictable and regrettable series of disasters. The partners step on each other's toes, entangle each other's legs, trip each other up, and launch into opposing and unsynchronized directions. This results in repeated collisions, falls, injuries, arguments, and reprisals with each other and with surrounding dancers.

This already disastrous dance is rendered even more preposterous if *both* partners are unawakened and, therefore, unconsciously fixated in the past. This is often the case, since humans tend to attract like-minded partners. These reciprocally-matched and hand-in-glove unawakened lovers stage competitively/synchronous and confusingly complex sadomasochistic scenes within their interpersonal dances, ... all in harmony with their fixated and reciprocal transferences. It's as if the phantoms of each of their extended families of origin are crowding invisibly into the ballroom, endlessly misunderstanding each other, loudly promoting their contrasting and incompatible agendas, and hopelessly confusing each original partner, who can't even hear each other over the din.

More paradoxically wise partners may give such hoodwinked and unawakened dualists a spin for a while, but they soon tire of such strange and dissonant dance scenes. Much as they're swept away initially by the amazing charms and charisma of this new lover, they just can't work up an enduring taste for these sadly ill-fated, disharmonious, and unworkable steps.

THE MORE REALISTIC DANCE OF OPTIMAL PARTNERS

Paradoxically wise partners sometimes manage to find their way to each other. These fortunate partners don't dance in such childish and dissonant choreography with merely self-projected shadows. These optimal mates live in the personal present moment, not the past. Their invisible families of origin aren't even invited into the room.

Such paradoxically wise pairs have the capacity to dance somewhat smoothly, harmoniously, non-transferentially, and seamlessly with similarly mature, profound, and paradoxical partners. They synchronize fully, personally, authentically, considerately, specifically, and lovingly with each other. Their love is characterized by balance, nuance, accuracy, harmony, compromise, tolerance, respect, kindness, honesty, constancy, and mutual autonomy.

Conflicts inevitably still occur between such optimally integrated adults, as they do between all humans, but they're quiet, brief, non-rejecting, non-brinksmanship-like, non-ultimatum-laden, non-symbiotic, non-delusional, and non-abusive. Such matched integrated lovers are able to recover much more quickly from argumentative set-backs, in order to resume their harmonious dances.

Moreover, integrated partners learn to use conflicts as opportunities to enhance their closeness and understanding, not to blow things apart. They argue in order to deepen their enduring love, not in order to merely win the day's unimportant and often childish battle. Above all, they don't throw each other under the bus. Chapter 15 will expand on optimal love.

SYMBIOTIC, UNCONDITIONAL LOVE: THE ILLUSION OF FUSION, OF WOMB SERVICE

It's such a profoundly tragic aspect of human nature that the most utopian and idealistic model of symbiotic love also happens to be the most wildly, preposterously, and impossibly unworkable. It's based on the well meaning, but disastrous illusion and promise of pure and unconditional love. If only such idealistic declarations could be true. Such perfect, utopian, and seamless harmony between humans actually exists only to a brief and primitive extent in the non-thinking womb. Intrauterine existence is truly the ultimate in effortless, soothing, floating, and heroine-like bliss. It's literally "womb-service." Even there, however, the fetus begins to manifest its innate developmental drive towards eventual freedom and autonomy when it tumbles, stretches, and kicks.

Life after birth can't possibly compete with any average mother's unconscious and seamless uterine care-taking. During the child's subsequent infancy, even the most optimal, devoted, and well-meaning parent operates amidst inevitable delays and mistakes, as he or she tries to decipher and fulfill the infant's needs. Deep down and at the most immature levels of our infantile unconscious minds, we all long for a return to this womb-service illusion of fused "oneness," ... to this mindless, effortless, warm, soothing, and endless caress of passive bliss, satiation, and rapture.

The urge to return to a state of oneness with mother, long known to analysts, remains as a permanent fundamental of character structure.
                                                                R. Stoller

No human being can understand us fully, ... give us unconditional love, ... offer constant affection, ... enter into the core of our being and heal our deepest brokenness.
Henri Nouwen

A century ago, Helmuth Kaiser called this "the illusion of fusion." Others call it the quest for a symbiotic feeling state of "oceanic oneness." This is the unconscious objective of those who get high, whether it's natural, hypnotic, or drug-induced. It's been described within the metaphor of "the hungry ghost."

When such symbiotic demands are unfulfilled, dualistic types throw giant hissy-fits, which, of course, they attempt to justify as reasonable, rational, and tolerable adult outrage. In effect, they're attempting to impose their preposterous and childish illusion of fusion upon the adult world. Their audacious goal is to improve on reality and transform it into a purely loving and all-indulgent uterus. This amounts to the wish to be an eternal child or "puer aeternus." It sentences them to a life of being hungry ghosts, searching endlessly and in vain for that which can never fill their enlarged, voracious, and insatiable bellies.

Collaborative, hard-working, and realistic adult love is inherently imperfect, compromised, conditional, and differentiated. Conflicts and misunderstandings between autonomous adults are inevitable. Adult love can thrive in the setting of predominantly positive circumstances with mature, integrated, motivated, cooperative, compromising, good-hearted, forgiving, honest, committed, energetic, and skillful loved ones.

In contrast, adult love will understandably dissipate over time if unawakened partners lie, cheat, steal, infect, reject, blame, manipulate, abuse, betray, squander, take the easy way, make impossible demands, and so on. This disharmony is inflamed even further if one or both partners of such couples abuse alcohol and/or drugs.

SYMBIOTIC RANTS

The standard, self-justifying, unapologetic, angry, repetitive, demanding, and entitled rant of the insatiable, disappointed, immature, and symbiotic partner goes something like this:

> What do you mean that you'll love me, "*if?*" That's not nearly enough! You're supposed to love and adore me totally, without exceptions or conditions, no matter how immature, irresponsible, and unreasonable I am! None of this "if" crap! You owe me! You promised to love me totally and forever, remember? That means without conditions. That means that when I slip up, you must gladly forgive me and even love me more.
>
> If you fail this test, then I guess you're just not capable of that pristine and unconditional love that someone as special and unique as me needs, are you? I'm a self-designated, special, and elite lover, don't you see? I have "special needs." I'm a certified rescue human. You're just like all the rest. They couldn't measure up to such a rare and fascinating challenge, either.
>
> I'll try to be patient. I'll try to forgive you, since you're so stunted in these matters. I'll even try to give you remedial lessons, but you're so far behind. I'll test the true quality of your love with my special brand of heart-and-soul-breaking argumentativeness and brinksmanship from time to time, just to see if you can step up to the plate, elevate your all-so-inferior game, and really love me enough; ... that is, unconditionally.

It's all for your own good, don't you see? After all, *I'm* the one who's special, here. You'd be nothing without me. I'm the one who gives your life meaning, intensity, excitement, passion, and interest. Without me, you're just ordinary. I'll deign to love you, but only if you live up to my understandably high [that is, impossible] standards of love. I set the rules! Don't ever forget that.

This imperialistic and impossible demand for unconditional love can't be satisfied, of course, in the real world by real people, because it's inherently insatiable. It provides endless quantities of needed and useful disappointment to feed the unconscious, self-defeating, and never-ending sadomasochistic contract between consenting and equally duped symbiotic lovers.

Addicts in twelve step programs indirectly refer to this never-to-be-satisfied hungry ghost illusion of fusion by saying that they're "just trying to fill a hole," a hole which can never be filled, of course. That pretty much says it all. If you're fixated in an adolescent and wildly idealistic type of symbiotic extremism, nothing will ever be enough.

> *To love, for him, means to ... merge with another ...*
> *and ... to find a unity which he cannot find in himself.*
> *... The quest for unconditional love ... is a demand for*
> *love ... regardless of ... [his] provocative behavior. ... Only*
> *if the other person sacrifices everything for the neurotic*
> *can he really feel sure of being loved...*
> K. Horney

> *Neurotic girls cannot love a "weak" man because of their contempt for any weakness; but neither can they cope with a "strong" man because they expect their partner to always give in. Hence what they secretly look for is the [strong] hero, ... who at the same time is so weak that he will bend to all their wishes without hesitation.*
> K. Horney

THE ILLUSIONS OF PERMANENCY AND INVULNERABILITY

Other favorite and impossible symbiotic love demands are the illusions of permanence and invulnerability. These are childish attempts to assuage and deny the terrifying elements of impermanence, insecurity, vulnerability, and risk amidst any realistic adult love relationship. Most of us can recall those youthful tremblings when we first risked our fresh new hearts for love. Adults try to place reasonable rules, protections, boundaries, and guarantees on love, in order to reduce this inherent risk. Non-paradoxical individuals, on the other hand, go far beyond this striving for reasonable reassurances and arrangements. They even attempt to house themselves and their lover in an all-protective and womb-service prison.

> *The cruelty of love (like that of reality) resides in the paradox ... affirming as lasting that which is ephemeral ...*
> C. Rosset

THE ILLUSION OF SUPERIORITY/INFERIORITY

Another illusory, and, therefore, futile effort to avoid the risk of loss in matters as elusive as love is to enter into a basic assumption of inequality. According to the terms of this unconscious interpersonal contract, an unawakened lover considers himself or the other to be vastly superior or inferior in matters of real or imagined power, wealth, attractiveness, fitness, fame, accomplishment, intelligence, cleverness, knowledge, astuteness, coolness, humor, strength, rebelliousness, unconventionality, courage, and so on.

This presumes that one must be especially superior or inferior, dominant or submissive, in order to be loved. This is a supreme example of either-or extremism. As we've discussed in the last chapter, either extreme actually seeks to extort the exact same generic group of larger-than-life, secret, and illusory victories. They only appear to be opposites.

This superiority-inferiority fallacy is a transference. It's an unconscious effort to return to the stability and nurture of childhood's realistically unequal parent-child dynamics. It unconsciously creates the naive illusion of womb-service security for both adult partners in their mutually created sadomasochistic scene, both the giver and the taker, the parent figure and the child figure, the savior and the supplicant. Both dare not leave such self-contrived, stable, and reassuring arrangements of inequality.

Despite inevitable cycles of rejection and reconciliation, which create loud, impressive, exciting, and required thunder, lightening, deception, distraction, brinksmanship, and melodrama; such tumultuous relationships can actually be surprisingly stable and enduring. In fact, it's often nearly impossible to pry these perfectly reciprocal, mutually destructive, desperately well-intended, on-again-off-again, and sadomasochistic partners apart.

> *We are programmed to receive. You can check out any time you like, but you can never leave!*
>
> Don Felder, Don Henley, & Glen Frey

CRUEL LOVE AND THE ILLUSION OF POWER

Self-aggrandizing masochists or sadists unknowingly sentence themselves to the task of hauling around these heavy, inflated, and costly self-esteems. The "superior" partner sometimes goes to the extreme of thinking that he or she must avoid any appearance of being kind or tender, since it makes him appear to be weak, subservient, small, vulnerable, or, even worse, merely equal. He leaves these more vulnerable feelings to the designated masochist. Superior types walk around with a permanent look of smug, self-satisfied, self-aggrandized, holier-than-thou, entitled, chip-on-the-shoulder, sullen, gruff, aggravated, and frustrated disdain on their faces.

Both of these reciprocally power-hungry lovers put each other into the "safe-keeping" of an artificially split-up, unequal, and sadomasochistic enthrallment, prison, or dungeon, ... in order to ensure themselves against any possibility of an esteem-shattering rejection. In fact, their very demand for what seems so idealistic as unconditional love actually amounts to mutual, reciprocal, and synchronized cruelty by its very nature. At the end of the day, such unconscious sadism does far more damage to themselves than to others. The impossible quest for absolute love corrupts absolutely.

> *To love ... is to be vulnerable. Love anything, and your heart will certainly be wrung and possibly broken. ... You must give it to no one. ... Wrap it carefully around hobbies and little luxuries; avoid all entanglements; lock it up safe in the casket or coffin of your selfishness.*
> C.S. Lewis

In contrast, paradoxically wise love is strong, mature, confident, and self-assured enough to be tolerant, gentle, patient, non-coercive, equal, sweet, considerate, honest, and kind. Awakened men and women can dare to risk the vulnerability of authentic tenderness, non-aggression, and non-coerciveness.

CHAPTER 13

ROMANTIC LOVE'S ILLUSIONS

PART TWO

PROVOCATION: WARMTH THROUGH FRICTION

The serenity, closeness, and stability of paradoxical love both terrifies and bores those who are fixated in loud and unpredictable sadomasochistic scenes. To them, equality and tenderness are intolerable. Their unstable and inflated sense of self is rooted in an effort to feel either superior or inferior, which we can now discern through our paradoxical lenses to be equivalents. They define their fragile sense of self by sadistically or masochistically banging up against others. That way, they know where their skin is, ... where they start and others stop. Otherwise, they risk the stark terror of being either swallowed up or abandoned.

This compulsively sadomasochistic style is no mere casual choice. It's a matter of stark, innate, and compelling desperation. Having given up on trying to master the subtleties, compromises, uncertainties, and complexities of integrated, gentle, equal, centered, and kindly love; sadists and masochists derive a backwards and perverted sense of pleasure and stability by keeping it intense, extreme, frenzied, melodramatic, competitive, abusive, combative, ever-changing, and provocative.

This literally tactile and desperate sense of self is called "warmth through friction." These types prefer this loud and volatile heat of abrasiveness over the quiet, authentic, centered, non-competitive, peaceful, harmonious, free, demure, and enduring warmth of tenderness. This is their perverse and stable safety zone of interpersonal conflict. They need a nearly constant and reassuring state of conflict and tumult.

Sadomasochists are able to feel intense and abundant passion, outrage, need, terror, grief, and pity; but not integrated, compromising, nuanced, centered, and serene love. They can tolerate a small and brief measure of tender closeness, but only within their predominantly abrasive, provocative, and self-defining comfort zone. Otherwise, they feel desperately antsy, like they're about to fall apart and disappear, entirely. They're like young boys. You can tell if they like you, because they tease, insult, ignore, pinch, or slug you.

These are the compulsive arguers, debaters, and "Bickersons" of the world. They're born trial attorneys, legislators, social advocates, or defenders of the world's victims. Such types thrive amidst a good fight, controversy, or argument. In fact, they constantly seek out and provoke conflict. Fights and melodramas make them feel comfortable and amorous. It's the only way they can get sufficient supplies of desperately-needed, self-defining, self-aggrandizing, and self-protective attention.

Not being integrated enough to trust that they can inspire something so ephemeral, complex, vulnerable, and terrifying as love by using gentle, positive, non-punitive, non-coercive, and non-suffering techniques; ... sadomasochists settle for the childish effort to provoke and/or experience admiration, terror, dependency, and submission. If there's no exciting, passionate, competitive, terrifying, combative, status-promoting, and sadomasochistic melodrama going on, they feel nothing's happening.

> *[The] patient's need for input ... cutting, burning, fighting, ... and arguing all serve the function of providing for self-definition as well as for [tolerable] connection.*
>
> R. Lewin & C. Schulz

This need for the amped-up intensity of provocation and suffering contrasts with healthy and integrated individuals, who have the luxury of a stable and integrated sense of self, with reliable and durable boundaries. This is what we call mature "self-object differentiation." They're able to feel differentiated, intact, self-assured, gentle, and modest enough to relax and avoid fights, whenever feasible. They're fortunate enough to possess the intrapsychic equipment necessary for integrated and wise love.

THE "I OWN YOU" ILLUSION

Sadomasochistic lovers don't trust a process which allows a differentiated other to have their own sense of restful autonomy. Instead, they attempt to literally own or be owned, engulf or be engulfed, and imprison or be imprisoned. They try to overwhelm and obliterate their or the other's separate identity. To justify this, they refer to their divine, religious, or ethical "right" to possess or be possessed, to command or be commanded. In fact, this preposterous and self-centered "right" remains the formal law in many primitive parts of the world. Even in so-called civilized cultures, this sadomasochistic inequality was the literal law until a mere century ago. Equal rights are a preposterously recent and infrequent event in the history of humanity. In fact, truly tolerant equal rights rather rarely persist in the shabby and volatile affairs of humankind.

Sadomasochistic lovers tend to be or prey on real or imagined victims, who feel powerless, unlovable, and disadvantaged. Victims are ripe for the picking. They gladly agree to enter into such enslaving interpersonal contracts. They often have very little realistic choice in the matter. Sadistic lovers literally terrorize their unconsciously and all-too-cooperative masochistic partners, thus soothing and hiding their own stark terror. "You can't leave me," or "I can't leave you." "I own you," or "You own me."

> *Love is a rose, but you better not pick it,*
> *Only grows when it's on the vine,*
> *Hand full of thorns and you know you've missed it,*
> *Lose your love when you say the word "mine."*
>
> Neil Young

THE NEED-FEAR DILEMMA

These highly troubled adults have failed to master the early childhood developmental stage of basic trust. Their predominant feeling states are aggression, sadism, fear, terror, superiority, inferiority, grief, and passion. Where tenderly loving feelings are absent, the natural drive for harmonious closeness becomes perverted and attached, instead, to the quest for clashing sadomasochistic power in the form of reciprocally equivalent dominance and submission.

In some instances, these troubled individuals were raised by a highly immature and symbiotic parent, who tried to use their child to finally attain the illusion of pure and unconditional love for the first time in their own young adult lives. Such symbiotic parents alternate between an idealistic, overly-gratifying, smothering, and stifling type of fused-at-the-hip over-closeness, on the one hand;

and a withdrawing, rejecting, cold, frightening, and cruel type of abandonment, on the other. They're either suffocating the child, or they're throwing him or her out into the cold. Understandably, neither dramatic extreme comes across to the child as having any resemblance to authentic, reliable, and personal affection. Rather, both are experienced by the child as equally cruel, abusive, cold, and unloving.

The child in this predicament naturally grows into an adult who fears any semblance or hint of closeness. To him or her, any form of love feels ominous and terrifying. Closeness signals a dreadful return to childhood's equally intolerable cycles of smothering or abandonment. They'll have none of that!

Such an individual is fixated on the horns of a "need-fear dilemma." Because of his or her over-all deprivation and abuse during childhood, he craves for inordinate degrees of love, but he also fears it. He can't tolerate what he needs most. Being immature, he's left with no alternative. He must fling himself into either the smothering quicksand of engulfment, on the one hand; or into the terrifying abyss of abandonment, on the other. He can't find the soothing, integrating, and healing middle ground. For him, it doesn't exist. He must, therefore, be an overly-intense, thrill-seeking, ever-anxious, provocative, self-contradictory, and sadomasochistic extremist. There's no other way out.

His or her behavior reverberates between extremes. He desperately seeks out others with whom to fuse, and then he unknowingly and inevitably blows the whole thing apart. When he feels too much suffocating closeness, he rushes to preemptively reject or be rejected, first. Once alone, he feels the intolerable pain of abandonment, so he desperately runs back into the arms of his rejected, aggrieved, and confused lover, and they start the whole sadomasochistic cycle, again.

These unconscious, fear-based, and mutually cooperative fusion-abandonment cycles go on and on. Sadomasochistic and symbiotic adults act out these endless cycles with all partners, all the while blaming and convincing each specific partner of the inadequacy of his or her depth, maturity, constancy, and quality of lovingness. This amounts to a wholesale, preposterous, self-deceptive, reciprocal, reverberating, and convincing projection.

These men and women are children grown tall, desperately trying to fill a hole which was not filled in childhood, and which, in adult years, can never be filled. In fact, they now unconsciously and compulsively recreate these bottomless pits. We call these types by the term "borderline personalities," who reverberate endlessly on the border between fusion and aloneness, suffocation and abandonment, psychosis and sanity. It's all a mutually dis/satisfying and un/intended con-game.

Symbiotic, "smother-mother," and sadomasochistic partners can't realize that they, themselves, are the ones who promote and stage the entirety of these impossible, melodramatic, repetitive, and sadomasochistic scenes. Such cycles have very little to do with their current and ever-confused partners. Such rumblings originate and resonate from their deepest unconscious inner workings. It's an inside job.

They all engage while repulsing ... so that neither the threat of fusion nor the threat of loss becomes too great.
R. Lewin & C. Schulz

B.E.COMING AN OPTIMAL LOVER

Unawakened lovers look to the outside. They use projection and externalization. They remain fixated in a permanent and adolescent shopping mode. They long to be loved by that ideal someone out there. Like an infant, they crave a perfect mother-other whose metaphorical breast will soothe and calm their terrible and intractable inner turmoil. This is, of course, yet another instance of their dualistic, compulsive, insatiable, externalizing, and projective acquisition mode.

These men and women fail to realize that the real objective is to gradually find and grow into their own integrated and differentiated center, ... to have an epiphany and **B.E.**come, thereby, an optimal, though flawed lover, themselves. As always, ultimate resolutions of life's deepest enigmas come from within, not from the outside. This is all the more true about even this most profoundly intimate, interactive, interpersonal, and collaborative of all human endeavors.

SWITCHING THE SCRIPTS

The pursuit of love is so very intense and frightening that it stimulates an enormous regressive pull towards the universal illusion of fusion. The non-integrated type of lover switches the scripts in his or her sadomasochistic play. The previously adored partner now becomes a supremely annoying and endless source of aggravation, since his or her every gesture, posture, action, expression, and word is now endowed with a negative interpretation or spin. His every charm now becomes an alarming, ominous, and unendurable source of disdain and repulsion. He's become the perfect recipient of the sadomasochistic lover's projected inner shadow.

Previously smitten and insatiable symbiotic lovers become constant and intolerable fighter-rejector-arguer-complainers. Anything that goes wrong is depicted as the partner's fault, no matter what the objective facts of the situation might be. After all, there's no reality that can't be "spun" just a bit. It only takes a two percent distortion of the actual facts to accomplish this wholesale, melodramatic, and convincing projection, especially in the retelling.

Until I got married, I was my own worst enemy.
                    Anonymous

If it weren't for marriage, men and women would have to fight with total strangers.
                              Anonymous

Love is what happens to men and women who don't know each other.
                              W. S. Maugham

Love is blind, and marriage is a real eye-opener.
                              Anonymous

Marriage is like a besieged fortress. Everyone outside wants to get in, and everyone inside wants to get out.
                              Quiitard

ONE PARTNER MUST BEGIN TO LOOK WITHIN

The bond of unconscious sadomasochistic glue often prevails, nevertheless, in these unfortunate and all-too-common pairings, even to the eventual amazement of the two lovers, themselves. The key factor which can lead to change takes place when one or the other experiences enough head-banging pain from this rug-pulling relationship calamortunity to start to get curious about taking a deeper look into his or her own inner and unconscious dynamics and illusions. This is more likely to occur if he or she remembers, experiences, or witnesses a taste of more optimal, paradoxical, personal, and profound love.

It's an inside job. This can start the slow and difficult process towards upgrading his or her own game from chess to checkers. It won't be easy. There will be many setbacks along the way. After all, his external symbiotic lover and his own illusion-driven part-self are eminently persuasive and deceptive. Nevertheless, and at this point, inner dynamics can really start to improve.

Notice that I say "one or the other," and not "both." I say this for statistical reasons. Remember my little Brenner Rule of Nine Out of Ten? If one out of ten individuals ever wise up and awaken to any degree of paradoxical wisdom, then the odds are that only one out of a hundred couples will consist of two partners who eventually manage to predominantly awaken to such uncanny regions. Although this sounds discouraging, it's actually cynically/optimistic. On a larger scale, one out of a hundred isn't that bad. It's just the way life is. It could/not be otherwise.

THE STAY-OR-GO DILEMMA

These newly awakening individuals are fragile and have a long way to go. They're left with a difficult dilemma. Do they stay and try to preserve and nurture the love, family, and mutual enterprises to the limited extent that's possible within such unsatisfying and sadomasochistic arrangements? Do they make do with occasional, impersonal, transferential, adolescent, and superficial spurts of closeness; or do they try for something more enduring, satisfying, constant, personal, paradoxical, and profound? Do they dedicate themselves to raising and nurturing the kids within as stable an environment as possible, without disrupting the kids' fragile and vulnerable sense of stability and security? Do they bide their time and make do with a profound and satisfying *internal* integration with their own paradoxically wise part-self? After all, this is the primary objective, whether they stay or go.

Do they go against the odds and try to help their dualistic partner to awaken, or do they go? Of course, they're afraid that if they finally give up on such an unlikely rescue project, that they might find that they gave up too soon. They fear that another awakening partner will latch on; take advantage of all their prep work; close the deal on converting the dualistic partner into a paradoxically wise individual; and claim, thereby, the idyllic rewards of an expanded love that the original awakening partner could have had, ... had he or she only persisted a bit longer. Such a possibility can be safely disregarded as merely a painful remnant of their self-defeating and what-if catastrophizing. Unfortunately, such unrealistic thinking can cause a newly and partially awakening individual to stay in a terrible relationship for a lifetime.

Despite well-intended promises and starts, their unconsciously fixated sadomasochistic partners usually continue to resist any thorough-going and strenuous efforts to awaken and change. The odds are that they're just not able to decipher the cosmic con-game for themselves. Maybe they don't possess the intrapsychic equipment to do so. They're just too committed to a symbiotic and projective way of thinking. Most newly insightful and awakened partners choose to stay, persevere, manage, and adapt to their fixated chess partner's problematic ways, as well as possible. After all, they carefully and unconsciously casted him or her as a costar of their original sadomasochistic scenes.

In many ways, such a dis/satisfying compromise is workable, at least to a limited extent. It's often the best possible overall solution for the children, finances, structure, properties, in-laws, society, and other parties. Certainly most friends and family correctly agree that love inevitably requires compromise and perseverance. Outsiders often have no idea, however, just how disturbed the couple's private dynamics really are, behind closed doors.

After all, this newly awakening, insightful, and as yet only occasionally paradoxically wise individual has no real proof, yet, that he or she will eventually have the skill and luck that it takes to find and succeed to any profound degree with the enigmatic project of authentic, equal, and enduring love with another unusually integrated partner. This is merely a theoretical, hopeful, and far-away possibility, at this point. What if the original awakening partner is the one who winds up alone and obsessed with coulda-woulda-shoulda regrets and envy. Life's a gamble. Does he or she squander what he has for the merely one-in-a-hundred promise of what theoretically could be? It's a tough call.

"It takes two to fight," so while he or she chooses to stay in this troubled relationship, can the newly awakening lover learn to unilaterally take matters into his or her own hands and learn diplomatic techniques to calm down the incessant bickering and provocation as much as is possible, especially in front of the kids? After all, it's the more insightful, maneuverable, and collaborative "smaller boat" which can avert an impending collision with a cumbersome larger boat in a tight spot, even if the smaller boat has the "right of way." Although this grates on the more integrating, awakening, and deflating partner's sense of fairness and fulfillment, it's often the most practical overall solution.

There are instances, however, when the more insightful partner chooses to end the relationship as gracefully, safely, and kindly as possible. Sometimes this decision is made easier if the fixated dualistic partner pushes crises too far by being too abusive, violent, unreliable, dishonest, philandering, infective, squandering, intoxicated, addictive, mind-blowing, psychotic, dependent, cloying, suffocating, repulsive, jailed, and/or obnoxious. In these instances, the non-insightful and fixated partner gives his or her more integrated partner practically no reasonable alternative. This is especially true if the non-awakened and dualistic partner fits the criteria for one or more of my "Big Five" fatally flawed types, which I'll describe in Chapter 15, part three.

It's an individual call. If the more integrated and insightful partner does leave, he or she can then either accept a life of predominant solitude, or he can attempt the risky project of finding a more profound, personal, and satisfying kind of love with a more paradoxically wise partner. It'll take luck and courage to accomplish this, but it's well worth it. Sometimes it's the unawakened partner who chooses to leave first. This can be a blessing in disguise.

CHAPTER 14

LOVE'S FIERCE TEACHER: THE MANIPULATOR

PART ONE

THE FROG AND THE SCORPION

Consider the parable of the frog and the scorpion. As a frog was preparing to embark across the river, a scorpion asked him for a ride, since he couldn't swim. The frog refused, of course, citing the scorpion's rather prominent and ominous stinger. The smooth-talking scorpion was ready for this and explained that a deadly sting during the crossing wouldn't make sense now, would it? It would be suicidal. This made sense to the naive and well-meaning frog, so he consented, and the scorpion hopped on.

The journey was going quite well, until the pair was midway across the stream. That's when the scorpion stung the frog, of course. The frog cried out in terminal agony, "Look what you've done! You've killed us both! Why?" The scorpion shrugged and replied, "I don't know; it's just my nature."

BEWARE OF CON-ARTISTS

Greater and lesser con-artists and manipulators are the scorpions of the world. Since they comprise at least four percent of all populations, most of us well-meaning frogs will have dealings with them from time to time. They don't all come with "BEWARE" warnings stamped on their foreheads. Their deadly stingers are either camouflaged, tucked out of sight, or prominently displayed and yet skillfully explained away. The best hiding place is out in the open.

Amidst the distracting demands of life, and due to their special charms and tricks, manipulators can be nearly impossible to detect. They easily dupe their fair share of naive and well-intended chess players. They intentionally and callously cause enormous pain to others, ... and themselves. In the end and despite the comforts of their free rides, they, too, drown.

Extreme con-artists lie about nearly everything. It's their calling, their nature. They start as children by using their unusually cunning and natural interpersonal skills and "gift of gab" to take advantage of family and friends. Early and easy success goes to their heads. Some say they've gone over to the dark side of human nature. Some say they're more or less born that way.

LACK OF LOVINGKINDNESS OR EMPATHY

The most extreme types of con-artists seem to be nearly entirely devoid of an essential ingredient of what it takes to be fully human. They're born without the capacity to feel tenderness, empathy, relatedness, attachment, love, guilt, or remorse. They have no discernible conscience. This reptilian nature makes them virtually untrainable, even as young children. This is not usually parents' faults. Being astute observers of human nature, these manipulative children learn to mimic tender feelings very well, indeed, but only to get what they want. Less severe manipulators have some or even abundant tender feelings, but they suppress, deny, or employ them in the service of their primary goal of exploiting others.

Back to extreme con-artists, they so lack any regard for others that they understandably think that the rest of us are merely faking tenderness, closeness, love, kindness, or genuine concern for others. Although they're ill-equipped to participate in the complex and enigmatic enterprise of genuine human lovingness; they're supremely endowed, nevertheless, for the tasks of deceiving and exploiting others without a trace of that inefficient stuff called guilt, remorse, or hesitation. It's their special affliction/endowment.

"WISE GUYS"

Career liars correctly sense that life is a giant con-game. They get partial credit for this insight. Nevertheless, they, too, fall for the cosmic con-game by seeing life as a merely two dimensional win-lose game between predators and prey, brutes and sissies, exploiters and victims. They decide, therefore, to throw in with the predators, brutes, and exploiters. This makes them feel much less vulnerable, and it preserves their grand illusion of personal superiority and power.

In effect, they pose as life's premier tricksters. Moreover, they have the arrogance to claim that they were never fooled by life in the first place, the way everyone else is. They even call themselves "wise guys." Exploiting a profitable portion of those other nine-out-of-ten fixated, naive, gullible, and unawakened chess players out there is, indeed, like taking candy from a baby.

THE REAL CON-GAME IS ON THEM; "TIME WOUNDS ALL HEELS"

Con-artists fail to grasp that they, themselves, are fooled by the split up dualism of the cosmic con-game, just like anyone else. In the end, their primary unconscious aim is to fool themselves. The real, immense, cruel, and painful damage they inflict upon others is merely collateral damage, in comparison with what they do to themselves. Their predatory way of life sentences them to an ever-deepening form of self-inflicted imprisonment, shallowness, impoverishment, desperation, and victimization, ... all inflicted by their own unconscious and sadistic five year-old con-artists.

They've sold their souls to their inner demonic part-self, in exchange for the mere smoke and mirrors of unfulfillable, grandiose, materialistic, and ever-receding illusion. Each day, their life becomes increasingly distorted and desperate, as their ever-escalating and addictive demands for power and wealth become increasingly impossible to fulfill. As their self-aggrandizing mirage recedes into the unreachable distance, they escalate their intricate deceptions to themselves and others all the more. Their victories become increasingly far-fetched, empty, and unfulfilling; and their intractable unhappiness grows even more desperate and unbearable.

In the end, they live out the paradox that the harshest deprivation is wholesale indulgence. They become the ultimate fools of their own con-games. Although all humans can awaken and redeem themselves on any pathway, career manipulators face even longer odds than most. This is because their dualistic cons are so abundantly gratifying and successful at a superficial and material level for so long, that they usually become increasingly and irretrievably alienated from their own paradoxically wise part-selves. "Time wounds all heels." They seem to be particularly prone to self-destructive addictions. We can feel compassion and pity for them, indeed, but we don't need to step in front of their bus, nor is it wise to give them a ride.

THE INNER AND ULTIMATE CON-ARTIST

It's an inside job for us all. An essential task in life is to awaken to the presence and influence of our own, inner five year-old manipulative con-artist part-self. He or she doesn't play by the rules. He takes advantage of being unperceived, so that he can exploit the conscious mind for his own illusory gain. In effect, he throws the conscious mind under the bus, every time. Until we catch on, he cons us into dancing like marionettes to his hidden, intricate, predatory, and sadomasochistic dances.

After all, no outside individual can fool us nearly as well. No one can con us unless we want to be conned; ... conned, that is, by the siren songs of our own unconscious five-year-old's naive illusions. Outside con-artists have simply learned to synchronize with their and our inner con-artists. They wave our own insatiable illusions before us. Until we awaken, we fall for the con-game every time, as long as we're still suckers for a "too-good-to-be-true" illusion. We like the magic show.

In effect, we unconsciously cast external con-artists as mere co-stars in our own, inner, and elaborate sadomasochistic scenes. After all, we're the unknowing playwrights of our own repetition-compulsions. We write the whole script. In effect, naive and compulsive masochists are actually conning the con-artist to play the role of "sadist" to their carefully written, contrived, and displayed "victim." Ironically, then, both the external manipulator and his victim have been in on, and victims of, the very same cosmic con-game, all along. What unending, reverberating, and reciprocal paradox!

We escape from external con-men and women only when we catch on to the cosmic con-game and awaken to our own previously denied dark sides. Only then can we heal our inner schism or abyss. Self-created external scams thus serve as pleasurably/painful calamortunities. Like all other rug-pullings, these predicaments can get our attention and open our eyes. Thus seen, hired con-men and women test the depth and durability of our own capacity for the most profound healing of detachment, insight, and wisdom. They can help us to deepen our paradoxical wisdom.

THEY'VE GOT US AT "HELLO"

Con-artists have honed their world-class, bedazzling, and manipulative skills from earliest childhood. It's their home field advantage, their turf. The rest of us haven't participated in as many years of dedicated practice and training. We're no match for them. We're truly out of our league if we dare to take them on, directly. Within seconds, they can easily and skillfully convert any disagreement into a resounding and guilt-provoking victory over us.

Their speech is total and duplicitous double-talk, disguised as clever, persuasive, charming, frank, fair, open-minded, and even honest discussion. They charm us with the larceny of their frankness. They've got us at "hello." If we fail to detect their reptilian incapacity for authentic closeness and conscience, and if we grant them the slightest credibility from the very first sentence, they'll have us doubting our own perception, memory, philosophy, religion, and even sanity. They're that good at subtly distorting and exploiting a story.

We may even know that they're putting on a mere magic show, but we're still enthralled and willing to pay dearly for the tickets. We so want to believe in magic. Maybe it gives us the illusion that we're "in on" the scam. This is why we need to develop the ability to detect con-artists as soon as possible.

I'm not exaggerating the danger, here. I'm not being melodramatic just to make a point. It's simply smart, humble, and necessary to be suspicious and astute from their very first phrase. It's best not to feel sorry for them. They'll do just fine without our impossible "beauty-and-the-beast" rescue ministrations. They'll quickly persuade the next hapless, well-meaning, and naive frog to give them a ride across the stream. In fact, they'll have an army of such frog-actors lined up at the stage door of the sadomasochistic theater, eagerly rehearsing their lines to try out for the coveted role of "victim."

BUILD AN INNER FIREWALL

Manipulators know that if we linger to argue or discuss, we're playing into their strong suit. We must train ourselves to never argue with them. They're just too good at distortion, distraction, projection, obfuscation, and bedazzlement. Once we expose them as liars, we must emulate Odysseus and simply and silently strap ourselves to the mast, harden our hearts, and sail on by those seductive Sirens on the cliffs. We must build an invisible fire-wall in our minds and hearts against anything they say or do.

Like the Sirens, manipulators are nearly irresistible. This is the way they make their living. There's literally nothing they can't talk themselves into or out of. Even after we expose them, if we pause to listen just down the waterway, or at the doorway, we're in grave danger of falling under their spell, once again.

These are the seductive voices of the night; the Sirens, too, sang that way. It would be doing them an injustice to think that they wanted to seduce; they knew they had claws and sterile wombs, and they lamented this aloud. They could not help it if their laments sounded so beautiful.

F. Kafa

ALWAYS ON THE CON

I'm not as benevolent as Kafka about how unaware these con-artists can be about their own manipulative, exploitative, conniving, and predatory motives. After many years and many mistakes, I've learned the hard way that at some level, these extreme types of con-artists are always conscious of and instantaneously deliberate in their cons. It's seamlessly built in to their well-rehearsed, automatic, and glib speech patterns. They're truly fast on their feet. They are consummately well-trained actors, liars, and cheats.

Even when they "earnestly" apologize and claim that they've merely made a mistake, or that they actually believed their now openly exposed and undeniable lies; this is just another part of their elaborate con, or "sting." This ruse of charming earnestness makes them even more convincing. It serves as yet another smokescreen. Amidst their highly convincing crocodile tears, they actually possess no measurable capacity for heartfelt ethics or remorse. It's all an act.

We give them far too much credit if we think they're ever really genuine, honest, taken aback, or remorseful, especially when they cry. Remember, con-artists are consummate liars, actors, and tricksters. They never break from character, even between "takes" or off the set. They're always on the con, even on their nights off. Unlike us, they've trained themselves to be able to lie without any tell-tale tics or blinks. They show no "tells" at life's poker table. Their con is seamless and endless. They can even fool the best of psychological testers and modern lie detectors. This will very likely always be the case.

OUR RESCUE ILLUSION

Rescue motives are for suckers. All con-artists know that our dualistic, lofty, self-righteous, and naive motives make us all the more exploitable. When they spot the approach of such a do-gooder, their mouths water. In fact, the manipulator's entire scam banks on our grandiose, naive, and hopeless illusion of rescue. Once we're involved in a sadomasochisitc enthrallment with them, we must turn our backs on our own well-meaning need to love, reform, and save con-artists and lessor manipulators. We must guard our heart and sanity; take our losses; do the best we can with our inevitably damaged psyches, bodies, kids, enterprises, bank accounts, properties, and other endeavors; go through the grief; avoid throwing good money, heart, and soul after bad; and have faith that we'll eventually recover, wise up, become deeper, and achieve relative immunity to their come-ons, and those of future con-artists.

We must create that firewall and never let it down! We must avoid making the mistake of thinking that they're not lying, this time; or that our grandiose, amateurish, and futile little heart-to-heart talk has now converted them, magically and instantly, into honest sorts. Manipulators silently laugh at such silly reformation-rescue lectures. In fact, while we're self-righteously going on and on, they're biding their time and devising their next manipulative come-backs and strategies. In effect, and while they seem to be taking our silly and futile sermons to heart, they're silently devising ways of using our moralizing lectures against us.

Despite the well-meaning and idealistic intentions and ministrations of guilt-ridden and social do-gooders, these sinister and unfeeling top-of-the-food-chain predators do not sprout consciences. When the great white shark has us in his jaws, he possesses no shred of inner hesitance or conscience to which we can appeal.

WE NEED TO BE STUNG

Paradoxically and seemingly preposterously, we actually need to be stung by such manipulative scorpions. In biological realms, for example, we build up protective, healing, and immunity-inducing antibodies in our blood systems in response to being infected. Such risky bacterial and viral exposures are good for us, if we survive. These calamortunities make us stronger. Infections are nature's way of boosting our immune system.

In the same way, we actually need to be fooled by one or two manipulators in our youths, so that we can develop protective antibodies of perception, insight, and experience. These teach us to recognize and expose con-artists, so that we can take astutely defensive measures against them and their kind. This makes us much more resistant, immune, and resilient. We become, thereby, grizzled and wounded veterans, who can maintain a good-natured and trusting/cynicism about others.

PARANOIA CAN BE ACCURATE

If you say that this sounds like paranoia, you have a point. These are the people we must avoid at first hints and at all costs. We can never trust a con-artist, especially a dazzling and charming one. We must never consent to give him or her a ride across the river. When we spot the scorpion's stinger, we must stop ourselves, right there. Thereafter, we know that we can't believe a word he says.

More importantly, we can't believe our own inner con-artist. Though we must accept him or her as part of our own inner congress, we must close our hearts, minds, and ears to his manipulations, too. Remember, his siren songs are irresistible, but only if we believe in magic. We must not fall for his considerable charms and charisma. He will take us down, every time. That's just his nature.

WHY WE LINGER

We linger at the threshold of escape in order to save face and in order to see the rest of the story. Unfortunately, this reveals that we haven't yet completely deciphered the cosmic con-game. We haven't yet realized that the conclusion of their tempting, seductive, exciting, larcenous, and nasty little story is not worth waiting to see. It never has the illusory, transformative, and happy ending which they promise, and which we so naively want to believe. Lucy will, indeed, retract that teed-up football at the last second, every time.

We linger after we've partially deciphered the con-game for eight other basic reasons. First, and perhaps foremost, we stay because we're seduced, pleasured, flattered, fascinated, and enthralled by the con-artist. We've never seen such a dazzling, amazing, beautiful, sexy, and pleasurable performance, before. We never thought we'd be able to attract such a beautiful and too-good-to-be-true specimen. We love being seen with him or her. We love the orgasms. We tell ourselves that we can, indeed, have the forbidden fruit; ... that we *can* fly too close to the sun. After all, we're special. We're the exceptions. We tell ourselves that we're not like those proverbial moths who are so self-destructively drawn to the fire.

Unfortunately, this reveals our enormous denial and our sad and grandiose illusion of superiority. It reveals that we need this mistreatment as an unconscious condition for love. We simply can't stop ourselves from being enthralled by their weird, captivating, abusive, and predatory sadomasochistic scenes. Such scenes don't even interest awakened and non-masochistic individuals.

Second, we linger because we're prone to self-aggrandizing guilt trips. We blame ourselves when things go wrong. This is an over-attribution of blame, due to our inflated illusion of control. In other words, if we think we're to blame for everything, we're unconsciously sneaking in that hidden illusion that we're so amazingly all-powerful as to be able to control all outcomes. This is, of course, a preposterous example of unconscious self-aggrandizement. Manipulators have learned to exploit this guilt-ridden narcissism and sentimentality to the hilt. This makes us highly suitable partner-victims. It's a perfect hand-in-glove fit. They make their living by blaming and manipulating, and we need to feel guilty and conned, all in order to support identically over-sized self-esteems.

Third, and while we're mentioning grandiosity, we linger because we subscribe to the illusion that we, among all others, can rehabilitate and even rescue the con-artist. We, alone, can recognize and cultivate this "diamond-in-the-rough." We've already discussed this. The con-artist senses and exploits this. By and large, these supremely calloused and unfeeling great whites are beyond rehabilitation. Besides, it's time we got over our naive and grandiose belief that we can single-handedly change all others for their own good.

Fourth, we linger, because we hope that we can beat the odds and escape, this time. We stay at the liar's roulette wheel, even though we know that the house odds are stacked against us. We suffer from the illusion that we, among all the other suckers of the sting, will manage to beat the odds, this time, and get back to even. We'll be "made whole." In fact, we fall for the even more implausible illusion that we'll be able exit the casino with a net profit.

Thus, like all gambling addicts, we throw good money after bad. It's a fool's game that every liar, manipulator, abuser, casino, and drug dealer knows and exploits only too well. They make their living by inviting us to entice ourselves to stay and/or return to the table, endlessly. This helps them to spin their manipulative web around us, all the more.

Fifth, we linger because we want "something for nothing." We still believe in the illusion of 100%, cost-free, all-or-nothing, black-and-white, "no-regrets" decisions. We want to sail through life without any second-guessings, or "coulda-woulda-shoulda's." We want to never have any regrets about life's larger and more challenging decisions. As we've discussed, all worthy and complex decisions in life are close calls. They're 52-48 decisions.

Of course we'll have regrets and costs, no matter what we decide about these difficult people. That's the negative "48%" factor of any worthy decision. The best we can do is to enjoy the 52% gains and mourn the inevitable 48% losses. Either way, there will be enormous grief! Of course our inner five-year-old will haunt us with regrets about what we miss about the manipulator, if we decide to leave. For this five year-old, nothing less than 100% profit will do. Besides, he wants us to remain in the clutches of one of his or her kind. We must admit that life with a con-artist has it's fair share of advantages. Nevertheless, we can't let the greedy, short-sighted, and naive inner child have the last judgment about the over-all wisdom of our choices. We can't let him or her drive the adult bus. He will sell us short, every time.

Sixth, we linger because we tell ourselves that things aren't really that bad. This is denial. We tell ourselves that we can handle it. We rationalize that all interpersonal arrangements entail compromise, so we may as well be flexible. We tell ourselves that we'll be able to reject the now fully exposed con-artist later, if things get really desperate. We tell ourselves that then we'll overcome our doubt and indecision, completely. Then, we'll be 100% certain. There's that illusion of certainty, again.

Con-artists exploit such grandiose and guilt-ridden doubt. Like casinos, they sprinkle in just enough minor pay-offs, especially to their hired casino actors, to keep us hopeful and on the hook. This is an essential part of the bait-and-switch carnival attraction.

Even most comparatively healthy and even paradoxically wise partners are unable to leave a committed and enmeshed relationship with a manipulator when they first realize that the negative factors only slightly outweigh the positives. This seems too close a call for them to make. Thus, most can't leave before things get really nasty. Sadly, most severe masochists can't leave, even then. They're still too attached and skillful at the subtle and self-deceptive art of self-defeat.

> *It seldom happens that a man changes his life through his habitual reasoning. ... He continues to plod along in old paths until his life becomes frustrating and unbearable - he finally makes the change only when his usual life can no longer be tolerated.*
>
> L. Tolstoy

Seventh, after we're so thoroughly enmeshed with a con-artist partner, complete with shared properties, enterprises, children, belongings, and such, we stay because we fear and dread retaliation and loss. If the con-artist senses that we're even considering walking away, he or she will use any available resources to force us to stay. He will, indeed, fulfill our worst fears by attempting to strip us of everything and by trying to turn our children and shared friends against us. We will be ostracized by some. His aim will be to take us down and strip us clean, no matter what the cost, even to himself. Indeed, we will be in for the fight of our lives.

We sensed that this was coming. We noticed his or her extreme "take-no-prisoners," "stop-at-nothing," and "make-them-suffer" revenge tactics for years. He's bragged to us about his ghastly, sadistic, damaging, and retaliatory measures. Sadly, we've even vicariously enjoyed being in on his or her ghoulish but self-justified and strangely fascinating acts of revenge. We were relieved, then, that we weren't the victims. We now correctly sense that this will be our fate, as well, if and when we choose to leave.

We even try to wait for the con-artist to leave first, in the vain hope that this will dampen his or her retaliation impulse, and to appeal to his non-existent sense of fairness. He usually waits us out. All too often, we never leave. We're just not willing to pay the exorbitant price for our own awakening.

> *... we are programmed to receive. You can check out any time you like, but you can never leave.*
>
> Don Felder, Don Henley
> & Glen Frey

Finally, we stay because we fear that in leaving, we'll lose aspects of ourselves that we can't do without. We inaccurately still believe the manipulator's dazzling "you-can't-do-without-me" con that he or she possesses superior attributes which we think we lack; or that he will deplete or drain us of essential parts of ourselves. We linger out of the fear that we'll be left as mere empty shells of ourselves, and that we'll be irretrievably disabled and ruined.

What we fail to realize is that we already have all the finest of resources within; that the calamortunity of loss is an indispensable part of growth; that loss is gain; and that we actually have nothing to lose. It's already gone. Enlightenment is free, but it'll cost us everything. We can grow to embrace this paradoxical and healing bounty of grief and loss.

CHAPTER 14:
LOVE'S FIERCE TEACHER: THE MANIPULATOR

PART TWO

WAKE UP, PAY THE PRICE, WALK AWAY

Anyone who begins to awaken to a measure of paradoxical wisdom and who chooses to leave a prolonged and enmeshed relationship with a con-artist must be willing to simply walk away with nothing at some point, no matter how exorbitant the cost may be. There's always a terrible cost. He or she must take the plunge into icy waters. They will never warm up. Indeed, they will chill him to the bone, but he'll eventually warm up, ... from within.

Such an icy plunge takes courage. Finding the way towards our sacred paradoxical soul is well worth the huge price tag. Besides, in any setting, enlightenment is free, but it costs us everything. This painful predicament is a truly "fierce teacher." There's never a good time to leave a con-artist. Ultimate life decisions are 52-48 choices. There are always endless obligations, circumstances, and details which can serve as impediments and excuses. This is part of any manipulator's plan. Indeed, although it's best to make careful contingency plans, there comes a "point of no return," when it's best to simply and quietly walk away, before it's too late to recover.

It's best to cease the masochism of throwing good heart, soul, money, effort, love, arguments, and rehabs after bad. Rescue missions merely escalate the cost. We must simply admit to having been fooled, and go on from there. There's no shame in that. It's best not to linger for the con-artist's inevitable, final, ghastly, gruesome, and further knife-turning machinations and script-changing acts. After all, we've been up against an Olympic quality liar.

Let others linger at the door and waste their precious time and resources by trying to punish, inform, rehabilitate, and/or change him or her. Let them try to go against the house odds and beat themselves bloody against the wall. It's better to just pick ourselves up and get on with life. We can recover; we can continue to try to resume the form of our paradoxically wise part-selves; and we can learn to be un/reasonably happy, as much as possible.

As we leave with regretful/relief and guilt-ridden/exhilaration, ... we shouldn't be surprised by that inevitable long line of willing and even enthusiastic applicants we pass at the sadomasochistic theater's stage door. These wanna-be's are enthusiastically rehearsing the very same lines that we naively recited so long ago. They're eager to take their turn to audition for our part in the manipulator's sadomasochistic play. For them, too, it looks like a really good career move. We remember how that felt. It's futile to warn them. We just keep on walking, while we appreciate the sad irony and savor the strawberry.

LEARN TO DETACH, OBSERVE, AND THINK LIKE A SHRINK

It's wise to train ourselves, as much as we can, to step back, observe, listen with the third ear, and think paradoxically, like psychotherapists. This way, we can look past the loud, distracting, and mesmerizing smoke and mirrors of a liar's seemingly heartfelt, carefully crafted, Olympic quality, shrewdly-scripted, highly seductive, ultimately bedazzling, and never-ending excuses and promises. A consummate liar always lands on his or her feet. They always find an instantaneous, plausible, guilt-inducing, and exquisitely convincing excuse, explanation, or accusation. These are siren songs to the ears of our gullible and manipulative inner five year-old part-selves.

In sessions, we therapists listen carefully and attentively, to be sure, as patients try to explain and justify their mostly self-created syndromes and predicaments. They don't know what they don't know, however. We're paid to not accept their conscious rationalizations at face value. We're paid to be tactful, diplomatic, and stealth confronters. We're not mere stenographers, suitable only for recording their subtly but drastically distorted tales.

We're listening for the unheard sound of patients' inner and unconscious five-year-old con-artists. We listen carefully in order to decode just how they trick the patient's ego into dancing to the unheard and repetitive marching songs of their childish and manipulative agendas, or repetition compulsions. We know how that goes. We've been there. They are us. They're just at a far earlier step on the spiral staircase of their potential awakening.

Amidst such astute, experienced, insightful, discerning, and shrink-like scrutiny, manipulators give themselves away, every time. The underlying repetition compulsions of their unconscious part-selves are on open display all the time, if we just awaken, detach, and observe.

We must remind ourselves that the definition of an "expert" is someone who comes from out of town, or better yet, from our own distant home town. They arrive with special, unique, and world-record-setting testimonials, recommendations, resumes, credentials, pedigrees, and status. They may even claim to know people and places we know. They've done their manipulative homework. It's so easy to do this.

This is how they gain our "*con*fidence." If they look and sound "too-good-to-be-true," that's because they are. They're just testing to see if we're still gullible enough to fall for such larger-than-life come-on's and scams. If we do, then such con-artists "have" us. If not, they simply and dispassionately move on, until they find just the right kind of sucker. There's always an all-too-willing sucker to be "had."

At their audition or free promotional luncheon, con-artists aren't attached to any particular potential victim. Despite their crocodile tears and protestations when we decline their too-good-to-be-true propositions, we're not really that personally important to them. Remember, despite their theatrics otherwise, they don't really have those feelings. They're just acting. They're just playing the casino's all-too-profitable and unfair odds. If this hand's a loser, they simply fold and wait for the next deal, the next frog. There are so many gullible frogs out there.

IMPEACH THE WITNESS

Once we've been lucky and/or skillful enough to expose a liar, we've managed to "impeach the witness," as lawyers say. We've exposed the immense underlying creativity of his or her spins, half-truths, omissions, and outright lies, as he presents his con-game.

The liar's entire testimony has been impeached, discredited, and thrown out. From this point forward, as in courtrooms, he or she can NEVER be believed, again. We don't need to collect a list of his numerous other lies and distortions. After all, we're not compiling a catalogue, here. One irrevocable life sentence is enough. Moreover, there's no need to try to convince, educate, or rehabilitate him or any of his past, present, or future all-too-willing victims. We don't have enough lifetimes for such a project. We've made the diagnosis, and it's best to stick with it, stand back, and get on with our lives.

We must then build a veritable firewall in our minds against believing anything these skillful and dazzling seducers say. We must realize that they're always on the con. While we're walking away, if we turn and linger to listen sympathetically at the doorway, we're setting ourselves up to be "had," once again. We should not merely walk away; ... we should RUN!

UP-FRONT TESTS OF CON-GAMES

If we catch on to the cosmic con-game; if we thoroughly expose our own inner con-artist; and if we graduate to predominantly paradoxical wisdom; ... we're able to recognize the external con-artist's maneuvers through the lens of balance, centeredness, kindness, compassion, and humility. His essentially imbalanced, sadistic, predatory, exploitative, and grandiose behaviors give him or her away, every time. With this perspective, focus, and insight, we can gradually become immune to the lure of his and *our* siren songs of lame rationalizations, excuses, externalizations, and counter-accusations.

There are many other tests, all of which the manipulator fails, almost every time. Just how does a substantially awakened and wise person act? In contrast to the manipulator, his or her paradoxical and kindly wisdom is positive, optimistic, open, patient, present, constructive, hard-working, diplomatic, centered, enduring, peaceful, supportive, attentive, conscientious, collaborative, gentle, liberating, yielding, quiet, listening, understanding, generous, insightful, tolerant, compromising, egalitarian, curious, intrepid, honest, principled, and amused. It's a **B.E. K.I.N.D.**, "boots-on-the-ground" brand of wisdom.

Again, once we've exposed the con-artist as a fraud, we're no longer under his spell. We've impeached his or her entire testimony. We know that literally everything he says or does is a part of his con-game. We now see through him. We're no longer vulnerable to even the opening lure of his scams or magic shows.

WE MUST BE TAKEN IN

Once again, it's important that we get "taken in" and fooled by one or more of these consummate liars and manipulators early enough in life, and hopefully in not too damaging a way, so that we can recover and learn. We must willingly take the vaccine of bad experience and expose ourselves to the toxin, so that we can develop a protective immunity, as a result of our new awakening.

Wisdom requires its fair share of negative and failure-ridden experience. An epiphany is simply the process of finding out what kind of fools we are. Without such curative experience and insight, we'll disregard all the early warning signs and waltz right in to the next predator's trap, every time. In that event, each time we attempt to escape without insight, we set the stage for yet another audition for the next costar-con-artist, and the next, all within our own unconsciously devised and victimized play. Our inner sadomasochistic scene will then go on and on. You can't con a truly awakened individual.

I wish we could preemptively teach our children about all this required, cosmically preordained, and self-arranged hoodwinking. Unfortunately, they, too, must learn the hard way. They, too, must line up at the theater's stage door, as the erstwhile hero-victim-star departs in shame and ruin. They, too will be eager to show their stuff, try to vanquish the now demonized ex-hero, and audition for the con-artist's sadomasochistic play.

Like us, they must discover their own unconscious repetition compulsion. They, too, must find out what kind of fools they are. It's just the harsh way the cosmos teaches us all. It could/not be otherwise.

We're all so very fooled by the cosmic con-game and its inner and outer con-artists at first. After we become painfully experienced and initiated, we go on to detect many other such well-disguised liars and cheats throughout life. They're everywhere. There's no utopian "con-artist-free-zone." They test just how well we've learned our lessons. That's their cynical job within the larger scheme of things. They harmonize with our own inner con-artist. It's our job to become thoroughly disinterested in their dazzling, forbidden, and larger-than-life propositions. It's important that we disappoint and bore them, so that they lose interest and move on to others.

PROMINENT CON-ARTISTS

Some con-artists eventually become political, corporate, professional, educational, religious, or other types of prominent leaders. Their lack of empathy and conscience makes them supremely well-suited for positions of power. Such is the way of the world.

When we hear the slightest hint of their projective, paranoid, rabble-rousing, and "us-against-them," prejudice, we can discount such leaders in our own minds, no matter how intelligently, learnedly, beautifully, persuasively, powerfully, and even charmingly they speak. They're exquisitely well-trained and practiced at the intricate art of such world-class deception. They methodically create false, projective, and decoy enemies. In this way, they can easily trick us into fervent, patriotic, corporate, professional, spiritual, or ecclesiastic war, in order to solidify their own power and fortune. It's all an elaborately idealized and camouflaged con-game.

These are the paranoid cult leaders who plant the virulent

seeds and infective pathogens of destruction, suspiciousness, delusion, persecution, war, genocide, terrorism, atrocity, and madness in any society. It's best not to believe them. They've sold their and our souls in exchange for the right to indulge their illusion of god-like power.

Nearly all newly exposed and prosecuted celebrity criminals claim to be entirely innocent of all charges. Banking on their fame, they blame accusers, police, witnesses, prosecutors, and, of course, even the victims, themselves. That's just a con-artist's standard and well-practiced damage control measure. They've done this for years. It's their glib, reptilian, and scorpion-like nature.

Their well-staged, skillful, and persuasive press conferences are full of half-truths, subtle spins, and outright lies. They construct defensive and evasive counter-attacks with the most convincing, intimidating, deceptive, and self-justifying of accusations and smokescreens. Within seconds, they can reduce any justified and damaged accuser into a guilt-ridden and anxious puddle. They've consistently backed down all confronters all their lives. They consider their wounded and complaining victims to be merely easily dismissible and manipulatable hecklers in the crowd. This is their stage, turf, expertise, and home field advantage.

If we dare to take them on, we had better be ready for the fight of our lives. They are really good at this. We have no idea what we're up against.

CALL IN THE PROSECUTORS

In contrast to private life, where people have their hands full with life's many demands, prosecuting attorneys' offices have the extensive governmental personnel and resources at hand to take their time and get the laborious job of confronting criminals done, no matter how long it takes. It's their full-time job. Teams of prosecuting attorneys and paralegals doggedly and systematically do the drill, over many months. They quietly and politely share the burden, follow the rules, study the evidence, take depositions, and gather evidence. Even with such extensive resources and back-up, they often fall short.

Ideally, prosecutors slowly break down the celebrity criminal's endless denials, delays, decoys, counter-accusations, tricks, and lies with the growing weight of objective, factual, and undeniable evidence. This is a truly daunting and enormous job. This enables them to impeach the criminal's testimony and to so expose him as a liar that nothing he or she says can be believed. This takes a village.

Sometimes, in the face of an overwhelming case against him, the con-artist and his lawyers see the writing on the wall. They "reluctantly" make a deal with the prosecution and accept a plea bargain. They altruistically proclaim that they really could prove their innocence, but such a prolonged and terrible trial would be too costly and stressful on their families, on their organizations, and on the government. They're really good spin doctors. They're gambling that they can later retrieve their reputation by staging further public lies and manipulations. All-too-often, they're right.

"MEA CULPA" SWITCHING OF THE SCRIPTS

Sometimes the celebrity con-artist caves in and admits to his or her guilt. Beware! This is the sound of his finest, well-honed, melodramatic, and self-serving "Mea Culpa" act, his switching of the scripts. It's just another con. Remember, a con-artist is always on the con. He never really comes clean.

It wasn't really his or her fault, don't you see. Underneath his systematic, willful, sadistic, and illegal behavior, he was really the victim, here. You should feel sorry for him. He then "reluctantly" abandons his heroic reticence and now openly displays his pitiful and crocodile-tear-laced story about how he was traumatized by his own abusive, disadvantaged, deprived, over-indulged, or traumatic childhood, or by some other semi-truthful or wholly fabricated sad tale. There's always a kind-hearted and well-meaning group within any society which falls for such skillful malarky. Behind the scenes, family and friends of the celebrity con-artist who know the truth find such a ploy laughable.

In time, he or she usually goes on to repeat the exact same types of compulsive misbehaviors, over and over, in this or other settings. They're like wind-up toys. You can count on it. Like the scorpion, it's just their nature.

ONCE AGAIN, IMPEACH THE WITNESS

Now let's return to a consideration of private lives. Such career and world-class manipulators also operate in normal families and between individuals in matters of love. If we manage to catch a new lover in two or three small lies, we've managed to "impeach" his or her testimony. Once we've exposed them as the career liars that they are, we can stop right there. We don't need their confession, confirmation, apology, or promises. We won't get them, anyhow. They're always on the con, remember? Nothing about them is honest or genuine. If we give their well-practiced manipulations any credence at all, they will take us down, every time.

As private individuals, we can't command huge governmental legal resources in order to prosecute them. In fact, most nations around the world can't afford such a luxury. We may as well accept that we've been thoroughly and grievously hoodwinked. It's best to simply wise up, take the hit, walk away, and recover.

LOVE 'EM, BUT LEAVE 'EM

I've tried, mostly without success, to treat these extreme types of con-artists in psychotherapy for years at a time in the office. By and large, they're nearly completely immune to any healthy, humbling, and transformative influences from others, therapy, or life experiences. As is true for any group of humans, there are occasional exceptions to this general rule, but their numbers are so small that we can reasonably disregard such a remote statistical possibility.

If, on the other hand, they experience a true and life-changing epiphany, suspend their excuses and guilt trips, take full and painful responsibility for their crimes, learn to **B.E. K.I.N.D.**, and start to speak and walk humbly within paradoxical wisdom, ... that's when we can be hopeful that they've begun to change. We've learned the hard way to believe behaviors, not words. Even then, it's best to double-check their stories.

Con-artists usually come to my office only when they're coerced, or when they're in the process of yet another manipulation. These mostly incurable reptiles are just not going to grow normal feelings of tenderness, love, remorse, and guilt, no matter how eloquently and tearfully they make claims otherwise. They're simply not interested in such a profoundly introspective, strenuous, frustrating, disillusioning, egalitarian, and deflating project.

Once we detect extreme types of con-artists, we must never, ever have the hubris and bad judgment to enter into any business or romantic transactions with them. It's permissible and safe to enjoy them as pure and distant entertainment, only. After all, they are dazzling, and they tell the best stories at parties. They never miss the party. We don't need to put them entirely out of our hearts. We can sympathize with and even pity them, but we must choose to escape, nevertheless, with our hearts and lives intact.

MOST OF ALL, BEWARE OF THE INNER CON-ARTIST

Ironically, outer con-artists and manipulators are fierce teachers, because THEY ARE US. They teach us about our own inner five year-old con-artist. He or she likes the company of his own kind. These outer allegiances with manipulators constitute our inner con-artist's distracting way of consolidating his own secret power over our conscious minds. This is his primary goal.

This inner, consummate con-artist is the real danger. It's always an inside job. Outside con-artists can't even come close to exacting the damage that he or she does to us. External manipulators are merely projections of our own inner con-artist. We've hired them to participate in our unconscious and self-imprisoning sadomasochistic plays.

CHAPTER 15

PARADOXICAL ROMANTIC LOVE

PART ONE

We've come to my audacious attempt to discuss optimal and paradoxical love. Such an enduring, romantic, erotic, and faithful love relationship is perhaps the crowning, ultimate, and most challenging of all human endeavors.

For one human being to love another: that is perhaps the most difficult of all tasks ...
                                        R. M. Rilke

Paradoxical and profound romantic love is quite different from the dualistic, illusion-driven, and manipulative model we've discussed. Although it's not prevalent, it's possible, and it's not that rare. These four brief chapters can't possibly convey its full complexity, majesty, mystery, and magic. Perhaps only poets can approach this. After all and ultimately, a paradox remains a paradox.

A PARADOXICAL TYPE OF LOVE

Although one can stumble into an optimally loving partnership by chance, it's usually possible only for those brave enough to embark upon a quest for disciplined, integrated, and paradoxical wisdom. Moreover, optimal lovers must also be astute and lucky enough to find another such unusual and "out-of-the-box" individual, with whom to learn. This usually occurs only to those who train themselves to settle for nothing less.

Paradoxically interpersonal love is essentially an individual, inside job. Until we decipher the cosmic con-game, embrace our illuminating disillusionment, and start to make progress towards paradoxical wisdom; we unwittingly and repeatedly write, direct, and act out our sordid, miserable, and unconscious sadomasochistic scenes, over and over. Only when we begin to experience a deep inner awakening will we realize that enlightenment is free, but it costs us everything, that is, all our illusions; but it rewards us with a quiet, humble, authentic, and exponentially more satisfying serenity and relatedness. It transforms the win-lose, oppositional, competitive, bickering, melodramatic, conflicted, mostly miserable, and occasionally ecstatic flat screen of dualistic relatedness into the cooperative, collaborative, kindly, serene, multidimensional, stable, quiet, and unreasonably joyful hologram of paradoxical love. This is a fully-committed, paradoxical type of love.

> *Love is both the most cruel and ... healing of all instruments in tearing away the illusions by which we try to ease our pain.*
>
> Monica Furling

> *...real love hurts; ... makes you totally vulnerable and open; will take you far beyond yourself; and therefore real love will devastate you.*
>
> K. Wilbur

Integrated love quietly synchronizes with the centered, entered, and integrated paradoxical wisdom within ourselves and the universe.

> *Your task is not to seek for love,*
> *But merely to seek and find*
> *all the barriers within yourself*
> *that you have built against it.*
>
> Rumi

By and large, optimal lovers tend to be non-dramatic and non-ostentatious. They've learned to keep their secrets. After all, and as per the cosmic con-game analogy, it's not smart to let on that you've switched from chess to checkers, remember? This stirs far too much envy, rejection, and retaliation, ... in any setting.

THE PRIZE: INNER LOVINGKINDNESS

In youth, we're innately driven to search for that particular mate out there to complete us. What we fail to grasp is that the real prize isn't being loved. Rather, the prize is the internal reconciliation with our own integrated and paradoxically wise part-self. We learn, thereby, to **B.E.** an ultimately profound lover, ... of ourselves and others.

Any unawakened individual can shallow out to a lifetime of lugging around an oversized self-esteem. Such a type compulsively stages repetitive sadomasochistic scenes, wherein he or she attempts to capture mere, elusive, and external illusions of love. These larger-than-life extravaganzas are never satisfying, reassuring, stable, or fulfilling enough.

It's the inner pathway, not the outer destination, that's important about a paradoxical type of love. Our paradoxically wise and loving part-self has been waiting to be discovered. This requires the rigors of years of experience and training, which are substantially informed through the epiphanies made possible amidst those wrenching calamortunities of love's heartbreak and failure.

…what is important is that one is capable of love. It is perhaps the only glimpse we are permitted of eternity.
Helen Hayes

The young are just beginners … and the art of loving matures with age and experience.
Isaac Bashevis Singer

The greatest thing
You'll ever learn
Is just to love
And be loved
In return.

Eden Ahbez

Compassion is probably the only antitoxin of the soul. Where there is compassion even the most poisonous impulses are relatively harmless.
E. Hoffer

IT'S ALL WITHIN/IT'S ALL IN THE CHOOSING

So, while it's true that the most profound project is the strenuous cultivation of our own paradoxically wise lovingness; nevertheless, our choice of mates is also crucial. Not one, not two.

Choosing a partner who has the requisite courage, strength, insight, and stamina to even begin to seek his or her own paradoxically wise self makes all the difference. We can't forge an optimal relationship with an attractive, sexy, exciting, self-confirmed, grandiose, and misguided horse's ass. On the other hand, we can, indeed, make do with any degree of sub-optimal love, as long as we're willing to pay the exorbitant price.

> *The happiness of a married man depends on the people he has not married.*
> O. Wilde

> *People marry happily with their own kind. The trouble lies in the fact that most ... marry at an age when they do not really know what their kind is.*
> Robert Davies

If we persevere in the quest for our own paradoxically wise part-self, optimal love can grow, deepen, and flourish, within. Nevertheless, it's never easy. Even optimal lovers inevitably present significant and difficult challenges, indeed. All humans are difficult to live with. That's life. Nothing worthwhile on this planet is easy.

Indeed, an optimal love relationship will make our lives supremely and "unreasonably" fulfilling and enjoyable, despite the struggle and vulnerability, and despite the inevitable criticism and disapproval of many well-meaning, but unawakened others all around. "There's no accounting for taste." Most are simply not up to the wonders and mysteries of experiencing an enduring love relationship with a strong, independent, authentic, and paradoxically wise individual. In fact, they often reject such prized lovers with a self-aggrandizing flurry of derision and contempt.

THE ULTIMATE AND INTIMATE CHOICE: LOVE OR POWER

In contrast to folly, the deepest of paradoxical wisdom is quiet, humble, and safe, not loud, self-aggrandizing, and daredevilish; subtle and gentle, not bombastic and rough; happy and sweet, not miserable and provocative; considerate and kind, not self-absorbed and argumentative; positive and cynically/optimistic, not negative and nihilistically pessimistic; inclusive and egalitarian, not exclusive and status-seeking; centered and tolerant, not extremist and competitive; constant and stable, not impulsive and fleeting; cooperative and coming together, not combative and splitting apart.

This gulf between fearful, abusive, and self-aggrandizing folly; as opposed to peaceful, kindly, and humble wisdom; ... this gulf usually widens with age. In the long run, we must choose. It's always a choice. Will it be power, or will it be love? Will we sell our souls to the extremist, resentful, grandiose, abusive, and foolish five-year-old part-self; or to the centered, loving, humble, kindly, paradoxically wise, and integrated part-self? It's that simple. It's a deliberate and methodical choice.

As with all things enlightened or not, choice comes with a cost. All significant decisions on this planet are 52-48 close calls or dilemmas, remember? There's no cost-free pathway, even on enlightened parkways. It's inevitable that nine out of ten choose the easy pseudo-invulnerable protections and projections of unawakened levels of either-or hatred, prejudice, aggression, power, and disdain.

In addition, the initial, essential, and nearly indiscernible differences between love and power are like the sometimes subtle initial contrasts between wisdom and folly, sanity and madness, or good and evil. As with all dualistic and artificially split-apart extremes, love and power may start from positions separated by a mere micron of distance, but they eventually lead to wildly contrasting, separated, and irreconcilable galaxies. That initial, seemingly tiny, and apparently insignificant four percent "path less taken" makes all the difference, ... and yet the improbable truth is that all pathways can eventually lead to the same generic and paradoxical wisdom.

LOVE HEALS US

The essence of paradoxical wisdom, itself, can be seen as a choice, ... a choice to be predominantly kind, compassionate, collaborative, and loving. Thank goodness we've arrived, after eons of intricately and impersonally haphazard evolution hard-wired with these marvelous, baffling, primitive, and complicated sex drives. They're as built-in as was the original, unfathomable, and replicative chemical property of the first intertwined and "hooking-up" precursor RNA strands in the primordial ooze.

We still have no idea how this marvelous biochemical magic happened and happens; that is, how a mere mix of chemicals and energy creates the imponderable, inexplicable, transient, messy, and replicative magnificence of life. In fact, we still have no precise scientific definition of just what life is, essentially. It's always been an indescribable dance between fusion and separation, love and hate, inhale and exhale, coming together and blowing apart. The resolution of a paradox remains a paradox.

Extremist aggression and hatred are literally dead ends. It's hard to talk the wounded, desperate, terrified, grieving, impulsive, furious, vengeful, self-important, and opposing inner and outer armies into trusting each other long enough to lay down their weapons and reconcile their differences. Only love, kindness, tenderness, humility, and forgiveness can bring us together in such a sublime, rapturous, and symphonic reconciliation.

Love and harmony replace hatred and war. Internal and external enemies become what they were all along: kindly and identical twin brothers and sisters. Apart from the one percent of superficial and rather inconsequential differences between us, we're all the same. Such healing and paradoxical love-transformations aren't prevalent, but they do occur, and they're well worth the effort and perseverance.

Love tames us and helps us to emerge, one person and couple at a time, from the collective, horrid, and barbarous side of human nature, with its eons of wired-in and survivalist brutality. We didn't arrive at the top of the food chain by being nice, philosophical, fair, or serene. By and large, our species tends to chose the all-or-nothing, extremist, "wipe-out-the-other-side," and "take-no-prisoners" type of strategy. We're very dangerous.

Love enables us to realize that our extremist, brutal, alienating, and war-like rages are obsolete. It helps us to transcend the illusions of the inevitably infantile, self-aggrandizing, and self-defeating side of human nature. Customary and sanctioned education often merely arms the self-aggrandizing/small self all the more. Awakening to love is what enlightens, enlarges, deflates, centers, tames, relaxes, humbles, and disarms us. In concert with the paradoxical wisdom of the cosmos, love heals with forgiveness and tolerance.

> *Three things in human life are important. The first is to be kind. The second is to be kind. And the third is to be kind.*
> Henry James

> *Being kind is more important than being right.*
> Anonymous

PARADOXICAL DIPLOMACY

In this hectic and aggravating world, it's far more elegant and skillful to be a diplomatic, humble, and kindly gentleman or woman than it is to be an angry, inflated, and hateful brute. Sometimes, we can calm a situation with a kindly jujitsu maneuver, converting the contention of aggression into the collaboration of love. Diplomacy can take on a modest, meek, seemingly weak, yielding, sometimes fumbling, and seemingly "uncool" appearance. This belies an ultimate, skillful, and practiced inner eloquence, agility, strength, respect, and dignity, all of which originate in the quietly astute, loving, and paradoxically wise part-self.

A paradoxical type of diplomacy allows for the other person, as well as for the inner parts of ourselves, to save face. This is world-class tolerance of differences. This art of kindness promotes harmony and cooperation. It disarms aggression and resistance. Except in dire circumstances, we usually have a choice. Whenever possible, it's best to start with kindness.

Indeed, there are times when extreme assaults from others require firm, desperate, aggressive, premeditated, and even deadly self-defense. Reality is not utopia, and humans are not always angelic. Nevertheless, and whenever feasible, ... gently/powerful kindness is the most astute and profound initial strategy. It often averts needless violence and injury.

If we take the trouble to cultivate the astute and strategic capacity to delay exercising that lethal little three ounce muscle in our mouth; then we can pause, delay, consider, and reconsider our options. We can choose to escort a contentious situation into more peaceful waters. We become the better man or woman, or, more importantly, the better part of ourselves, our paradoxically wise and integrated selves, as much as we can.

An over-all strategy of strenuous kindness is far more ultimately and subtly clever. It allows us to bypass the reflexive, lazy, and self-destructive trap of pre-paradoxical, linear, win-lose, and superior-inferior tactics. It enables us to keep others in our hearts. It allows us to see the aggressor as redeemable, himself. He or she is us. We remember how that felt. It's almost never too late for him, too, to awaken. Seen in this way, kindness is simply more realistically grown up, accurate, prudent, strong, and compassionate.

SUDDEN AWAKENINGS, ENDLESS SETBACKS

When we break through and enter into this ultimately kindly, compassionate, and paradoxically wise part-self within, it can be a sudden and life-changing breakthrough. An underlying, vast, and complex three-dimensional world emerges from the merely two-dimensional surface pattern. Life becomes an immensely enlarged, enriched, and enjoyable hologram. This is what we've been hanging around for, … to have such a healing and expansive awakening.

We're only human, however. We often fall back many times into habitual, reflexive, familiar, defensive, self-justifying, unloving, and immature habits. After all, our inner five-year-old part-self has to win some of the time. He or she entices us to write and act out yet another exciting, melodramatic, frightening, and foolishly pleasurable version of the same old self-inflating and ultimately self-defeating sadomasochistic scene. We can't begrudge him his fair share of hollow, futile, and illusory victories. Nevertheless, the trend can become a saw-toothed and failure-ridden pathway towards more predominantly wise lovingkindness.

DISILLUSIONED, CENTERED, DEFLATED

The paradoxically wise lover integrates lofty ideals with his or her baser and more primitive dark side. He embraces the fullness of his "all-ness," his inner congress. As such, he's ultimately, intimately, and gloriously disillusioned, deflated, humbled, compromised, tolerant, centered, and healed. He's gone far beyond childish, overly-idealistic, split apart, heroic, and all-or-nothing pursuits. He's become so much smaller, in order to become so much larger, enriched, and authentic. Less is more.

ACCEPTANCE OF SEPARATE/CLOSENESS AND VULNERABLE/STRENGTH

Paradoxical love has the capacity to reconcile and integrate the futile wish for fused and symbiotic oneness, on the one hand; with an accurate acceptance of our irretrievable and utter separateness, on the other. As in nature, it's an intricate and seamless balance and rhythm between fusion and fission, closeness and separateness, symbiosis and aloneness, attraction and repulsion, inhale and exhale, and so on. As such, paradoxical love reconciles the maddening need-fear dilemma in the only way that it can be reconciled. The answer resides amidst the integration of paradox, always in the centered and entered middle. Not one, not two. That's where enhanced fulfillment can be found.

Achieving a measure of paradoxical love is like spending years to master a musical instrument, so that we can then cease the self-absorbed, showy, and narcissistic solo; take our seat with colleagues in the orchestra; and consent to playing a mere part within a much more magnificent, multi-dimensional, cooperative, harmonious, and inspiring symphony; ... a symphony which is possible only if we play in concert, in an integrated way together, and in a way in which the listener can no longer discern the separate instruments, harmonies, and musicians. We lose/and retain our separate identities in order to promote the larger symphony and synchrony of paradoxical love.

It's so paradoxical that the most deeply harmonious brand of interpersonal and cooperative intimacy must also cultivate, embrace, cherish, and even revere the counter-balance of stark separateness, solitude, and individuality. To be entirely fused is to be confused. Symbiotic over-closeness is a well-meaning, but suffocating and extremist form of tyranny. Paradoxical lovers celebrate each other's independence, autonomy, initiative, and self-reliance, ... amidst an inner strength which has the capacity to risk the vulnerability and loss of control inherent within truly equal intimacy. In fact, gentle and paradoxical vulnerability makes possible the most profound levels of strength.

> *It is the separateness of two partners that enriches the union.*
> M. Scott Peck

> *... let there be spaces in your togetherness*
> *... Love one another, but make not a bond of love*
> *... Even as the strings of a lute are alone*
>   *though they quiver with the same music.*
> K. Gibran

> *... a firm identity ..., risked in the closeness of intimacy where vulnerability is strength ... Only the self absorbed cannot leave the safety of their fortress.*
> C. Hampton-Turner

> *To contain our own experiences, we must be separate ... not so fused with others as to be too confused with and by them. ... Relationship is ... not entirely together and not entirely separate, but in between.*
> R. Lewin & C. G. Schulz

CHAPTER 15

PARADOXICAL ROMANTIC LOVE

PART TWO

ENDING PROJECTION; OWNING THE SHADOW

Paradoxically wise lovers can own, tolerate, embrace, and integrate with their dark side; and yet they don't let it drive the bus. In the same way that our paradoxically wise part-selves are essentially the same, the dark sides of all humans contain seeds of the same despicable attributes. Witness the grizzly attacks, injustices, and atrocities that ensue whenever the thin veneer of civilization disappears anywhere in the world during times of mob rule, anarchy, genocide, terrorism, and war. We're all capable of the worst atrocities of hatred, prejudice, and destruction; as well as the most sublime feats of kindness, tolerance, and achievement. It's our choice.

There's no need to indulge in a one-eye-blind, "not me" projection of our dark sides onto others. This all-too-human tendency to disown and project inner evil may well constitute our most intense manifestation of evil. It replicates the very splitting up of reality into dualistic opposites which keeps us so imprisoned, unawakened, and miserable. This projection onto others takes place almost constantly in any group, as we complain and gossip about others, especially about absent others. Don't get me wrong, here. Illuminating group discussions can also be supportive and helpful methods whereby we establish and develop badly-needed and safe group solidarity and cooperation, while we expose and manage bad actors and tyrants.

> *We all straddle the abyss. If we don't look down, how do we know who we are?*
>
> O. Wilde

> *Everything that irritates [you] about others can lead [you] to an understanding of [yourself].*
>
> C.G. Jung

THE TOLERANT/REJECTION OF TENTATIVELY/PERMANENT LOVE

This acceptance of our own beautiful and terrible inner congress allows us to exercise the fine-tuned and paradoxical balance between commitment and rejection. The strenuous and ambitious project of cultivating an enduring and paradoxically wise love relationship requires the capacity to tolerate and forgive a lover's flaws, but only to a point. We humans fall in love so quickly, but, thereafter, we must pause and evaluate the relationship gradually and objectively over time.

Tolerance and forgiveness are necessary, but they don't amount to blanket and permanent absolution in matters of paradoxical love, at least not at first. Let's be practical. Let's not get carried away by the limitless enthusiasm and intensity of any new and passionate love. Our blood circulation, itself, seems to divert its flow to a region other than the contemplative brain during the sexual frenzy of new and romantic love.

After we tentatively fall in love "forever," it's best to give ourselves two years or so to evaluate and determine if a wholehearted, practical, and permanent commitment is wise. It's best for us to avoid even thinking about a commitment before then, even though every seventeen-year-old wants to run off to the chapel the morning after the first love-intoxicated night together. This totally committed/probationary period can be condensed at times for those over the age of forty-five, but not by much.

It's best to take our time. Indeed, even optimal and paradoxical love is foolish, impulsive, passionate, blissful, and voluptuous at first, ... and hopefully, forever. Nevertheless and thereafter, we must pause and settle into our more profoundly, paradoxically wise, and integrated self. It's best for us to get to really know and become best friends with our new lover. Thus, in the long haul, we must practice ultimate shrewdness and judgment, amidst impulsive and ecstatic love. Not one, not two. In harmony with the universe, we become foolishly/wise and impulsively/methodical. This enables us to love with the deepest and most wondrously constrained/abandon.

It often takes time for lovers to reveal their fullness, for better or worse. This is because hidden, more extreme, and even divorce-worthy "fatal flaws" can be lurking, undetected, below the surface, especially while we're enjoying the early stage of being passionately fused fools for love. Sometimes, these flaws are so severe as to indicate that despite the new lover's abundant, pleasing, well-intentioned, passionate, and winning positive aspects and assets, ... their underlying character structures simply can't bear up under the natural stresses and adversities of enduring and profound love.

Such flawed lovers haven't done enough of their internal homework towards the never-ending project of graduating from linear to paradoxical reason. They're not yet ready for prime-time love. At times of pressure and adversity, they break form all too readily and resort to their old, childish, frightened, neurotic, dualistic, addictive, aggressive, combative, capricious, and abusive habits.

Depending on the paradoxically wise lover's depth of experience and perceptiveness, such severe flaws in the new partner will inevitably become apparent, sooner or later, usually during the first few fused and ecstasy-laced months. The fixated dualistic lover can't help but reveal themselves to the discerning and paradoxically informed eye. The most experienced and savvy are able to detect such fatal flaws during the first weeks, days, encounter, or even within the first two sentences.

The more integrated lover then has to courageously break both their hearts and walk away during this two year probation. Break-ups are risky, indeed. Both will then endure and perhaps learn from the disappointment, grief, and loss. Perhaps the paradoxically awakening lover will learn to choose more astutely, next time. He or she will be able to discern the warning signs of dualistically fixated lovers a bit sooner.

After the parting, the unawakened partner usually soothes and defends his or her damaged self-esteem by using the self-justification and projection of blaming the other. Thereby, he stunts his growth and misses this calamortunity to expose his own illusions, to decipher the cosmic con-game, to look within, and to find out what kind of fool he is. He remains imprisoned within his own repetitive, self-created, self-aggrandizing, self-justifying, and self-defeating sadomasochistic scene. As a result, he can't change. He continues to sabotage subsequent love relationships.

AS A RELATIONSHIP BEGINS

Another rule of thumb: As a relationship begins, that's usually how it continues. If it begins unethically, aggressively, selfishly, abusively, or perversely, that's how it tends to continue, only more so. An overtly and obviously bad start is a bad omen, indeed. It's the elephant in the room. It's best to avoid falling for the usual self-aggrandizing conceit that we can be the one-and-only who can manage to just waltz in and magically reverse such an exciting but ill-fated beginning.

It's best to leave idealistic "beauty-and-the-beast" and rescue fantasies where they belong, within works of fiction, and, better yet, within children's stories. Our merely realistic love is humble and limited, remember? It can only do so much. It can't overcome unworkable, distorted, incorrigible, unethical, or illusory beginnings. Even a more optimal start can still take a bad turn under stress, thereafter, as hidden, unconscious, unresolved, and self-defeating tendencies emerge.

BEWARE THE LURE OF AFFAIRS

An all-too-frequent example of such an ominous bad start occurs when the relationship begins as a clandestine affair. We love to sneak. We humans are suckers for the seemingly enhanced forbidden fruit of such erotic larceny. One or both paramours are thus demonstrated, collaborative, and non-paradoxical types, who lie and cheat; and who telegraph, thereby, that they'll likely betray each other, as well. They need to cheat. Each still artificially splits up reality into illusory, either-or, win-lose, competitive, dualistic, and projective camps. Each needs to imagine a "bad" and "inferior" other, on whom to project their own denied and disowned dark side.

Each cheating paramour has unconsciously written, staged, and re-staged so many versions of their respective, hand-in-glove, and sadomasochistic plays. Each is now amidst yet another well-practiced Act III switching of the script on their current and now cuckolded partners. Each is holding a joint secret tryout for a new and reciprocal co-star. The resulting blending of their sadomasochistic scenes puts their unconscious stage productions onto an inevitable collision course with each other and with reality.

If one or both paramours eventually divorces their present mate, and even if they then commit to being faithful, henceforth, to each other; ... they'll likely continue to unconsciously operate within the same hopelessly self-defeating, reciprocal, and now merged sadomasochistic plays. They'll likely eventually turn their projective and critical machine-guns away from their former and now thoroughly discredited and discarded mates, ... and onto each other.

In effect, each will then secretly switch the scripts on each other during their forthcoming Act III's, just as they did with their ex-mates. In turn, they each will then continue to see themselves as needing to escape into the arms of yet another idealized and heroic understudy or new actor, and so the ever-recycling, never-ending, dualistic, and shopping-mode sadomasochistic play goes on and on.

I know, ... exceptions exist to all rules involving such enigmatic, unpredictable, complex, and multidimensional mammals as humans. Sometimes couples actually do go against the odds and grow and learn from their mistakes. Sometimes an affair serves as their mutual awakening calamortunity to such a healing extent that they both have an epiphany; decipher the con; come to terms with themselves; relinquish their dualistic logic; detach from their illusions; abandon their entire sadomasochistic productions, altogether; and enter into the realm of paradoxical love. This doesn't happen nearly as often as people claim, promise, and believe. The odds that both will have such simultaneously transforming and enlightening awakenings are so remote that such a possibility may as well be discarded, altogether.

We humans can talk a far better game than we can play. In fact, it's probably wise to pay attention to our own and a new lover's behavior, only. It's astute to disregard our and their most serene, earnest, eloquent, heart-felt, profound, and well-meaning words. After all, most paradoxical awakenings take place at times of self-deprivation, solitude, and loss; not amidst those avalanches of larcenous over-indulgence which characterize new and secret affairs. Moreover, and as always, enlightenment is measured more by what we lose than by what we gain.

JUDGE OURSELVES AND OTHERS IN THE WORST OF TIMES

A related principle comes to mind. It's wisest to emulate nature and judge our own and another's strength and depth of character during the test of one of life's inevitable bad times. The universe hurts our feelings with rug-pullings to see if it can knock us off center and reveal whether there's any authentic depth to our paradoxical wisdom. Anyone can be gracious, kind, humble, and magnanimous during and after victories, triumphs, successes, and gratifications. How does a new lover behave during defeats, setbacks, and frustrations? In those trying times, can they manage to just **B.E. K.I.N.D.**?

Stress exposes underlying, tragic, and dualistic character flaws. That's nature's survival-of-the-fittest way of separating the men and women from the boys and girls. That's when unawakened and non-paradoxical types unravel and revert to their underlying, unfortunate, self-aggrandizing, self-limiting, self-defeating, and dualistic illusions. They're telegraphing what a future with them will be like. When the going gets tough, as it inevitably does, these unawakened cookies crumble into puddles of dualistic, impulsive, and frenzied futility. Despite their considerable charms, and despite the make-up sex, this will get old, indeed.

At such a juncture, the smart cookie does the "Brenner Ole Tactic." That's when we observe and accept a fatal dualistic flaw in our new lover, relinquish our fondest urges to rescue him or her, choose to break our own hearts, and just let this non-insightful and, therefore, likely unchangeable "toro" pass on by. We let him or her butt up against another, and another. There's always another willing bullfighter-hero-heroine-understudy in the wings.

The paradoxically wise lover is able to handle life's inevitable, never-ending, and ever-increasing stream of adversities and conflicts with some degree of patience, grace, and kindness. He or she doesn't expect life to be a cake-walk. He understands that frustrating misunderstandings, challenges, failures, adversities, roadblocks, limitations, and tragedies are just part of the gig.

AS THEY'VE DONE AND DO TO OTHERS

Another glimpse of the hidden dark side of a seemingly ideal and perfect new lover occurs while each lover is more or less subtly and surreptitiously trying to gather an investigative background history on the other. They're understandably trying to size each other up. They want to confirm that this new lover is the genuinely deeper and more reliable sort of individual that they've been searching for.

The most profoundly predictive evidence, however, is present behavior. To those with astute insight, no further history is necessary. Present behavior encapsulates both past and future behavior. Nevertheless, accounts of the past can be very revealing, ... often all the more so in terms of what's left out.

The new lover sometimes sheepishly admits to, or, even worse, blatantly brags about, what awful things he or she did to deal harshly with and even to "retaliate" against those supposedly "awful" past others. He reveals, thereby, his fixation within dualistic, projective, and non-paradoxical reasoning. By and large, we can silently disbelieve his inaccurate assessments of those others. He hastens to add that he certainly would never resort to such extreme tactics with us, of course.

In this way, he's telegraphing precisely what he'll do to us, too, during the inevitable bad patches and conflicts to come. Whatever dirty tactics he's done to others, and whatever switchings of the scripts he's arranged, he'll pull these same sadomasochistic scene tactics on us. Unbeknown to him, it's been a well-practiced, intricate, and internal hatchet-job, all along.

On the other hand, if our new lover describes past relationships in a more balanced way, while owning up to his own past and contributing mistakes and illusions, from which he or she has learned; ... then such an unusual individual "passes" this history test. He's done his internal, insightful, and paradoxical homework. He's demonstrated that he knows it's an inside job. If, in addition and more importantly, he can walk the walk, then this one may well turn out to be a keeper.

CHAPTER 15

PARADOXICAL ROMANTIC LOVE

PART THREE

In the midst of the compromised mixes of closeness, distance, talents, deficits, assertions, and yieldings entailed in the imperfect, complex, and often bewildering enterprise of romantic love, we humans can make even the most dysfunctional types of relationships work, if we're unawakened, unambitious, distracted, preoccupied, patient, tolerant, naive, inexperienced, uninformed, mistaken, idealistic, dualistic, guilt-ridden, determined, trapped, desperate, and/or masochistic enough. My forty-four years of professional experience and my seventy years of life have led me, however, to identify what I call "The Big Five." These are the most extremely fixated types of individuals with whom I consider it to be nearly useless to try to sustain anything approaching an optimal, ambitious, awakened, or profound type of closeness.

Any of these "Big Five" types are the new lovers from whom a paradoxically wise lover would be reasonably justified to kindly, gracefully, strategically, and astutely withdraw, ... without waiting for any excuse or outer confirmation. Their considerable charms are not worth the inevitable disasters. Although it's best to keep these extremely unworkable Big Five types of individuals in our hearts; and although it's kind to wish them well in the future, as they attempt to attain whatever degree and form of compromised love that they have the capacity and good fortune to achieve; ... nevertheless, ... it's best to quietly, kindly, humanely, and firmly depart, as soon as possible.

On the other hand, if it's taken us five or ten years of committed and enmeshed relatedness to finally discern that our long-term partner qualifies for one or more of the Big Five categories, then we'll find ourselves in quite a challenging dilemma, indeed.

"THE BIG FIVE"

Just what are these supremely unworkable "Big Five" types? I categorize them as:

1). *PSYCHOTICS*: who are blatantly, chronically, and/or episodically unable to stay in confirmable reality. Sometimes, less severe, subtle, and/or borderline psychotic types are hard to detect at first. Some can even be intelligent, charismatic, and well-placed enough to enlist uninformed, inexperienced, untrained, and unsuspecting others to support and promote their subtle delusions.

2). *PSYCHOPATHS*: career criminals, pathological and compulsive liars, and more or less gifted minor manipulators. We've discussed this type. The most extreme such types simply don't possess the intrapsychic equipment it takes to learn to engage in profound relatedness.

3). *PERVERTS* (this category does not automatically include or exclude those who prefer same sex partners): whose interests are centered on highly specific and compulsive objects, acts, sensations, strangers, and children.

Their psychosexual development is stuck or shallowed out at much earlier infantile and childhood levels and issues. These have little to do with fully integrated and related adult sexuality. They're not actually interested in, or capable of, the infinitely more strenuous and profound project of relating at any truly authentic, personal, and enriching depth to the specific and complex adult partner in their lives. As a result, and as per their own deeply unconscious repetition-compulsion, their perverse sexual functioning parallels their limited and pathological interpersonal skills. They wind up missing the mark and settling into an impersonal, self-absorbed, self-centered, inflexible, compulsive, stereotyped, distanced, and highly dualistic style.

Nevertheless, gullible, tolerant, passive, entrapped, limited, and/or reciprocally-matched perverted partners can try to make a go of it with such types. It may well be the best compromise these partners can manage. For example, a fixated masochist needs a sadist.

4). *ABUSERS*: the violent and extreme physical and emotional types, not just mildly frank, annoying, inconsiderate, and undiplomatic critics. Predominant, persistent, and argumentative disdain can be considered as a subtle, but significant form of abuse.

5). Active, incurable *ADDICTS*, not those fine individuals who attain stable, one-day-at-a-time recovery, and even paradoxical transformation.

NO NEED TO STEP IN FRONT OF THE BUS

Supremely pathological and dualistic types of new lovers sometimes qualify for several of these Big Five categories. Once we detect that our newly beloved is one or more of these, it's best to break our own hearts, humbly play the cosmic casino's odds, and gently walk away. There's no shortage of challenging relationship work to do in normal and less extreme types of suboptimal pairings. Moreover, significant challenges occur even in the most fortunate of optimal relationships, as well.

We can be compassionate and loving without choosing to remain aboard such a Big Five type of runaway train. We can let the teeming numbers of unawakened, idealistic, and naive others waste their time by volunteering to get involved with such inevitable train wrecks.

BEWARE OF THE "IF YOU REALLY LOVE ME" PLOY

As you've likely noticed, sadomasochistic scene entrapments are usually presented and promoted in the form of overly-idealized, carefully crafted, and well-rehearsed guilt-trips. They often take the implied or overt form of "If you really love me, ..." ploys:

> If you really love me, you will: ... overlook my infidelity, lies, kookiness, impulsiveness, perversion, delusion, abuse, addiction, intrusive mother, compulsive self-defeat, irrational fears, and so on. I can't help it, don't you see? Humans make mistakes. I really love you. We've got great chemistry. That's all that really matters. You can't just walk away from all that!
>
> You promised to love me forever. That means you must overlook and forgive anything I do. That's the proof that you really love me totally and unconditionally, don't you see? You need to step up to the plate, here.

Immediately after a mutual love declaration, such unawakened guilt-trippers pander to our self-inflating illusions by claiming that our special, unconditional, healing, and even magical love has now set them free, as no one else has ever been able to do. It sets them free, indeed, ... free to misbehave in harmony with their customary, well-practiced, pathological, and unconscious sadomasochistic scenes. In the name of unconditional love, we're supposed to tolerate and forgive all these seemingly normal, unimportant, and repetitive transgressions.

If we "fail" this "love-me-totally-as-I-am" test by requiring that this new and guilt-tripping partner must change and embark on an inner pathway towards paradoxical wisdom, we're then accused by him or her as being cold, distant, rigid, unfeeling, self-absorbed, demanding, perfectionistic, abusive, and "love-'em-and-leave-'em" types. These accusations are self-confirming projections.

We can't win an argument with them. They doggedly stick to their scripts. They're simply too practiced and skillful at writing, editing, and switching the scripts of their internally and unconsciously conceived sadomasochistic plays. They inevitably convince all the other actors. They often convince us, as well.

After all, we're unusually vulnerable to and suitable for believing this guilt-trippers' particular brand of reality-bending. That's why we casted them into our erstwhile sadomasochistic scenes. We're filibustered at great length to set aside our new-found more modest, balanced, profound, and paradoxical principles; in order to adopt the flawed lover's much more extravagant, extreme, superficial, symbiotic, self-absorbed, grandiose, impossible, impersonal, and ruinous model of closeness. In reality, this amounts a worthy test of the resilience and depth of our own growing paradoxical wisdom.

It's vital that we bite the bullet, at this point, and that we carefully and diplomatically choose to "fail" these theatrical "if-you-really-love-me" tests. In fact, it's best that we build a fire wall of inner defenses, in order to head off a wholesale regression back to our own five year-old part-self's hero or heroine role.

THE "LOVE-ME-OR-I'LL-DIE" PLOY

The "if-you-really-love-me" ploy can take an extreme twist when it escalates to a more or less implied threat: "You must stay with me, or I'll kill myself, and then you'll be sorry, and everyone will see that it was all your fault." This popular, adolescent, melodramatic, and highly effective ploy may well be the ultimate and most hostile and vengeful of all guilt and responsibility trips. It reflects a lover who endorses a disastrously unhealthy symbiotic model of love. These types of lovers think that this "I-can't-live-without-you" maneuver is, itself, convincing proof of the true authenticity, intensity, depth, and virtue of their love.

Nothing could be further from the truth. Real love isn't demanding, angry, irritable, impatient, melodramatic, ultimatum-generating, brinksmanship-inducing, punitive, or symbiotic. A paradoxical lover has the capacity to stand on his or her own two feet, while simultaneously risking the vulnerability inherent within the pursuit of real intimacy. This infantile "I'll-die-without-you" ploy offers a loud, brinksmanship, and self-defeating type of dualistic love, instead of the quiet, humble, and profound constancy of paradoxical lovingness.

This "love-me-or-I'll-kill-myself" maneuver reveals that this lover falls into several of the "Big Five" types. It usually means that he or she suffers from significant and often hidden mental illness. Such an ultimatum appeals only to dedicated masochistic types, who remain preoccupied with staging their reciprocal, savioristic, repetitive, long-suffering, and sadomasochistic plays. Awakening individuals simply won't put up with such nonsense.

This sick ploy requires great compassion and skill on our parts. It's best to take our leave with kindness, sympathy, understanding, love, patience, gentleness, care, and timing. Remember that these are highly vulnerable and troubled individuals. Tragically, some of them do, indeed, make good on such desperate suicide threats. Sometimes they're so profoundly mentally ill and on such an irretrievable collision course with reality that suicide is an inevitable and consistent finale to their long-chosen and self-destructive sadomasochistic play. Some of them even turn the gun on us.

52-48/TOTAL COMMITMENT

This is where the paradox of "52-48/total commitment" really shines. Choosing a new mate always involves an intricate balance of compromise and assertiveness, of acceptance and rejection. All humans arrive with more or less reasonable loads of baggage or flaws, to be sure. There's always a price to pay for any pairing, even an optimal one.

It takes exquisite, independent, and often unpopular judgment to determine just which of a lover's flaws are reasonable and acceptable, and which are unworkable. Sometimes the difference between such extremes is paper-thin, indeed. I narrow down the most extreme and unacceptable flaws into the above "Big Five" categories. Of course, any unawakened lover can list a host of much less significant or even imaginary flaws to justify breaking up with any new, challenging, or even optimal lover.

Sooner or later, hopefully after two years or so, there will come a time when we have to make a tough, 52-48 determination about whether to commit. Life requires that we make such close call, predictive, and risky judgments and estimates. Life's a gamble, even with an optimal type of mate.

Nevertheless, once such a commitment is made with a thoroughly tested, worthy, self-reliant, and growingly paradoxical lover, ... that's when we can begin the practice of tolerating and even overlooking the inevitable and permissible negative forty-eight percent portion of any such love equation. All humans, enlightened or not, are hard to live with. Nevertheless, once the two year vetting process is completed, we must elect to burn the bridges of our all-too-easy escape routes.

> *Keep your eyes wide open before marriage, half shut afterward.*
>
> Anonymous

> *The alchemy of unconditional love that heals us only takes place when [partners] ... finally accept what is unacceptable in the other, burn their bridges, and close off their escape routes.*
>
> Sam Keen

LOVE AS EARNED/GRANTED

This leads us to the "earned/granted" paradox. As we've discussed, a paradoxical type of love is earned through a two year, exclusive, more or less live-in, and probationary period of togetherness. Committed love is just that ... committed, but only after a long evaluation. It's both earned and granted. It's not one, not two.

Even more importantly, the most profound type of love is earned through each partner's years of internal hard work that precede this relationship. Past adolescent years, the skills required to make a mature relationship thrive don't just spring forth for the first time during or as a result of a relationship. Works of art and fiction depict such magical and spontaneous epiphanies and transformations. This is not how it really is in real, or "non-reel," life.

NO LOVE IS WASTED; LOSS IS GAIN

When we experience the sudden, unanticipated, and permanent loss of a cherished love relationship, we're often thrown into a deep and intense state of inconsolable grief, hopelessness, emptiness, and anger. We cry that we wasted all that time and effort. We feel all is lost, and that we'll never have a chance at love, again. We sometimes feel suicidal, ourselves. At such times, we forget that we humans have evolved to be resilient and persistent, even amidst the worst of tragedies and losses. We're built to survive and learn from these painful experiences.

It's important to let the process of grief take its time. It heals us. Trust it. Don't push the river. Allow for the healing S.P.A.C.E. of stillness and reflection. There's so much to learn while we're amidst such profound grief and turmoil. It's a calamortunity, a "fierce teacher." Deprivation is indulgence.

It's best to strive to arrive at a level of inner equanimity wherein we can welcome good and bad fortune equally. Unless we sustain enormous and painful loss and adversity very early in life, it usually takes us the better part of half a century to come to anything approaching paradoxical wisdom. It's best to choose to persevere with this never-ending learning and rug-pulling process called life.

If you're going through hell, keep going.
W. Churchill

The paradox here is that love inevitably leads to terrible loss to be sure, but at the same time, no love is wasted. Each attempt at love teaches us so much. We have the opportunity to shed so many more illusions during and after a love relationship. These include illusions of symbiosis, permanence, and guarantees.

We must remind ourselves that "experience" really means "bad experience." It inevitably involves the healing process of disillusionment. Losing an illusion hurts, but that's a good thing. It enables growth. Loss is a challenging and instructive calamortunity. Losses are needed, along the way. As always, enlightenment is measured more by what we relinquish than by what we acquire, especially since we lose everything in the end. It's already gone. The ultimate goal is to find out what kind of illusion-driven fools we are. We can emerge from such painful losses as deeper, enriched, and accepting humans. Paradoxically, loss/is gain.

A Big Five type actually does us a favor when he or she rejects us. Being unable or unwilling to try to change and grow, himself, he refuses to "settle" for deeper, more challenging, more rewarding, and non-symbiotic love. He's convinced that we're depriving him of that impossible oneness, fusion, or womb-service to which he feels so entitled, and in pursuit of which he's gone to such lengths out there to *not* find.

In reality, the unawakened lover deprives himself by refusing to settle for a realistic, balanced, paradoxical, deflated, and enlarged love, which is far more fulfilling, enjoyable, and possible; while he shoots for his silly, empty, exciting, symbiotic, and ever-receding mirage of the moon, out there. In leaving, he stamps his feet and insists on the unachievable. He or she unknowingly presents us with the healing calamortunity to learn from the experience, correct our own misassumptions, and find our way to a more awakened and optimal type of lover, who won't drag us through such useless, idealized, contorted, and gymnastic misery.

We're free to learn from the pain of this rejection. We now know more about those internal and external warning signs that we so doggedly ignored. Now we can better find our way to a measure of paradoxical lovingness. Seen in this light, each unsuccessful attempt at love is a valuable and even indispensable learning experience. It adds to us by shattering our illusions, not ourselves.

We need our illusions to be harshly, painfully, and abruptly shattered; so that we can discern the cosmic con-game, realize just what kind of fools we are, graduate into an all-too-small, but humanly possible measure of paradoxical wisdom, begin to resume the form of our paradoxically wise part-selves, and learn to simply and profoundly **B.E. K.I.N.D.**

CHAPTER 15

PARADOXICAL ROMANTIC LOVE

PART FOUR

ARGUMENTS - WITHOUT - END

Again, there are no perfect, "fully realized" humans. No one can totally understand and agree with another. After the honeymoon, there's no seamlessly symbiotic oneness, fusion, or or unconditional adoration between adults, especially amidst life's day-to-day challenges. If any two humans can misunderstand or disagree with each other, we will, ... even amidst the most fortunate, optimal, and even awakened pairings and settings.

Even optimal lovers enter into repeated and heated arguments, although theirs are not nearly as profoundly and permanently alienating as those in sub-optimal relationships. This chapter deals with the **B.E. K.I.N.D.** mitigation of these minor, but vexing disagreements.

Optimal lovers sometimes feel provoked, regress to their

own childish part-selves, and throw needless tantrums. These can stir their partners' argumentative part-selves to emerge with a flurry of their own defenses, counter-accusations, and attacks. Both blurt out ugly, dualistic, externalizing, and "I'm-right-and-you're-wrong" pronouncements.

What started as a small or insignificant tiff quickly escalates into a circular and unresolvable argument-without-end standoff. Both partners are stubbornly defensive. Neither angry, hurt, and/or terrified five year-old part-self has the capacity to stand back, really listen to the other side, back down, apologize, compromise, or make peace.

At this point, one or both partners assesses the predicament and is appalled at their mutual over-reaction. He or she gives in, apologizes, becomes silent, walks away, or hangs up, … sometimes in angry and door-slamming frustration, complete with counter-productive and regrettable epithets about the other's impossible and unreasonable character, lineage, history, and sanity.

Both wounded and grieving partners then pout and sulk for hours or days, nursing their wounds, and longing for some sort of reconciliation. Each comforts him or herself by retelling increasingly distorted, self-justifying, and self-pitying versions of the argument, to the applause of inner and outer manipulated audiences.

At some point, both optimal partners miss each other, give up the right-or-wrong blame-game altogether, and begin to look for any reasonable and face-saving opportunity to initiate a reconciliation. Eventually, one or both invites his or her own paradoxically wise part-self to step in, resume driving the relationship bus, really listen to the other side, prioritize the larger needs of the relationship, and negotiate a compromised and lasting peace. This enables both partners to just let go of the needless, unimportant, small-minded, and illusion-driven hostilities. The couple can then forgive each other and resume their optimal love. After all, love is the glue which has embraced and preserved their fallible, yet enduring rapture.

Each five year-old part-self goes back into the dungeon of the unconscious. Both partners agree to "not go there;" ... that is, back to the original disagreement, since it only re-ignites the same painful, circular, and unresolvable argument-without-end. All seems to go well, ... for a while.

ENSUING SADOMASOCHISTIC SCENES

Nevertheless, the fight doesn't really disappear. That's just a "sweep-it-under-the-rug" type of wishful thinking. The couple *does*, indeed, "go back there," from time to time, and revisits the same old argument. This is because each partner's unreasonable five year-old part-self remains bitter about what he or she considers to be an unjust, humiliating, ill-advised, and cowardly compromise. He feels that the peace-making ego didn't listen, caved in, and sold him out. He's dedicated, therefore, to re-staging the original fight, so that he or she can properly and definitively make and prove his case, this time, by God, and score a come-from-behind, all-or-nothing, and total victory. None of this murky compromise stuff will do.

While the lovers bask in their resumed, peaceful, considerate, and optimal love; the still resentful part-self works on editing and perfecting his ancient sadomasochistic scene, adding new, more distorted, and more overwhelming arguments. He thus prepares for the time when he can ambush and trounce his illusory opponent, this time, at the slightest opportunity of real or imagined injustice.

On such a cue, which is usually self-contrived and self-created, ... he seizes the opportunity and the stage, activates the newly updated C.D. of his sadomasochistic scene, and delivers his well-rehearsed new lines. This child part has vastly underestimated his or her partner, however. He doesn't realize that his partner's unconscious and resentful counterpart has been similarly scheming and enhancing his or her own arsenal of enhanced counter-arguments, within his own highly repetitive sadomasochistic scene. He's thus rehearsed and prepared the partner's ego for this new ambush. When the same old argument is revisited, it meets with updated, heavily reinforced, determined, and effective opposition. What follows is an even more circular, angry, and unresolvable argument-without-end.

> *Holding on to anger is like gripping a hot coal with the intent of throwing it at someone else; you are the one who gets burned.*
> The Buddha

Finally, one or both partners puts a merciful end to this particular episode, and the same sequence follows, ... of sulking, silence, resentment, alienation, longing, reconciliation, forgiveness, recovery, "sweeping-under-the-rug," "stiff-upper-lip" resumption of love, and unconscious updating of arguments to even further escalate the next version of the argument. This inevitably self-defeating ritual recurs over and over through the years, between relatively long periods of optimal love.

THE MERELY HUMAN RESOLUTION

Unfortunately, during the course of these episodes, and within the workings of the inner congress, one or both partners can use his or her "underestimate-o-scope" to make the mistake of deciding that their proven optimal lover has now transformed into one of the dreaded Big-Five unworkable types. This opens the possibility that he or she will begin to turn away from a truly misjudged and wonderful mate.

The misassumption, here, is that an optimal lover should be a perfect, imperturbable, and single-minded demigod. This illusion ignores the reality that even optimal partners can't jettison their entire inner congress of unawakened part-selves and graduate, thereby, to permanent, utopian, purified, single-minded, and paradoxical wisdom. Whether we like it or not, our all-too-human, split-minded, and argumentative inner congress remains. Nothing about the self goes away.

The most optimal partner is still trying to arrange for his or her paradoxically wise part-self to preside over the ever-present, uncooperative, and argumentative inner congress, for as large a portion of time as is humanly possible. The crucial difference between optimal and sub-optimal couples lies in how quickly both optimal partners can dampen the "reactivity" dial on their reciprocal hot buttons, recover from such a damaging regression, relinquish a bit more of their abiding and all-too-human self-absorption, take an objective look at themselves, get over themselves, achieve a deeper and enhanced level of insight and perspective, and refocus on the larger priority of mutual love.

EMERGENCY B.E. K.I.N.D. AND "BE BLIND" TIME

We can manage to mitigate and sometimes even graduate altogether from this intermittent cycle by training ourselves to regard the very start of any argument as an opportunity, or calamortunity, to enhance and enlarge the love relationship, rather than seeing it as an opportunity to win or lose the unimportant and superficial argument. We can regard it as the start of an interesting, welcomed, mind-opening, and illuminating debate, much as scientists are supposed to do at professional conferences, where their new theories and concepts are presented in order to see if they can withstand the test of severe, but necessary, worthy, learned, and detached peer review, ... which means arguments. This is how scientists willingly stage a collaborative crucible of confrontation with each other, in order to test and move objective knowledge a bit forward.

We can accomplish this mysterious jujitsu by using our **B.E. K.I.N.D.** mantra-mnemonic, as soon as possible. At the first sign that we're taking offense, it's important to immediately immobilize or even paralyze our self-defeating, impulsive, provocative, feisty, and "don't-tell-**ME**-what-to-do" five year-old part-selves, so that we can enhance the love, rather than the animosity. It's time to "think twice, before you say nothing." Anyone can take the easy way and lash out.

During this emergency pause, we then use the three emergency, cool-down, and "talk-yourself-down-off-the-ledge" letters of **B.E. K.I.N.D.**, ... the "**K.**," the "**I.**," and the "**E.**" It's time to head off conflict by pouring on huge doses of abruptly soothing and healing **KINDNESS, INSIGHT,** and **EMBRACING**.

With resumed and abundant **KINDNESS**, we can return to our usual gratitude for having such an unusually wonderful, but reasonably flawed and sometimes exasperating partner. In fact, we can get back to the realization that this more profound and paradoxical type of partner is the best that anyone can have. All-in-all, and among mere humans, no one can do better.

When we add emergency doses of **INSIGHT**, we're able to put away the provocative and ever-handy "projectoscope;" ignore the superficial argument, altogether; emerge from our temporary setback into right-wrong concepts; become "BLIND" to the outside; look within; regain our proximity to and harmony with our paradoxical center; and return to our ever-patient and **KINDLY** lovingness. This prevents our usual externalizing reflex of stirring our partner's unreasonable, reactive, and argumentative part-self, who loves any excuse to emerge and flex its self-defeating muscles.

THE HEALING STRATEGY OF DELAY

While we're using **INSIGHT** to focus within, we can realize that sometimes it's wise to "win" an argument later. If a lover is annoyed with us, and if he has angrily rejected our first couple of explanations, then we know that our partner's just not very receptive in this heated moment to hear our annoyingly contradictory point of view. Anger has a way of turning off all the collaboration neurons of the mind. He or she's only human. His mind is closed, and he's reverted to his more dualistic, angry, and right-wrong self. Sometimes it's best to say, "I see your point," and let him calm down. Just because we can always manage to see the point of any opposing argument doesn't actually infer that we agree.

Sometimes during such an insightful delay, we can pause, reflect, and reconsider. We may become more open to the possibility that, in this instance, *we* are the ones who are incorrect. If, on the other hand, we see that we are, indeed, the ones on the correct side of this particular issue, we can bide our time and practice patience and good timing. We'll be just as correct at a later time. Maybe then, we'll be able to seize a collaborative and loving moment, when our partner's at his or her best. Then, we can resolve the misunderstanding in a skillful, humorous, ironic, and wily way.

AN ALL-EMBRACING S.P.A.C.E.

At this point, it's time for each optimal lover's paradoxically wise part-self to take the wheel and give the inner and unreasonable child his or her S.P.A.C.E.: **S**ilence, **P**ause, **A**cceptance, **C**ompassion, and **E**mpathy. It's time to invoke the third emergency letter, the "**E**." It's time to EMBRACE and ACCEPT the inner child and give him a good listening to, as he rants about feelings of outrage, pain, fear, injustice, humiliation, and so on. In this way, we tenderly welcome and EMBRACE him or her, like an old friend. The inner child can thus have a spacious, unlimited, unimpeded, sympathetic, loving, and comforting hearing, where he can make his case in the safety of the internal court. He can thus experience a healing catharsis.

The child part-self now feels heard, understood, loved, and satisfied. He can calm down. This lowers his need to nurse his wounds and resentments between spats. This kind of compassionate, **E**MBRACING, and **A**CCEPTING S.P.A.C.E. is a third emergency element of the **B.E. K.I.N.D.** mantra.

FURTHER B.E. K.I.N.D. HEALING: A PARADOX REMAINS A PARADOX

The paradoxically wise part-self has thus consolidated his or her role as the centered, healing, and diplomatic leader of the inner congress. He has cooled down the external crisis, substantially. Having already provided emergency supplies of **K**INDNESS, **I**NSIGHT, and **E**MBRACING, he can supply the remaining four elements of the **B.E. K.I.N.D.** method: **B**ALANCE, here-and-**N**OW presence, **D**ISILLUSIONMENT, and **D**EFLATION.

In this way, the wise part-self can teach and encourage a **B**ALANCED and PARADOXICAL way of reframing the disagreement. The awakened lover can talk himself off the extremist ledge, get back to center, and return to the most important project in life, that of harmonizing with his or her paradoxically wise part-self. He or she is large enough to step back and consider both sides of the argument.

Perhaps we could take a page from the Stoics and Samurai about this. Despite their separate and disparate cultures, their ideal was to train themselves to remain in their earnestly/indifferent balance, center, and composure at all times, and especially under fire. This is called "equanimity."

The test of breeding is how ... [we] behave in a quarrel.
G. B. Shaw

The paradoxically wise part-self can stay in the centered **N**OW of the situation, instead of trying to correct, undo, and avoid all past and future wrongs. Further, he or she can undergo the healing process of **D**ISILLUSIONMENT, dispelling illusions of perfection, utopia, smooth sailing, womb-service, unconditional love, and the like. Finally, he can **D**EFLATE the child's unreasonable, entitled, self-absorbed, and larger-than-life demands for attention, power, consideration, indulgence, coddling, special privileges, and so on.

Optimal lovers need to remind themselves and each other that a paradox remains a paradox. It doesn't offer a clear-cut, right-or-wrong, and thus illusory type of solution or vindication. It goes far beyond that. Lovers need to realize that when one or the other's angry child part emerges, as it always does, it's best to emulate the paradoxically wise self and universe by pausing, remaining silent, and refusing to respond in kind. After all, the child's tirades are nothing personal. They're derived from ancient and unconscious scenarios.

STEALTHY, KINDLY, OR COLLABORATIVE/ASSERTIVENESS

Even though an astute and optimal lover realizes that arguments and fights are usually not in his best interest, he also realizes that there are times when he must be able, nevertheless, to gently, kindly, firmly, and diplomatically stand up for him or herself. He realizes that the best way to do this is by employing the jujitsu of a diplomatic capitulation. The best way to assert is to lead with kindness and listening, to always be mindful of the larger objective of fostering the relationship.

We gain much more by yielding and by using the partner's momentum. In this instance, however, the deceptive and effective leverage of jujitsu is used in order to foster closeness, love, cooperation, and success for both partners; rather than as an effort to split, oppose, exploit, defeat, and dominate. It's a benevolent form of manipulation. This is stealthy, **KINDLY**, loving, or collaborative/assertiveness.

More often than not, the authentic "winner" is not the one who gets his or her way immediately in a conflict or argument. Rather, it's the one who gives in and apologizes, first, ... even if he knows that he's not entirely wrong. It's often best to let the other person win or appear to "win." It's prudent to be the smaller, more maneuverable, and more astute boat in the narrow, turbulent, perilous, and difficult channel of love. At times, it'll make us appear to be cowards or doormats. Often, this giving-in will cost us dearly. In the long run, however, such wise, kindly, and humble jujitsu is far more loving, skillful, astute, and mutually advantageous.

Most quarrels amplify a misunderstanding.
Andre Gide

Education is the ability to listen to almost anything without losing your temper or your self-confidence.
R. Frost

You can better quell anger in others by listening to what they have to say.
Anonymous

Whenever possible, it's best to just be quiet and listen, especially when we're angry. That little three ounce muscle in our mouths can land us in lots of trouble when it starts moving before we've paused, consulted with our paradoxically wise selves, and thought it through; ... and especially before we've succeeded in letting go of yet another of our own most cherished and self-defeating misassumptions or illusions.

If we find ourselves in dire need of telling another person off, it's usually best to think again and give ourselves that healing pause of S.P.A.C.E. Otherwise, we're prone to make the mistake of stamping our feet and demanding to have one of our illusions gratified. This will only land us deeper in self-defeating misery. "Think twice before you say nothing." Look within, instead. That's where we find the most realistic, loving, balanced, profound, and astute **B.E. K.I.N.D.** solutions.

The first duty of love is to listen.
                                        Paul Tillich

Speak when you are angry and you will make the best speech you will ever regret.
                                        Ambrose Bierce

Talk slowly, think quickly.
                                        Anonymous

We have two ears, but only one mouth, so that we may listen more and talk less.
                                        Zeno

He who tells the truth says almost nothing.
                                        Porchia

It is only the intellectually lost who ever argue.
                                        O. Wilde

Don't talk unless you can improve the silence.
                                        Anonymous

There are very few people who don't become more interesting when they stop talking.
Mary Lowry

The voice of experience keeps its mouth shut.
Anonymous

A closed mouth gathers no foot.
Anonymous

If A equals success, then the formula is A equals X plus Y plus Z. X is hard work, Y is play. Z is keep your mouth shut.
A. Einstein

The empty vessel makes the greatest sound.
Shakespeare

It isn't the whistle that pulls the train.
Anonymous

See everything; overlook a great deal; correct a little.
Pope John XXII

The time to win a fight is before it starts.
Frederick W. Lewis

We need silence to be able to touch souls.
Mother Theresa

Soft of eye and light of touch, speak you little and listen much.
The Wiccan Rede

Humility collects the soul into a single point by the power of silence. A truly humble man has no desire to be known or admired by others.
Isaac of Nineveh

All this talk, ... turmoil, ... noise, ... movement, and desire ... [are] outside the veil; inside ... is silence, ... calm, and peace.
Abu Yazid Al-Bistami

THE HEALING OF GOOD-HUMORED FORGIVENESS

From this enlarged perspective, arguments serve as calamortunites which can deepen our paradoxical wisdom and agility. We can now further realize that regressions are inevitable among mere humans; that our five year-old part-selves, illusions, and sadomasochistic scenes will persist; that even the wisest among us have a lot to learn, indeed, and break down occasionally into foolish and childish tantrums; and that the finest resolution will not only be a **BLINDNESS** to what we mistakenly judge as outside provocations, but also an abiding **INSIGHT** into and a **FORGIVENESS** of our essentially mistaken, argumentative, and uncooperative human nature.

This allows us to enjoy paradoxically wise lovingkindness amidst regrettable, aggravating, inner, and outer congresses and realities. It's all so enigmatically forgivable. A paradox remains a paradox.

Now we can maintain a detached, engaged, and gently ironic sense of humor, even amidst an argument. After all, an accurate measure of paradoxical wisdom is the degree to which we can maintain a considerate and subtle sense of humor, even when we're on the hot seat. We can wink at and even gently tease and cajole our own and our partner's irascible five year-old part-self, when it emerges. We realize that its tantrums are nothing personal, and that arguments are mere decoys.

We get the cosmic joke, and we're thus able to more thoroughly decipher the cosmic con-game. We've learned to use and even **B.E.** the reliable and good-humored **B.E. K.I.N.D.** method. This enables a much more profound, stable, enduring, intrepid, realistic, imperfect, enriching, playful, kindly, and forgiving type of love. The adversity of arguments is one of our finest and most illuminating pathways to a more enriched, multidimensional, and profound rapture.

CHAPTER 16

FINAL MUSINGS

The projects of letting go of our illusions, deciphering the cosmic con-game, looking within, realizing what kind of fools we are, owning our inner playwright, reuniting to some small degree with our paradoxically wise part-selves, continuing to abide and forgive our split and conflicted minds, and growing into an increasing and balanced harmony with the universe's counter-intuitive and paradoxical wisdom, ... these take so much time and require so many unanticipated, painful, frustrating, foolish, and yet enlightening rug-pullings and setbacks. Adversity, loss, and failure become our finest teachers. Like anyone else, we must make so many and repetitive rookie and even veteran errors along the way, until, and even after, we get the hang of it.

HALF A CENTURY; 85 YEARS/YOUNG

It takes so long to grow young and wise. It's never too late for us to awaken. For most, it takes the better part of half a century. Even when we're eighty-five, we still have so much to learn. The patient, enlightening, and rug-pulling calamortunities from the universe never cease. If anything, they escalate with age. They provoke us to re-evaluate, think out of the box, change directions, grow, and relinquish even more false notions, ... even to the last moment. Ultimately, we need endless patience with our enduring human folly. It's beyond patience, really. It's a celebration!

I am not young enough to know everything.
O. Wilde

The latter part of a wise man's life is taken up in curing the follies, prejudices, and false opinions he had contracted in the former.
Jonathan Swift

If you would live in health, be old early.
Spanish proverb

Wait for that wisest of all counselors, Time.
Pericles

To be seventy years young is sometimes far more cheerful and hopeful than to be forty years old.
O. Holmes

Ah, but I was so much older then, I'm younger than that now.
Bob Dylan

The young should love life like the old.
Anonymous

If I had been told when I was twenty-one that I should be as happy as I am now, I should have been sincerely shocked.
Christopher Isherwood

If you enjoy old age, then you've won the game.
Anonymous

But the adult is not the highest stage of development. The end of the cycle is that of the independent, clear-minded, all-seeing, [and well-trained] Child.
Benjamin Hoff

The closing years of life are like the end of a masquerade party, when the masks are dropped.
Schopenhauer

What do you want? It gets harder to answer as you get older. The answer gets subtler and subtler.
John Jerome

In the midst of winter, I finally learned that there was in me an invincible summer.
Albert Camus

Youth is so sure the rules have changed. Age is sure they haven't. Youth feels it knows how far it can go. Age is deeply aware of the danger. Youth feels it can always apply the brakes in time to save itself. Age knows it isn't always so.
Richard L. Evans

It is high time for me to depart, for at my age I now begin to see things as they really are.
Le Bovier de Fontenelle

GENTLE PARADOXICAL TRUTH IS PERFECTLY SAFE

Centered, poetic, diplomatic, and paradoxical truth is perfectly safe. We can engage in the generous practice of quietly, gently, kindly, tactfully, and humorously speaking centered and paradoxical truths to anyone at any time. Nine out of ten don't believe us. They usually think we're kidding or mad. We remember how that felt. Perhaps our more balanced and ironic concepts will echo, later, within their minds, if they attempt to comprehend our words. We can be patient. We're planting seeds. There's plenty of time, really, ... even a present moment/eternity.

If you want to be thought a liar, always tell the truth.
Logan Pearsall Smith

I am old enough to tell the truth. It is one of the privileges of age.
Georges Clemenceau

On the other hand, we might be fortunate enough to run into an occasional other who just happens to be open to the lifelong process of paradoxical awakening. They've already begun their internal journeys by using calamortunities to catch on to the cosmic con-game and to grope towards an ever-growing reunion with their own paradoxically wise part-selves. Dancing in harmony with such an individual's awakening is great fun. It adds to our own paradoxical wisdom, as well.

BLIND/VISION

Enlightenment is an "endarkenment," too. We gradually become wise enough to be predominantly blind and deaf to those bright, sparkling, impressive, and seductive siren song illusions from within. They no longer call to us. After all, they produce merely extremist and ever-receding mirages, while they render us increasingly lost, desperate, and miserable. It turns out that we lose nothing, really, when we give up on smoke and mirrors. Imagine! We have nothing to lose! We can give up on this misery-inducing project of "suffering from illusion," all in the service of preserving our precious illusion of being larger-than-life.

This new endarkenment is a quietly ecstatic blind/vision. It illuminates vast and previously obscure vistas. It's mostly a solitary thing, but it's also wondrous to share it with another. It couldn't be otherwise.

> *Be grateful for the darkness. That's when you can see the stars.*
> Anonymous

> *Shut [your] eyes in order to see.*
> P. Gauguin

> *Vision is the art of seeing things invisible.*
> J. Swift

THE FINEST SELF IS YET TO COME

Paradoxical wisdom hides in the best and most unexpected places, amidst the capacity for sustained humility, modesty, simplicity, stillness, pause, delay, silence, solitude, perseverance, resilience, openness, curiosity, courage, compromise, balance, suffering, deprivation, loss, grief, failure, defeat, confusion, foolishness, disillusionment, kindness, tenderness, gentleness, love, forgiveness, acceptance, tolerance, equality, vulnerability, yielding, leisure, humor, obscurity, unpopularity, paradox, mystery, and enigma. Paradoxical wisdom will never be popular.

> *Be patient toward all that is unsolved in your heart and try to love the questions themselves ... Do not now seek the answers, which cannot be given you because you would not be able to live them. And the point is, to live everything. Live the questions now. Perhaps you will then gradually, without noticing it, live along some distant day into the answer.*
>
> R. M. Rilke

This ultimate paradoxical awakening isn't what we had in mind. It's all so terribly/beautiful, frantically/serene, foolishly/wise, confusingly/clear, engagingly/detached, primitively/sophisticated, painfully/blissful, cynically/optimistic, un/comfortable, un/confirmable, and "CON/FUSING." It's the calm, multidimensional, ever-deepening, and ever-expanding center of the spiraling maelstrom. Even out at the speeding edges of the periphery, we can manage to gradually prevail against the centrifugal force of illusion, make our way to the center, and enter into increasingly paradoxical realms.

We *can* get there from here, right here and now, especially as we embrace our immense and enduring folly, and even at the last moment. If we stay alert, flexible, and humble, we can't miss it. We can remember that in all things, the opposite is also true. If we can contradict ourselves with a gentle, forgiving, and ironic sense of humor, we know we're on the right and "wrong" track.

We can embrace the full and glorious enigma and deception of the cosmic con-game. We can enjoy the journey towards paradoxical wisdom, and we can begin to resume the form of our own integrated selves; ... if we take the trouble to pause, question our assumptions, stay curious, enter into present moment/eternity, give ourselves S.P.A.C.E., keep a sense of humor under fire, and just **B.E. K.I.N.D.** Namaste.

ABOUT THE
AUTHOR & EDITOR

Born in Paris, France, and raised in the U.S., Dr. Sayers Brenner was educated and trained at Tulane University, Tulane University Medical School, University of Texas Medical School at San Antonio, and Sheppard and Enoch Pratt Hospital in Baltimore, Maryland. He has been in the private practice of Psychiatry since 1974. He has served as a training staff Psychiatrist at Sheppard-Pratt Hospital, head of Towson State College Mental Health Clinic, Chief of Staff of Sarasota Palms Hospital (a former psychiatric hospital), and head of Psychiatry at Sarasota Memorial Hospital. His first book, *Suffering From Illusion, the Secret Victory of Self-Defeat*, was published in 1988. Over four plus decades, he has developed expertise in the application of paradoxical, integrative, cognitive, Eastern, and existential concepts to the practice of insight-oriented psychotherapy, about which he travels, trains, and lectures.

Charlotte Brenner has a Bachelor of Fine Arts from Maryland Institute and a Master of Fine Arts from University of South Florida. She has taught in the Fine Arts departments of Maryland Institute, AACC in Annapolis, Maryland, and Ringling College of Art and Design in Sarasota. She is an award-winning painter, who has shown her art in various galleries. In addition, she has established two art venues for charitable fundraising.

The Brenner's have lived, loved, and worked in Sarasota, Florida, since 1977.